Email: glloyd@ahistoryofpoint.com

Website: www.ahistoryofpoint.com

Copyright © Gower Lloyd, November 2017

ISBN: - 978-0-9934140-1-5

All rights reserved. No part of this book may be reprinted, reproduced or utilised in any form or by any electronic mechanical or other means, not known or hereafter invented, including photocopying and recording, or in an information storage or retrieval system, without the permission in writing from the publishers.

British Library Cataloguing in Publication Data.

A catalogue record for this book is available from the British Library.

Designed by Gower Lloyd.

Printed by PPG Print Services Limited, Portsmouth.

Portsmouth Point

A Commercial & Cultural History

Panoramic view of Portsmouth Point c.1825 from the old Semaphore tower – painted by Francis Spencer Smyth, Commander R.N., later promoted to Admiral.

Portsmouth Point in 2015

Contents

Chapter

	Acknowledgements	iv
	Introduction	v
	Location Map	vii
	General maps of Spice Island	viii
1	Life on Point	1
2	Fraser & White	32
3	Pickford & Co	49
4	W.G.Lucas & Son Limited	66
5	Grogan's	75
6	Portsmouth Sailing Club	80
7	The 1st Portsmouth Sea Scouts	108
8	John Patrick O'Halloran Ashdown (1905-1979) (1st October 1905 – 12th March 1979)	134
9	A.R. (Sam) Loader (1897 – 1985)	156
10	The Last House on Point (The story of 102 Broad Street (1656 – 1960))	167
11	Advertisements	187
	Bibliography	202

Acknowledgements

The author would like to thank the staff at the Portsmouth History Centre, Central Library for the assistance given to him whilst undertaking the book research.

In addition, acknowledgements are given to the work of numerous authors of the Portsmouth Papers, a wonderful collection of historical information published about Portsmouth.

Thanks are given to my daughter, Nicky, for painstakingly reading my early drafts and providing suggestions to improve and enhance the book and I extend my gratitude to my friend Derek Lines for so professionally undertaking a great deal of work in enhancing photos, newspaper advertisements and providing original art work during the preparation of the book.

Graham Hurley, local author and an old friend kindly provided information about Sam Loader, much of which I have reproduced and Peter Lucas has been very helpful in explaining the history of his sail making company.

The Chapter about the "last house on Point" was prompted following my discovery of its history published by the late Tim Backhouse on his excellent website: www.historyinportsmouth.co.uk. Much of that article was extensively researched and written by Cynthia Sherwood who lived in the house when she was young and I was very fortunate in meeting her and being allowed access to her original notes.

During the time I have been researching this book, many people have allowed me to photograph their pictures and copy their personal records and for this I am extremely grateful. The provenance of some items is unknown, but where the origin is known it is acknowledged beneath the picture. If I am notified of any omissions I will update the picture credits in any further reprinting of this book.

Finally my eternal thanks are given to my wife, Yvonne, who assisted in proof reading and endured all the time I spent researching and writing the book and to my father for providing historical information for inclusion in the book and personal comments about Jack Ashdown.

Others, too numerous to mention have also helped me and for their contributions I am truly grateful.

Introduction

On reflection, after writing my first book, "A History of Point- Portsmouth's Spice Island", I realised there were more untold stories to research and write about this unique area of Portsmouth.

Whilst growing up on Point in the 1950s and 1960s, I recall some local organisations and businesses which had existed for many years on Point and their stories needed to be told to keep their memories alive since they significantly added to Point's rich history.

In this book I have included an initial chapter about "Life on Point" through the centuries, describing living conditions for poorer people with the overcrowding and generally dreadful unhygienic situation that existed for many, causing numerous deaths from diseases as a result. It also refers to some of the businesses and trades that existed in the area throughout the centuries and examines population patterns.

Furthermore, the Camber, so influential to life on Point throughout the centuries is described, including its development and trade, daily events and customs, together with its fishing industry.

Commercial organisations that operated from Point for more than 100 years included the firms of W.G.Lucas & Son, Fraser & White and Pickford & Co, together with Grogan's, the well-known cafe/restaurant, which opened its doors to customers for more than 50 years. These businesses are still etched in the memories of many people today and their histories warrant being recorded in writing for the benefit of future generations.

Two non-commercial organisations that have existed for the best part of 100 years and are still going strong on Point are the Portsmouth Sailing Club, formed in 1920 and the 1st Portsmouth Sea Scouts formed circa 1907. Their history is of great interest to the city as they have both helped in the training of many youngsters and adults in seafaring skills, particularly the Sea Scouts that trained many local children, who later became Captains in both the Royal and Merchant navy and served their country over the years in these professions.

Many local characters have made their mark on Point throughout the centuries and a couple of twentieth century characters are described in detail in my book.

Firstly there was John O'Halloran (Jack) Ashdown, who, although not living on Point, was heavily involved with many people's lives on Point since circa 1918 when he joined the 1st Portsmouth Sea Scouts as a young Sea Scout under the guidance and influence of the famous marine artist, W.L.Wyllie. He later became their Scoutmaster for many years until his death in

1979, having earned a reputation, second to none, for the first class standard of seamanship and nautical training he provided to youngsters, many of whom lived on Point. He was also a member of the Portsmouth Sailing Club throughout his life.

Another local character was Sam Loader, whose father had opened up the Temperance dining rooms in the late nineteenth century in Broad Street and his local upbringing on Point in the early twentieth century helped shape his life. After moving away from the area, he later returned to live in Broad Street making a positive contribution to many people's lives.

One chapter of the book is dedicated to Cynthia Sherwood who lived in the "Last House on Point" at the northern end of Broad Street between 1935 and 1951. She personally researched the amazing history of this property some years ago and I have based this chapter on her writings and research and for that I offer my gratitude.

Some of the information about life on Point has been obtained from numerous adverts that were published in the local newspapers of the day and they provided a wealth of information about local businesses and activities that occurred on Point.

Since these adverts, from the eighteenth, nineteenth and twentieth century are so informative, I have included them in a final chapter of the book. Collectively they describe life in great detail during that period and help provide an insight into everyday life on Point.

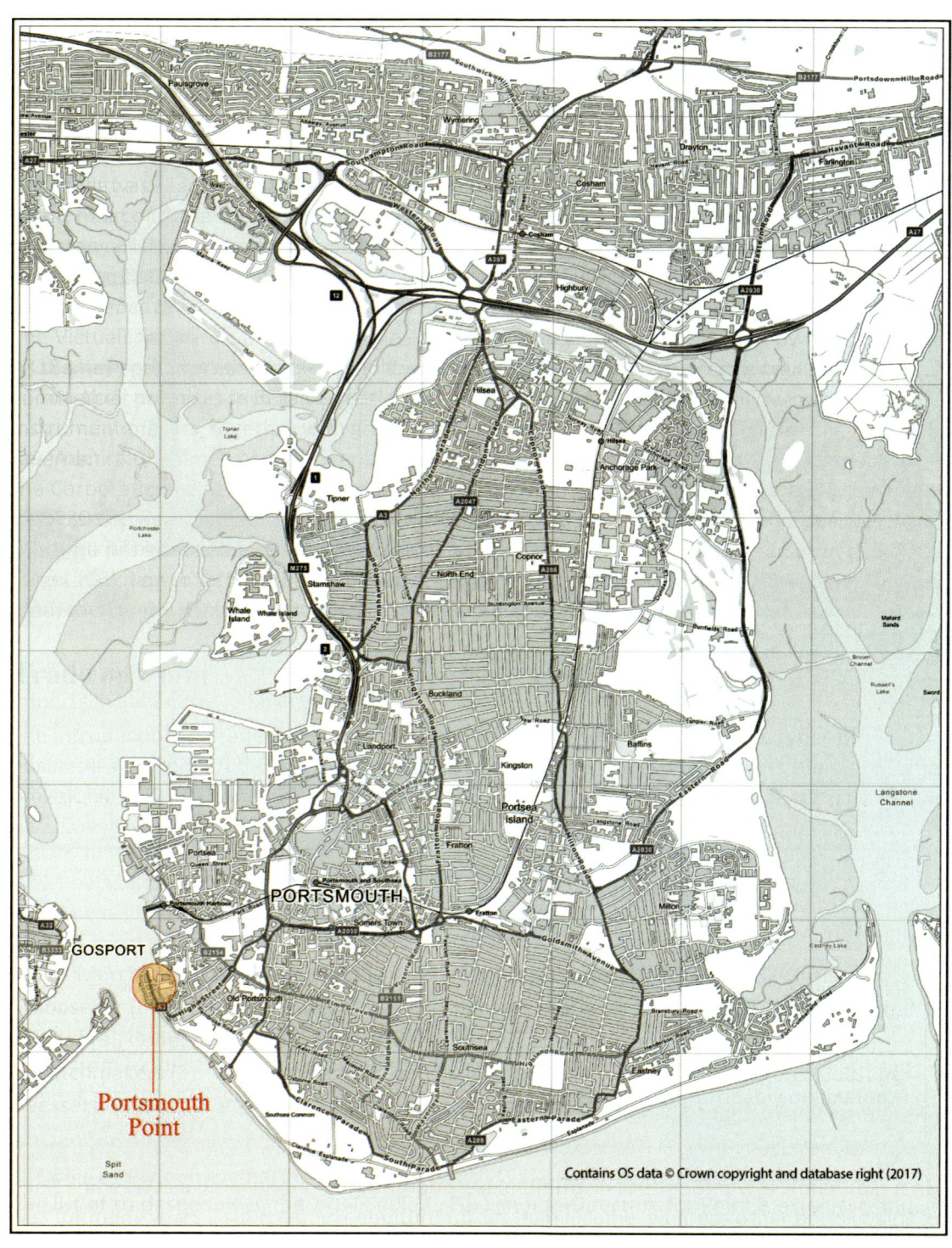

Location map of Portsmouth Point

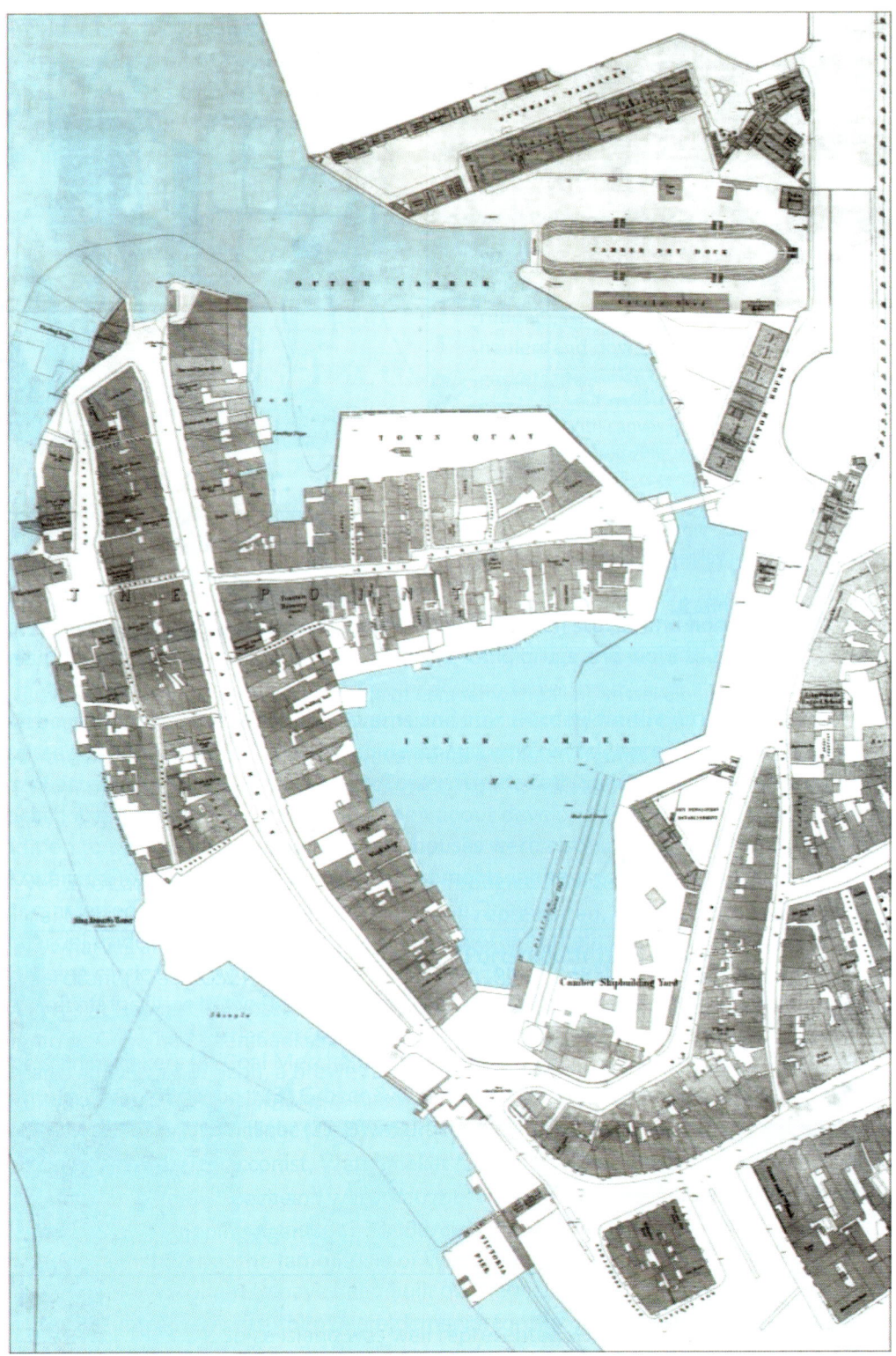

This map of Portsmouth Point (Spice Island) is part of an original map that was engraved and published at the Ordnance Survey Office Southampton in 1867, and supplied to the author by the University Library, University of Portsmouth.

It shows the area at that time, including important locations and buildings. However, some buildings and sites referred to in this book were established post 1867 and have been added to the map. The purpose of this master map and the maplets that follow, together with their respective keys, is to provide the reader with an idea of the geography of the area.

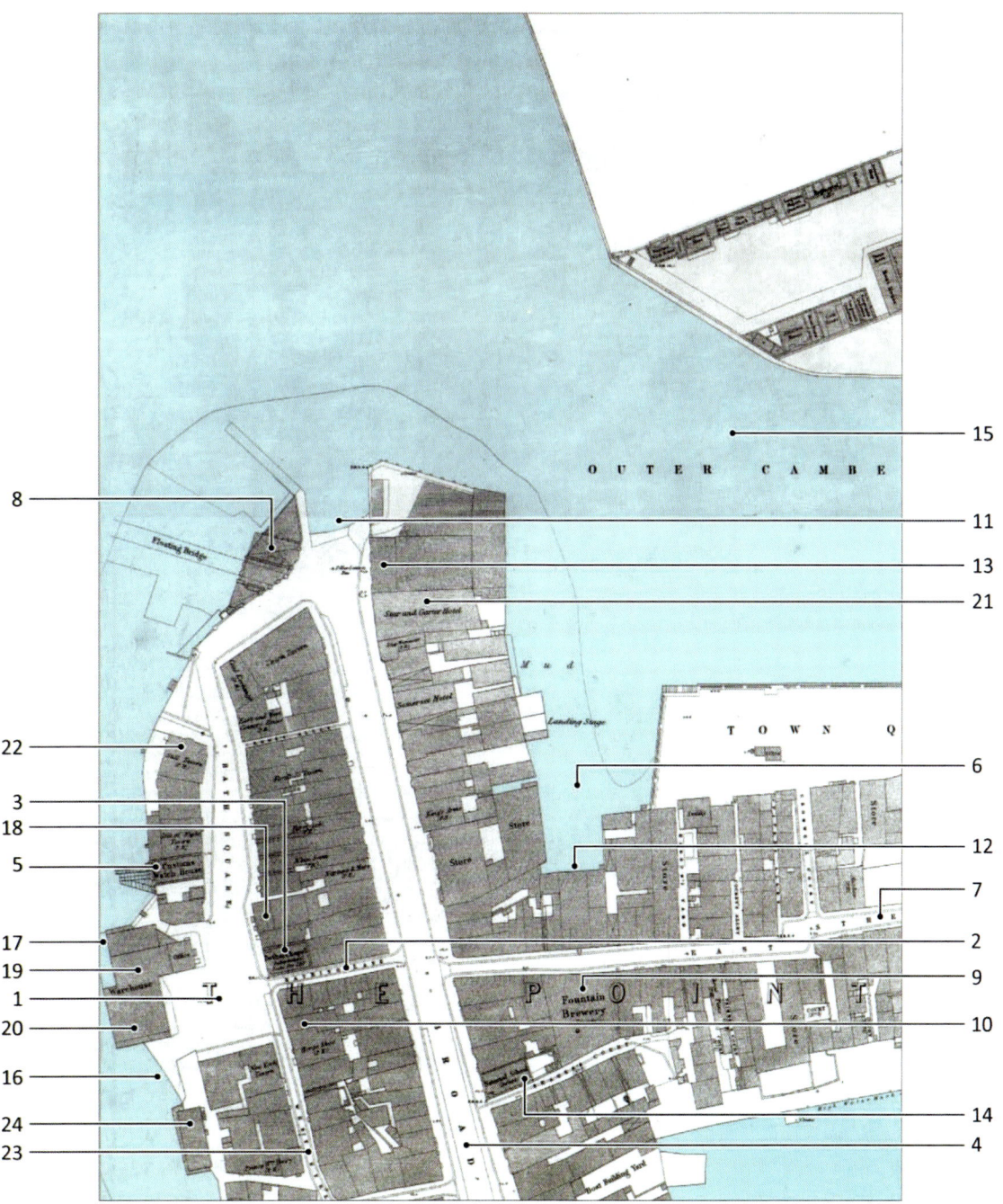

Key

1. Bath Square.
2. Bathing Lane.
3. Bethel Chapel.
4. Broad Street.
5. Customs Watch House.
6. Dirty Corner.
7. East Street.
8. Floating bridge office.
9. Fountain brewery.
10. Harry Feltham's yard.
11. IOW Car ferry slipway (pre 1961).
12. IOW Car ferry slipway (1961)
13. Last house on Point
14. National School.
15. Outer Camber
16. Pickfords beach.
17. Pickfords quay.
18. Portsmouth Sailing Club.
19. *Quebec Hotel*.
20. Quebec House.
21. *Star & Garter Hotel*.
22. *Still & West*.
23. West Street.
24. Weeke's wharf

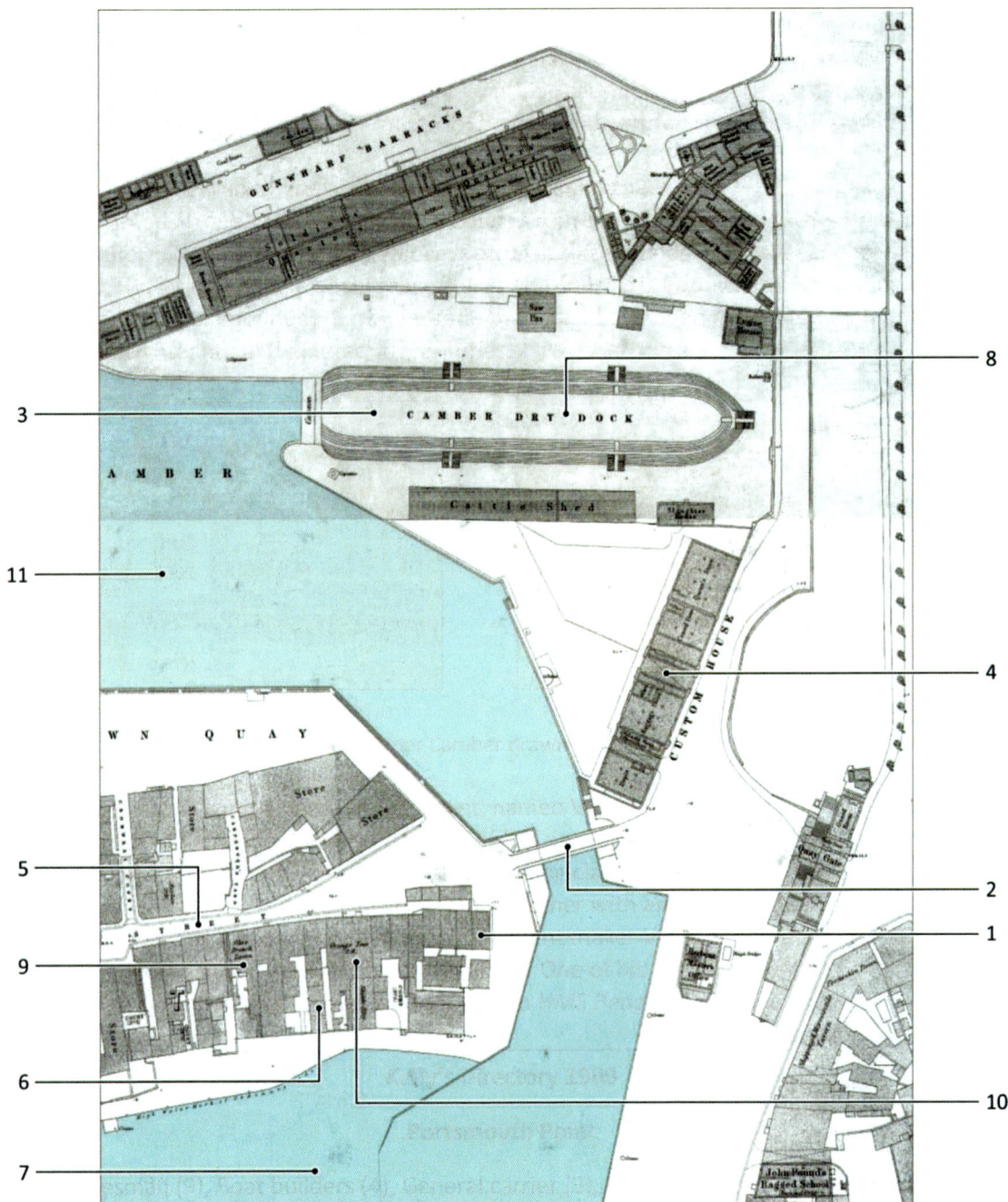

Key

1. *Bridge Tavern*.
2. Camber Bridge.
3. Camber Dry Dock.
4. Customs House (1828).
5. East Street.
6. Fraser & White coal bunker.
7. Inner Camber.
8. IOW Car ferry (existing).
9. *Olive Branch tavern*.
10. *Orange Tree Tavern*.
11. Outer Camber.

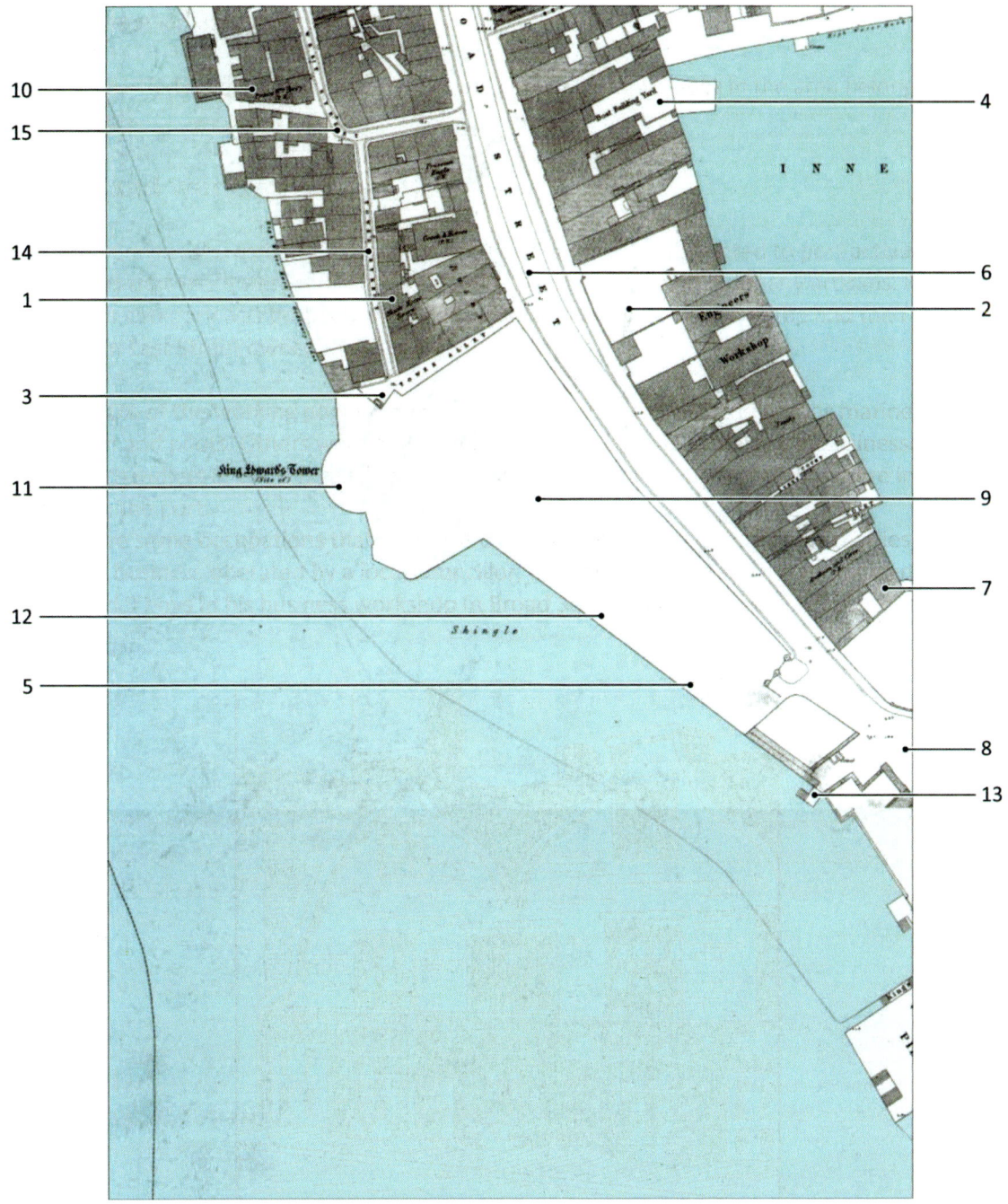

Key

1. *Black Horse Tavern*.
2. *Blue Posts Hotel*.
3. Capstan Square.
4. Clemens boatyard.
5. Eighteen Gun Battery.
6. Fisherman's Row.
7. George Feltham's boatyard.
8. King James's Gate.
9. Point Barracks.
10. *Prince William Henry*.
11. Round Tower.
12. Sally Port.
13. Sally Port (original).
14. Tower Street.
15. West Street.

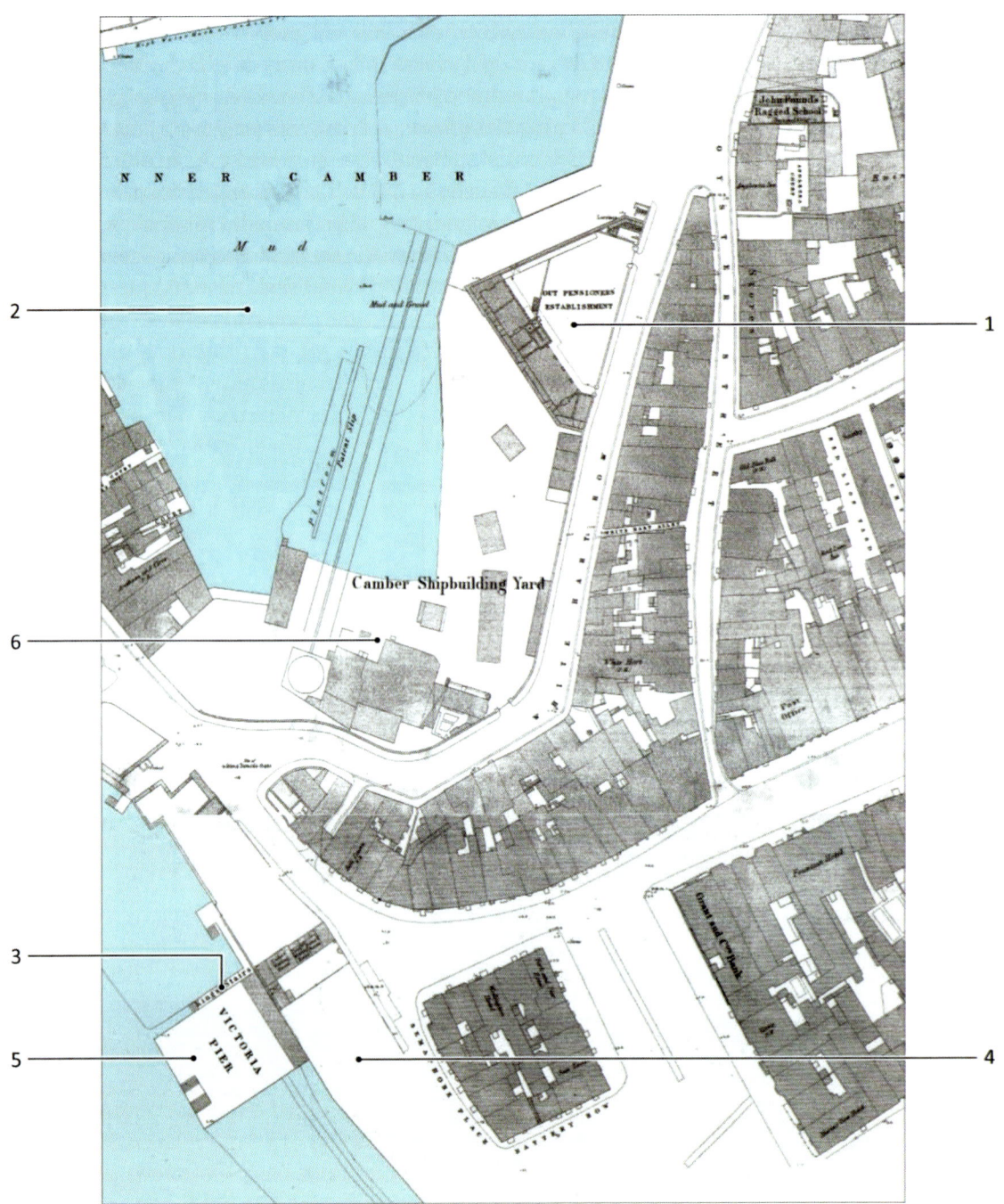

Key

1. Camber Bastion.
2. Inner Camber
3. Kings stairs
4. Square Tower.
5. Victoria pier.
6. Vospers boatyard.

xii

Chapter 1

Life on Point

POINT as described in "The New Portsmouth Guide 1835"

Broad Street begins on the outside of King James's Gate and ends at the water's edge opposite to Gosport. Having passed the gate and bridge, a short turning to the left leads to a sally port, communicating with the beach outside the harbour's mouth where watermen ply for passengers to Spithead and the Isle of Wight. From this sally port the line of batteries as having been built by James II begins and ends at a newly renovated Round Tower. In a small square near the tower, called Capstan Square are the remains of a capstan, originally placed there for the purpose of raising the "mightie chaine of yren", part of which may still be seen on the beach at low water. This square may also be reached by the first cross street from the east side of Broad Street. About midway down the Broad Street, on the north side, stands the *Blue Posts Hotel;* a little further down on the opposite side, a turning leads to Bathing House Square where are the *Quebec Hotel*, the Navy Post Office, a sea bathing establishment and a landing place for passengers from Ryde and a short distance onward what is termed the Point Beach, a general landing place for persons coming by water to Portsmouth, especially from Gosport. Near the beach are the office, wharf and stores of Mr Lindegren (agent for the East India Company) and the *Star and Garter Hotel*. Returning through King James's Gate to the High Street nearly opposite the *Fountain Hotel* will be found Oyster Street, branching off on the north and extending to the Quay Gate.

Sketch of Point from Portsmouth Harbour entrance drawn by W.H.Snape in 1897 in which can be seen the *Still & West* pub and Floating Bridge sheds on the left. *"Illustrated History of Portsmouth"* by W.G.Gates. Reproduced courtesy of The News, Portsmouth.

When Point was first inhabited during the reign of Queen Elizabeth I, it didn't take long before a significant community was established. Being a peninsula it soon developed its own unique character and with the construction of King James's Gate and the resulting access restrictions, the area became notorious, being outside the fortified town of Portsmouth.

The first development on Point would have been in the late sixteenth century when foreshore was leased to construct storehouses and wharfs and in addition pubs and taverns started to appear.

As the area grew up from the sixteenth century, a street layout was developed, together with associated housing and in some areas of Point the housing conditions were very cramped and deplorable, leading to severe illnesses and deaths.

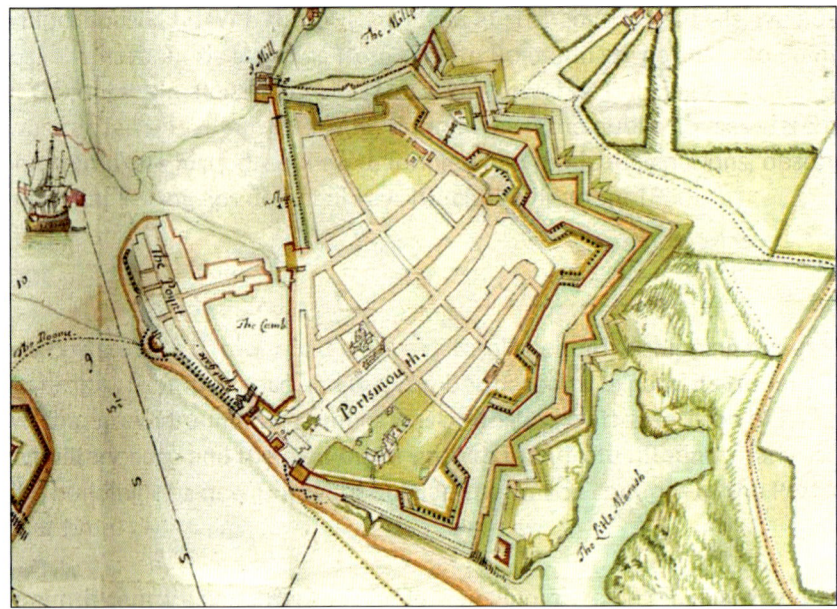

The early road layout on Point can clearly be seen on this 17th century map of Portsmouth.

Because Point was outside the town and its fortifications, the inhabitants enjoyed many privileges which were denied to the citizens of Portsmouth and among these was the fact that many of the pubs and taverns were kept open practically all day and night, resulting in much lawlessness.
King James Gate, located at the approach to Point, was closed at certain times and there was a drawbridge with moat beneath; it was the only route on and off Point by road, which effectively made Point an island and night time closures applied.

Within the first century since its formation, Point gained a reputation for being a dirty place and on March 26th 1653 the governor, Colonel N Whethem, wrote a letter to the Admiralty:

> My own sense of the sad effects that may come from the filthy nastiness of this place and the entreaty of others leads me to remind you of it. Nothing has yet been done nor is likely to be done in cleansing the town, paving the streets and making sinks and passages for the water and filth to pass through. The smallpox begins to increase and two or three have died suddenly this week.

Unfortunately, some of the population on Point not only refused to contribute to the cost of the necessary improvements, but actually stood out in opposition to it. However, it was reported shortly after the publication of this letter that thanks were given to the Mayor and Aldermen for "cleansing the town".

In 1674 it was recognised that there were 140 properties on Point, but many of these would have been storehouses.

In 1716 it was reported that there were 41 public houses, brandy houses and coffee houses on Point. Most of these establishments were located in Broad Street, East Street and Bath Square and many of the houses of entertainment on Point were named after great victories or celebrated fighting ships such as the *Royal George, Arethusa, Ship Worcester, Neptune and Mars, Quebec tavern, Roving Sailor, Lord Hood* and the *Ship Tigre.*

As the navy grew in size, Point served its needs and typically many maritime trades opened up commercial premises such as slop sellers, chandlers, riggers, sailmakers, tallow merchants, instrument makers, together with grocery stores, butchers, bakers and-of course-the inns and taverns.

By 1730 there were 159 properties on Point and by 1785 this had risen to 228 properties. At this time it is interesting to note the whereabouts of these properties: - Broad Street (97), East Street (66), Tower Street (42), Bath Square (16). When one considers the geography of the area, this clearly demonstrates that East Street and Tower Street were very densely developed.

Trade on Point

The introduction of Trade Directories from the 1780s provides a record of the types of businesses on Point. Although these directories list commercial establishments there are some omissions, but they nonetheless provide a good representation of business life at that time.

Sadler's Portsmouth Directory 1784

Portsmouth Point

Coal Merchant, Glazier, Merchant (2), Ironmonger & Brazier, Hairdresser (3), Grocer (4), Slopseller (8), Mercer (2), Butcher (4), Apothecary & Surgeon (2), Stationer & Silversmith, Baker (3), Cooper, Attorney, Brandy Merchant (2), Surgeon, Earthenware Shop, Taylor, Watchmakers (3), Cobbler, Dressmaker (5), Auctioneer, Coach travel, Waggons, Coasting vessels. Taverns, Hotels & Inns (47)

The list of tradespeople in the 1784 Sadler's Portsmouth Directory for Point is extensive, but mainly lists properties in Broad Street. It includes most of the expected businesses of the day, but it is surprising that some marine businesses such as sailmakers, ships chandlers, boat builders etc. are not recorded, although perhaps this is because many of these businesses were likely to have been located in East Street and Bath Square.

Slop sellers were merchants who traded in slops, which were ready made clothing, rough working dress or bedding sold to sailors and the high number of Slop sellers on Point at this time indicate the large numbers of sailors that would have been visiting the Point. Mercers were dealers in textile fabrics, especially silks, velvets and other fine materials, but most of these shops were based outside Point in areas such as the High Street or nearby.

In 1790 a company named Morgan, Mercer and Sea Draper, slop sellers located in Old Portsmouth had an advertising sign with the following poetic gem written on it:

Sailors rigged complete from stem to stern, viz, chapeau, napeau, flying jib and flesh bag, inner pea, outer pea and cold defender; rudder case and service to the same; up haulers and down traders, fore shoes, lacings, gaskets etc.

> With canvas bags
> To hold your rags
> And chests to sit upon;
> Clasp knives your meat
> To cut and eat
> When ship does lay along.

Coopers made or repaired storage vessels made of wooden staves and hoops such as casks, barrels, tubs etc. and apothecaries sold medicines and drugs and were the pharmacies of their day.

As can be clearly seen in the list, the taverns and inns were by far the most prolific of businesses at that time with 47 establishments and were widely spread on Point, being located in Broad Street, East Street, West Street, Tower Street, Bath Square and also listed as being on the beach itself.

In addition to taverns, hotels and inns, beer houses were also numerous at the time, so would have swelled the numbers of drinking establishments in the area considerably.

Pigot & Co Directory for Portsmouth 1823-24

Portsmouth Point

Boot & Shoemakers (3), Coal Merchants (4), Consuls (3), Cooper, Druggist, Fruiterer, Furniture Broker (2), Grocer (3), Grocer & General Dealer (2), Hatter (2), Ironmonger, Linen Draper, Merchants (3), Milliner (2), Pawn broker, Perfumer, Sailmaker (3), Ship Chandlers (8), Shipwrights (4), Tobacconist, Watchmaker (2), Rope maker, Basket maker, Slop seller, Anchor and Shipsmith, Coach and waggon travel to London & Brighton, Coasting vessels (UK and abroad), Shipping Agents (4), Tallow chandlers (2), Taverns, Hotels and Inns (47)

From the list of 1823-24, Spice Island was well represented with Carriers (waggons) travelling to places including London, Brighton and other destinations, with the *Blue Posts* in Broad Street being the main operating base. Also at this time, Pescott's waggons and vans went to London from 46 Broad Street, Cox's vans to London from 57 Broad Street, Matthews's waggons to Brighton and Garnett's waggons to Fareham.

There were numerous establishments where conveyance by water could be purchased such as at the *King's Head* in Broad Street to Cowes and Guernsey, the *Thatched House* in Broad Street to Lymington, the *Neptune & Mars* in Broad Street to Plymouth, the *Roebuck inn* in Broad Street to Poole, the *Cornish Arms* in Broad Street to Ryde, the *Neptune & Mars* and the *White*

Hart in Broad Street to Southampton and the *Quebec tavern* to Havre-De-Grace.

Other transport that existed on Point at this time included the coaches operating from the *Blue Posts* to London on a regular basis.

Some of the houses sited in Broad Street pre 1847 on the site of Point Barracks before it was built.
The Illustrated History of Portsmouth by W.G.Gates. Reproduced courtesy of The News, Portsmouth.

Broad Street was very well represented with an extensive range of businesses at this time, although it is interesting to note that the more affluent residents and professionals lived in the High Street, or nearby, which was a more upmarket area. Point was a much more working class area with many of the people who lived there being employed in the area around the Camber. General research of family names living in the area reveals many very large families, most of whom were engaged in maritime activities, be it watermen, boat builders, dockers or fishermen etc.

Broad Street catered for shipping and other maritime related activities, whereas the High Street and adjacent roads housed the types of businesses and professions more suited to the middle class. This is typified by the fact that Point had 3 sailmakers, 8 ship's chandlers, 4 shipwrights and numerous other marine related businesses, whereas the High Street had 11 academies, 12 attorneys, 6 booksellers and printers, 10 fire and life insurance offices, 3 physicians, 4 teachers and professors, 7 surgeons, 15 tailors and drapers and 7 wine and spirit makers. Again, as in the 1784 directory there were 47 hotels, taverns and inns on Point which must have resulted in a very crowded and noisy atmosphere, particularly at night.

Harrod's Postal and Commercial Directory for Hampshire, Portsmouth Section 1865

Portsmouth Point

Greengrocer (4), Grocer (7), Corn merchant, Boot & Shoemaker (4), Dining and eating rooms (3), Ships Chandler (4), Shipping Agent (2), Outfitter (2), Fruiterer (4), Painter & Glazier (3), Ironmonger, Basket maker, Glass blower, Tobacconist, Hairdresser (3), Gas fitter, Sailmaker, Confectioner, Baker, Butcher (3), Hardware store (2), Ship builder, Fish dealers (3), Hat manufacturer, Tailor, Beer retailer (7), Shopkeeper (8), Potato merchant (2), Consul, General carrier, Watchmaker, Mast and block maker, Shoeing smith, Coal merchant (2), Taverns, Hotels & Inns (31).

One of the main changes in this 1865 list compared to the 1823 list is the reduction in taverns, hotels & inns and this is primarily due to the demolition of a number of properties on the west side of Broad Street for the construction of Point Barracks, which included at least 7 drinking establishments: *Lord Howe & General Elliot, Bridge Tavern, Three Guns, Fortune of War, Prince of Wales, Vine and the Sun.*

In the mid-19th century there were more than 10 shipping agents on Point, almost all with offices in Broad Street. Four were listed as consuls representing many countries including Belgium, Brazil, Denmark, Sardinia, France, Portugal, Netherlands and Hanseatic towns and Hanover. The large numbers of shipping agents and consuls is hardly surprising when one considers the huge amount of maritime trade that must have been associated with the Camber port in the eighteenth and nineteenth centuries.

Views of the Inner Camber drawn by M.Snape.

In 1865 one of the companies in Broad Street, named Valentine Rumley & Co, were specialist army and navy tailors and there were also cobblers and other businesses dealing in garments. Although Point was certainly much more of a working class shopping area than the High Street, a couple of watch makers were based at Point together with an optician. At this time, George Stebbing is listed as being a mathematical instrument maker in Broad Street and a calibrator of ship's equipment, which was very highly regarded. One of his sons was appointed as the Librarian and chronometer keeper with Darwin on *HMS Beagle's* scientific voyage.

Kelly's Directory 1900

Portsmouth Point

Fish salesman (9), Boat builders (4), General carrier (3), Lodging house (2), Shipping agent, Consul building, Greengrocer (2), Engine oil manufacturer, Shopkeeper (8), Coffee and dining rooms (5), Coal merchant (3), Ice factory, Beer retailer, Builders merchant, Fruit & Potato merchant (2), Bonded store, Flour merchant, Butcher (2), Cork manufacturer, Sailmaker (2), Dairy, Hairdresser, Decorator, Shipping agent, Grocer (2), Musical Instrument dealer, Baker, Ironmonger, Chemist (2), Ship's chandler, Boot & shoemaker, Taverns, Hotels and Inns (15)

By 1900 the number of pubs had reduced considerably with only 15 taverns, hotels and inns in existence.

This is indicative of the reduction in activity in the Camber over this period and a reduction in the population. It is hardly surprising that the number of pubs had reduced and in addition, the general opinion of the Government of the day was that drink was a demon. The Beer House Act of 1869 was repealed in 1871, effectively preventing the opening of any new beer houses. Magistrates were reluctant to grant new pub licences, so often licences were transferred on the closure of a pub.

By 1901 the tied house system was in full swing and all but two pubs in the area belonged to the brewers.

Living and working on Point.

The 1851 Census shows that the main occupations on Point were related to port activities and also shows that there were not many professionals living on Point, but many artisans. Included within this category was probably the Shipbuilder of the time, Thomas White and the Fountain brewery in East Street owned by Joseph Knott.

At least 30% of the working population were in jobs associated with the port as mariners, watermen and pilots. Others were employed in shipbuilding, sail making or in businesses such as ships' chandlers and it is highly likely that a substantial number of other jobs were indirectly related to the port.

There were some occupations that were not directly associated with the port activities, such as one large business operated by a local councillor, Mr William Cavender, who employed 13 adults and 9 boys in his business workshop in Broad Street making and selling quality tobacco products.

William Cavender's shop in Broad Street – "*Portsmouth in the Past*" by William G Gates

The retail sector accounted for 104 workplaces and many of these were in pubs and taverns and also beer houses which were still very common on Point in the mid-nineteenth century. The vast majority of these beer houses were very small and cramped having low rateable values in the order of £9.

The largest drinking establishments such as the hotels were rated far higher. The largest was the *Quebec Hotel* in Bath Square at £105 where there were a number of live-in staff. The *Blue Posts* was assessed at £90, the *Star & Garter* at £73, but the normal pubs were rated at much less. Some of the very small pubs such as the *Plough* in Tower Street and the *Ship Worcester* in Broad Street had rateable values of £10 or less.

There were so many drinking houses on Point that it equated to 1 pub or beer seller to every 35 people, which is quite amazing. This very high concentration was much greater than in other poorer areas within the fortified town of Portsmouth, such as the Old Portsmouth quarter, where drinking house ratios were 1 for every 104 people.

One very surprising fact is that the 1851 Census lists 76 servants, many living in Broad Street and they were in fact the second largest employment sector after mariners, even in a working class area such as Point. Other facilities in the area included a laundry business run by local women to supplement their family income or just to make ends meet.

The Town School, Gunwharf Road

The State only began to acknowledge some responsibility for the conditions in which the poor and poor children lived and the lack of any educational policy at the beginning of the nineteenth century. The Reform Act of 1832 gave a million people the right to vote and revealed the utter inadequacy of England's educational provision. Education was very limited in the early years on Point until schools were introduced in the area. The Royal Victoria independent school was established in Bath Square in 1825 and some years later the Portsmouth Anglican infant school was built in 1846 in Broad Street. After these two schools closed down children from Point used to attend Portsmouth Town School in Gunwharf Road crossing the Camber bridge on their journey until its removal in 1924.

Point had much changed by the start of the twentieth century and the population had fallen from 1504 people in 1851 to 813 people in 1901. Although there were efforts made to improve facilities in the Camber and surrounding area this resulted in a large reduction in population due to the demolition of residential and business properties.
Fraser & White's expansion in East Street resulted in the demolition of many houses and by 1901 Vosper had demolished 8 houses in Broad Street. Further north, four former dwellings had become the premises of the sailmakers C Groom Ltd and at the northern end of Broad Street, Curtiss & Sons, carriers, had transformed three properties into their offices and store.

The Corporation demolished four houses in East Street to improve access to the quay and nine properties in Seager's Court were condemned by the health authority and were too expensive to renovate so were demolished at the end of the nineteenth century. Five dwellings in Camber Alley suffered the same fate.

Furthermore, the lodging houses in Tower Street had ceased to exist, as had others in both Broad and East Streets and there were now far fewer public houses that let accommodation reducing the population in the area still further.
With the reduction in the number of pubs, the ratio of drinking establishments to the residents

was now 1 to 51, a considerable decrease from that of 1 to 35 in 1851.

An analysis of the leading occupations in the area in 1901 showed a remarkable similarity to the figures relating to the total workforce in the 1851 Census.
Although retailing numbers contracted greatly over this 50-year period, some businesses increased. At the turn of the century the number of fish salesmen increased considerably, probably due to the regular early morning fish market held opposite the Still & West pub. There were 12 persons registered in this trade and at least half lived in Bath Square in 1900.

Tales from the nineteenth century on Point

In F.J.Proctor's book, "Reminiscences of Old Portsmouth "published in 1931 he writes of many past customs and the following tales relate to Point and the Camber area:

Cigarettes were taboo; indeed the rope's end awaited lads at home if a fag or nips of tobacco were found secretly stowed away in their pockets. This was the rule, whatever their station in Point society.
However, when a trading vessel from the Dutch ports brought to our Camber a part cargo of shag tobacco, most of our ordinary seafaring men had their pouches bulging, their pipes in full service or their stained teeth chewing quids of shag, the latter usually deposited within the crown of their hats on going ashore.

If a Point boy aspired to be a leader of his companions, he was expected to skate well on the moats during the long sharp winters of those days, to swim at low water across the harbour mouth from the Round Tower to Blockhouse fort, to dive from the Camber Quay, and to box, fence or otherwise qualify for the budding sportsman. The Point mothers, as a rule, bore healthy sons and daughters, whose almost daily exercise in the refreshing sea breezes made sturdy men and women of them.

There were always cosmopolitan characters buzzing around when a trading vessel was unloading in the Camber, in case the last crate of oranges would "accidentally" burst its sides, or a box of Jersey potatoes miraculously collapsed and the contents got scattered, as the privileges of nomads on the loot; for the skipper had handed his little son his oilskin coat to take home, with a bottle of cognac stowed away in the inside pocket or the lining stuffed with choice brands of tobacco. But men were not always the sinners, for women's "bustles" were often bulging at their backs, or their large pockets swollen under their voluminous skirts with smuggled silks from Lyon.

Likewise when a foreign ship arrived at Spithead and sent her boats to the Beef Stage by the side of Victoria Pier to load up with provisions, you could see the quaintest characters, sharp of eye, and as eager as seagulls spotting their prey.

Many years after the cruel sport of bull baiting, which used to occur every Shrove Tuesday in Broad Street opposite the *Blue Posts* had been banned, one of the sports which replaced it was that of catching a greasy pig let loose in Bath Square during regatta festivities. Only boys were allowed to compete and the only way they could secure the prize was by grasping a foreleg with one hand and finger looping the curly tail with the other hand.
Most lads seized the ears or curled their arms around the porkers neck, but this was invariably a failure, for the animal squeaked and struggled until the attackers clothes were smeared with grease and he was bowled over. Thereupon the excited pig tried to escape through the crowd, when women screamed with mingled fear of soiling their long dresses and as a vent for their

hilarious emotions. After poor chooky was pretty well scraped dry with strenuous handling a fortunate competitor managed to get his arms around the belly and triumphantly carried away the wriggling kicking screamer.

The next amusing event was on the beach where a long greasy pole was horizontally strung out with another spliced up vertically with a box at the top containing a Christmas suckling pig.

The adult or lad who could "run" the gauntlet and reach the upright pole, which was smeared profusely with tarry grease, had then to climb up, open the box, seize the squealer, slide down and jump into the sea and swim ashore. If safely landed, little chooky's throat was usually bleeding, a knack pigs have when trying to struggle out of the briny.

When the "duck hunts" were in full swing, the enormous number of pleasure craft extended from Point to Blockhouse and with the latitude given at such joyous festivals, we boys were allowed to cross the harbour by stepping from boat to boat and we got back to Point in the same manner. Of course the Regatta finished up with fireworks. Dancing to a band playing in Bath Square was carried on far into the night, during which the public houses were packed, but although the merrymakers jostled, squeezed, fondled and made assignations, observers even then had learned that kissing lips do not always touch the heart. (c 1850)

The Camber

In Roman times Portsmouth harbour had been a natural shelter for shipping but as ships grew in size Portchester lost its importance and the Camber began to expand its trade.
The small town that grew around the Camber was nourished by the decision of Richard I to develop it as a military base and the next major growth in the late fifteenth/early sixteenth century was the building of a new Dockyard outside the walled confines of the Portsmouth Township at that time.

By the late sixteenth century Portsmouth Point was beginning to be inhabited and was well established by the mid-seventeenth century. As part of this development the Camber became a much busier place.

Trade rapidly grew in the seventeenth century with the import of goods and livestock into the Camber in order to victual the East India Company boats.

Ship building also started in a small way and, of course, numbers of boats grew to deal with the demand for ferrying goods and people to many destinations, both home and abroad.
During the mid to late 18th century many East India Company vessels visited the port and the Camber would have been very busy. In August 1778 there were no less than six East Indiamen laden with tea anchored off Spithead and because of the importance of securing this trade a lookout was often posted in the cupola of St Thomas's church and later at the top of the Baltic Tower in Baltic Wharf.

By 1760 the East India Company had acquired storage and repair facilities in the Camber, Coal was readily imported and it is recorded that there were 15 coal merchants in Portsmouth in the 1780s and 1790s, three of whom lived in the Camber.
In the late 16th century the most frequent arrivals from abroad were vessels laden with wine and brandy from France and Iberia.

The largest group in the Camber in 1799 were the Customs & Excise, many officers employed presumably to curtail the act of smuggling. Some were crews in the revenue cutters that were berthed in the Camber and used along the south coast to apprehend smugglers.

William Burridge, originally a naval agent for Portsmouth had a bank at 13-14 Broad Street. He financed the construction of the Baltic Wharf in the Inner Camber, together with Burridge's tower nearby and became financially involved in some speculative timber contracts that turned out badly. His bank later failed and he reportedly later died in poverty. Baltic wharf was later purchased by the Corporation in 1879 for the sum of £1500.

The Victualling Board's premises on the east side of the Camber were bought by the Customs in 1828 after they moved to the Royal Clarence Yard at Gosport, thereby enabling the Customs to vacate their premises in Broad Street.

The Admiralty claimed control over both the Harbour and the mud in it, so that attempts by the Corporation to develop the Camber could not proceed without Admiralty permission. This was granted only if a thorough inspection by the Yard's naval officers ended in a positive report. It normally followed a rather convoluted procedure in which the Corporation had to agree in writing that there was no challenge to the Admiralty's rights over the Harbour and yet word the statement in such a way as to keep open the Corporation's claim to Harbour rights.

The Camber played a central role in everyday life for people and in 1836 an inventory of imports included the following:

58,862 quarters of grain
30,588 firkins of Irish Butter
19,191 bales of bacon
12,070 lumps and leaves of sugar
8,521 packages of eggs, poultry and apples from France
4,693 boxes of oranges and lemons
1,631 bags of Spanish nuts
2,854 casks of herrings and salt fish

In addition, large quantities of wine and spirits were imported.
Apart from food, other imports included coal, softwood, candles, soap, tallow, tar, slate and cement and most of these materials with the exception of the timber probably originated elsewhere in the UK.

The Camber was a drain on the Corporation's expenditure: in the 1830s it was stated that it was for many years a source of expenditure rather than income, whereas other ports could expect to receive income from rents charged.

In the nineteenth century the Camber saw a number of attempts at improvement, most of which ended in a qualified success. The first significant Camber improvement was undertaken by the Municipal Council some years after their installation in 1835, partly as a repudiation of the restrictive ways of the old Corporation.

Prior to these improvements the Corporation had already discussed the enlargement and repair facilities in the Camber, adding plans for a dry dock which had been drawn up by T. E. Owen. This initiative promoted by the Portsmouth Commercial Dock Co in 1838 did not gain sufficient financial backing to succeed, so was dropped.

Historical view of east side of Camber with sailing vessel alongside.

Initially the project for the Camber improvements was in the hands of a private Docks Company, but in 1839 the Company decided (perhaps because it was having problems raising the funds) to allow the Council to take over.

However, the Camber still had to be improved through a Private Act, which was opposed by the Local Merchants' Association. The Association represented, in effect, those who held existing wharves and stood to lose from competition. Its leading lights were Edward Casher, a wine merchant (1785-1852); William Atfield (1791-1846), a coal and timber merchant who took up wharves at Gosport in protest at the Corporation's tolls; John Lindegren, a shipping broker and importer who had been bankrupted in 1833; Richard Henry Rogers (1788 -?), a coal merchant; and Henry Deacon, a brewer and newspaper owner. Unfortunately for them, they were unable to block the improvements after royal assent was received for the Camber Improvement Act in 1839.

The Camber gained new wharves, was thoroughly dredged and now included a building slip together with new cranes at a cost of £30,000. The slip was rented to Thomas White of Gosport (1796-1863), a member of the famous Isle of Wight shipbuilding family.

After the 1839 improvements, there were demands for the new Council to apply the tolls equally upon all the users of the Camber (previously Burgesses had been exempt), to reduce charges and improve facilities, to keep the rates down in general and to pay only those Council employees who worked for the council.

On completion, the Camber improvements resulted in increased wharfage dues amounting to £4171 in the two years to April 1843.

After the improvement works the accounts were investigated and as a direct result of the discoveries found, the Harbour Master was dismissed for corruption and several Burgesses received claims for unpaid dues.

It was decided that in future, the tolls would not be applied for the use of a select body, but for the general benefit of the public, a proper and equal collection should be enforced.

The introduction of a swing bridge across the narrow entrance to the Inner Camber in 1842 made movement for the local people much easier, entering and leaving Point through Quay Gate to Portsea and Landport rather than having to pass through King James Gate.

However, it would seem from looking at historical records that this bridge caused a lot of problems over the years and although replaced with another bridge in 1906, that bridge was finally removed in 1924, opening up the free movement of water traffic in and out of the Camber with no restrictions.

In 1850 Portsmouth had five gates which historically were closed in the evening until being opened the next day accompanied by the sound of the morning gun. One of these gates, known as Key gate (later rebuilt in monumental style in 1734 as Quay gate) lead to the Town Quay at the Camber.

Key gate, built during the reign of Elizabeth I, is shown on De Gomme's map of 1668 within the fortifications suggesting that a masonry quay existed on the east side of the Camber at that time.
There was a wharf built especially for the use of His Majesty's Victualling store adjacent to Quay gate and the annual rental was £16 in 1730.

Quay gate or King George's gate located on the east side of the Camber.

Quay Gate, which faced the Camber was erected in 1734 in accordance with plans drawn by Inigo Jones and was known also as King George's Gate. It was later demolished in 1883. This very large masonry gate had space for accommodation and one Joseph England, who died in 1937 aged 81, recalled living there with his parents, remembering passes being written out by his parents for those whose duty took them through to town after closing time.

The business of the Camber no doubt increased as a result of improvements but remained largely limited to coal, timber and foodstuffs. Total dues (and rents after 1841) rose significantly in the 1840s (see table below), but the commercial activities of the port remained well below those of neighbouring Southampton.

At the beginning of 1850, for instance, there were 244 sailing vessels with a tonnage of 14,874 registered in Portsmouth while Southampton had 210 vessels of 13,498 tons.

In the more important matter of steam shipping, Southampton had 25 vessels of 2,428 tons and Portsmouth only had 4 with a registered tonnage of 174. In addition, with regards colonial and foreign traffic, Portsmouth did less trade than Southampton or Plymouth, let alone the larger commercial ports such as Bristol.

GROSS INCOME FROM CAMBER DUES AND RENTS   1830 to 1845

	£
1791-93 (annual average)	168
1830-32 (annual average)	1043
1834	1275
1835	1271
1836	1319
1837	1284
1838	1315
1842	2773
1843	3151
1844	3022
1845	3219

Further Camber improvements in the 1850s may have changed the situation slightly, but what is noteworthy is that the Council, despite their intention to let the dock to a private concern, were forced to operate it themselves.

The commercial activities of Portsmouth's commercial port took place on a smaller scale than at Southampton, where the port was dominated by the P & O line and by the Steam Packet Mail.
The mean tonnage of the Portsmouth registered vessels was extremely small and there was still a lasting reliance on sail, rather than steam. Most of the port's traffic was coastal with very little in the way of colonial and overseas traffic.

Supplies for the armed forces (except for servicemen living in the town outside the barracks) were provided by contractors and shipped onto the government quays at Portsea and Gosport.

TONNAGE ENTERING AND CLEARING MAIN SOUTHERN SEAPORTS IN 1849 (excl. LONDON)

	Coastwise	Colonial	Foreign
Portsmouth	129,044	12,810	29,105
Southampton	242,662	21,700	173,482
Plymouth	518,450	43,132	50,547
Bristol	755,133	107,022	99,537

When making comparisons with other commercial ports it must be realised that Portsmouth was primarily a principal naval port with its historic dockyard dominating the harbour geographically and preventing any significant expansion of the Camber area. Most other commercial ports were not restricted in this manner and were able to expand their commercial port activities and subsequently their trade.

The port's commerce tended to conform to a pattern of small scale economic activity and does not appear to have been particularly important as an employer. There were lightermen, seamen and labourers working at the Camber and at Flathouse quay but they did not appear to have been numerous.

It is interesting to examine records of imported goods and vessels visiting the Camber in the 1850s. In September 1853 the goods imported included timber from Southampton, oats from Ireland, potatoes from Havre and potatoes and eggs from Cherbourg. In January 1854 all the visiting vessels were sailing ships such as schooners, brigs, barques, ketches and sloops. Numerous schooners were in port carrying oats from Waterford, Youghal and Cork in Ireland, there were vessels carrying cargoes of stone from Swanage and Guernsey, coals from Sunderland, Shields, Newcastle and Hartlepool, potatoes from Montrose and boats from London with cargoes of general goods aboard. Surprisingly the most common cargo during this particular week was oats: nine vessels with cargoes of oats, all schooners, were either in or due into the Camber.

Regulation of Meters

During the nineteenth century the Corporation adopted the use of meters to ensure that visiting vessels in the Camber paid the correct dues for unloading goods.
The Borough of Portsmouth Byelaws for the regulation of meters dated 1869 stipulated the roles of the meters.

A coal meter had responsibility for measuring or weighing all coal or culm which was landed or shipped on the wharves or quays of the Mayor, Aldermen and Burgesses of the Corporation.
A general meter was responsible for the measuring and weighing of all corn, grain and potatoes in bulk and other articles that need to be measured or weighed.
The byelaws listed the rates of payment or remuneration at that time as being 3d per ton of coal or culm, 1d per quarter for corn and grain and 6d per ton for potatoes and other articles or produce of the like kind.

This money would have been paid initially by the Master of the vessel or owner of the goods to the Chamberlain of the Borough.
Work was not always available and the meters had to attend the office of the Chamberlain six days a week at 9am to see whether their services were needed. It was the duty of a meter to deliver in writing a daily account of the quantity of goods requiring to be weighed or measured.

There were also rules about the conduct of meters and also the penalties the owner of the goods would pay the Corporation for leaving them on the quay, after exceeding the allowed period of time to load them into transport.
Meter's jobs were highly sought after and for example in 1849 when adverts were placed for the appointment of 4 coal meters, 37 candidates applied and for 2 positions as corn meters, 6 applications were submitted.

Sometimes ship captains and owners broke the law when unloading goods in the Camber as they often undertook this work without requesting the services of a Corporation meter. If caught, this resulted in a visit to the magistrate's court, where the perpetrator was heavily fined, and these court hearings were regularly reported on in the local newspapers. In 1879 the Corporation had 28 meters in its employ: it considered this number adequate to cope with demand and therefore believed there to be no valid excuse for illegally weighing or measuring goods being unloaded.

Further expansion

In 1859 construction work on the new Camber dry dock commenced and the first vessel entered this new dock in 1863. This proved to be a very useful facility for carrying out refits and maintenance work on larger vessels.

The vessel "*Nordstern*" in the Camber dry dock in 1864

Throughout its history, ship building firms based in the Camber had built boats of relatively small tonnage, but in the mid-nineteenth century ship building facilities were improving and Thomas White upgraded his patent slip construction work to cope with ships of 3000 tons. However, things ended badly for him and he was declared bankrupt in 1857. John Read took over as the major boatbuilding firm with the largest boat built by him and registered in the port being 125 tons.

The best known Camber boat builder was Messrs Vosper & Co which initially started work in a small engineering workshop backing on to the Camber in 1869. The Company gradually expanded becoming the largest employer in the Camber, based in premises in White Hart Road and Broad Street with substantial facilities to build ever larger vessels. Initially they undertook small contracts building marine steam engines, then petrol engines but then as they grew in size they worked on building and maintaining large vessels. Much work was carried out for the Government.

Vospers yard in the mid-1950s

The size of the Camber and lack of available space to expand was a real drawback: its expansion was prevented by the location of the Gunwharf nearby.
Improvement works continued to be carried out in the Camber and the Inner Camber wharf was extended in 1877, but in the latter part of the nineteenth century the Corporation had a couple of wharf proposals turned down by the Admiralty.

In 1879 the Corporation acquired the Customs House from the Office of Works and later demolished it.

As world trade expanded it was very noticeable that the commercial traffic had reduced in the Camber due to a lack of space and facilities. Furthermore, the Camber, the city's main commercial port had no direct railway facility. Trade was being directed elsewhere due to economies of scale and the use of the railways.

One trade that did expand was that of coal and there were numerous coal merchants based in the Camber area. One Company that grew significantly was Fraser & White, who, in conjunction with the Corporation, was responsible for the demolition of numerous properties in East Street to construct their huge coal bunkers and overhead gantries which existed for many years.

As the years rolled on, facilities in the Camber were improving and in the latter part of the nineteenth century it was reported that to ease the movement of carcasses in the slaughterhouse an overhead monorail was constructed and a gutter built to assist the flow of liquids. A new urinal was built in 1887 together with an adjacent gaslight.

The Camber regularly suffered from siltation and 2,160 tons of mud were dredged out in 1888. In 1894 the new municipal power station was opened and electric lighting was introduced in 1896.

Inner Camber, back of East Street, by M. Snape.

In 1900 the following businesses were based on the Town Quay: Fraser & White (Coal merchants), J.T.Crampton & Co (Coal merchants and ship builders), W.P.Winter & Sons (Builders merchants), S & F Ash (Fruit and Potato merchants), E. Cook (Fruit and Potato merchant), E.G.Whicher (Bonded stores), Batchelor & Sons (Carriers) and Thomas Jas & Co Ltd (Flour merchants). In addition, the Customs House was situated there together with the Weighbridge, Wharfinger and Harbour and Dock Master's office.

At the beginning of the twentieth century, sailing vessels brought cargoes into the Camber from Scotland and France and vessels came from Norway with timber and ice. No ice was made locally at that time and great blocks were brought from the ice fields. Humby & Co were the leading ice merchants based in East Street and these vessels brought on average about 50 or 60 tons a day. The ice blocks were raised out of the hold and pushed down a slide on to the waiting trolleys.

At that time all cargoes were discharged by hand and potatoes and apples were shipped in bulk. Baskets were filled in the hold, emptied into a sack on a low scale and then carried on the backs of the men who walked the plank leading to the quay. Mistletoe and holly were imported from France at Christmas time.

Timber being unloaded in the Camber in the 1930s.

Colliers were unloaded by five gangs of men over a period of two or three days to unload 800 tons of coal. When cranes were later installed 800 tons of coal could be unloaded in 8 hours using machinery that replaced about 50 men.

Crampton's had several sailing colliers running from Newcastle, including a well-known vessel called the *Thorney Island* and general cargos were regularly landed twice weekly from Dublin and London. Some of these boats were too large for the Camber so the cargo had to be unloaded into smaller lighters. Guinness's stout arrived in Irish boats and was later distributed to other south coast ports.

It was being predicted at this time that the days of sailing ships were numbered as they were being slowly replaced by steamers that themselves were being replaced by more modern motor vessels.

In the 1920s the Camber was very busy with colliers regularly arriving with coal from the towns of Goole or Blyth in the north east or from South Wales with cargoes of 1000 tons of coal unloaded by the travelling cranes on the overhead gantries in the Inner Camber, or by the coal handling plant built solely for the Power Station. There were also cargoes of stone from the West Country and Guernsey, cement from Belgium, potatoes from Ireland and Germany and sugar from Kings Lynn. There were slates and tiles mainly from France, and big consignments of flour from London, Ipswich, Cardiff, Liverpool and Swansea.

In 1931 there was 683,000 tons of cargoes dealt with in the Camber. The boats visiting comprised 3753 steamers, 2481 motors, and 693 sailing vessels. These figures included 485 coasters and 244 foreign vessels.

In 1948 the *Pompey Light* was launched, following in the footsteps of her earlier sister ship the *Pompey Power* which had been built in Sunderland for the purpose of carrying coals from Blyth to Portsmouth Camber for use by the Electricity Department in the Power Station.

In the mid-1960s the Camber docks were busy, profitable but outdated. In 1965/66 the annual goods dues amounted to £43,000 and in the mid-1960s the tonnage of freight handled was about 210,000 tons per annum.

It was recognised that because of the difficulty of access, the limited space available and the environmental problems created, the Camber Docks were an anachronism. Since there was little or no possibility for significant expansion or improvement, the Council had resolved to develop a new City Docks complex in the harbour at Mile End to the north of the naval dockyard. By 1966 the work was well advanced and in February 1968 the new quay named Albert Johnson Quay was officially opened with the facilities being leased for the use of Commodore Shipping.

Another review of the port facilities was carried out in the spring of 1968 and further developments were planned for Flathouse and Mile End, including facilities for roll on roll off traffic and it was envisaged that by the mid-1970s all commercial traffic would have been withdrawn from the Camber Docks.

It was announced that the Portsmouth electricity generating station would close down, which it did by 1980, finally ending collier traffic at the Camber and that would leave only Vosper Thorneycroft shipbuilding activity, the Isle of Wight car ferry and the small fishing fleet as users of the Camber Docks.

The Council therefore considered alternative uses for the docks and by late 1970 appointed consultants to undertake a study of the advantages which would accrue from transferring all commercial activities to Mile End and redeveloping the Camber. This resulted in objections from the local fishermen and much discussion about development.

In 1974 the Camber Docks still remained in use, although a large proportion of the trade had been transferred to Albert Johnson and Flathouse Quays.
Commercial trade really began to increase in the north of the harbour with further reclamation works being carried out by the City Council. A new Continental Ferry Port was established with roll on roll off facilities being provided for ferries travelling to and from the Continent and the Channel Islands. These ferries catered for both commercial and leisure traffic.

As a result of all this expansion, the commercial trade in the Camber docks began to diminish and finally ceased apart from the Isle of Wight car ferry and the continuation of the fishing fleet.

The Fishing Fleet

A quay was initially thought to have been built on the mainland side of the Camber in the early sixteenth century and the naturally sloping foreshore in the Inner Camber would have been suitable for grounding vessels such as fishing boats.

It is likely that fishermen began to live on Point shortly after its initial development commenced, since one terrace of properties called Fisherman's Row or Middle Houses (four houses), existed in the middle of Broad Street near the *Old Blue Posts* coaching inn, but this was later demolished in 1771 to allow Broad Street to be widened.

The Camber has had a fishing fleet for centuries and in the mid-eighteenth century tier upon tier of boats lay alongside the dock walls discharging fish with men and boys leaping from deck to deck bearing heavy boxes and sacks as the few derricks available were quite inadequate to deal with the work.

Craft would worm their way through the pack of boats by means of warps and poles and farther out they would be making sail while some of the crew toiled with heavy sweeps to keep them moving. In through the crush would come new arrivals charging down furiously on the crowded ships into the narrow mouth of the Camber and then dropping their sails in a hurry at the last moment, often only just in time to check their way before they became entangled in the medley of outgoing craft. Such situations called for quick decisions and good judgement, but accidents were rare, for these men were splendid seamen.

This photo of the Camber is early twentieth century and portrays the typical crowded conditions showing fishing boats with their sails moored alongside each other.

When trade was bad the small craft turned their attention to fishing, spratting, trawling, drifting, together with oyster and scallop dredging and sometimes the fishermen were not above trying a little smuggling.

Life was hard for those fishermen who ventured farther afield across the Channel to France and the Channel Islands in boats sometimes only 30 ft. in length and often undecked, making them very vulnerable to sinking in heavy weather. These boats were of course totally reliant on their sails and ash sweeps and were crewed by men of real skill and much courage.

They used to tell of occasions when they have had to sit shoulder to shoulder across the stern of their craft and thus form a human bulwark to prevent heavy following seas from "pooping" her. They also told of times when they had to tear up the bottom boards and wedge them with tholepins round her sides in a vain attempt to keep out the lumpy breaking seas which curl up awkwardly in places like the Portland Race or Alderney Race.

Fishing in those days was a very dangerous occupation with no help at hand if they got into trouble and fishermen were often lost in bad storms if caught out at sea. Those men did not rely on charts, compasses or lead lines, but on their natural instinct and were known to boast that they could tell where they were in a fog or by looking over the side.

Many of these old seamen earned no more than three or four pounds a month in spite of all the hardships they endured but seemed happy and contented. The fishermen came from all parts of the south coast and often from France, as Portsmouth was a great market for distributing fish. In the mackerel season the Camber was congested with small luggers hailing from Rye, Hastings, Deal, Newhaven, Shoreham and even the West Country.

A large number of men were also employed in the cattle trade and the vessels engaged in this trade were small schooners and brigantines originally coming from the West Country ports where they were used in the fruit trade. Corunna in Spain was their principal market and they brought the cattle to the Camber where they were slaughtered in a covered enclosure which was sited at the head of the town dock.

The Camber fishing fleet dwindled over the years and by the late 1920s there were only a few small craft, about a dozen left, but the numbers were boosted in the summer with the arrival of the French onion boats from Roscoff.

Today the Camber in-shore fishing fleet is one of the largest on the south coast as far west as Plymouth. In 2016, 23 skipper owned boats fished out of the Camber giving employment to over 40 crew plus 30 non seagoing workers employed by Viviers, the fish market operators located in the Camber. Species landed include bass, mullet, plaice, sole, brill, skate and shellfish and large quantities of cuttlefish have been landed in recent times. 50% of the fish caught are sold to residents, visitors and the catering trade, with the other 50% going to Billingsgate fish market in London.

"Johnson Enterprises" a sales and distribution co-operative also buys the catches of local fishing boats, delivering the fish to restaurants, hotels and the retail trade across the south of England. In 2010 they began opening their very successful weekly fresh fish stalls in villages in Hampshire and Sussex.

Drownings

Throughout the centuries drowning was a real risk to the locals on Point as most people never learned to swim when young and often never learned in their adulthood.

On Point, the danger of falling into the Camber always existed due to all the hazards of a commercial port and small children were allowed to roam free in such a busy area. I can remember in my youth roaming around the Camber unsupervised in the late 1950s: even then it was very busy and I recall incidents of people falling in and being rescued, particularly one occasion when a cyclist and his bike fell into the Camber and he was fortunately rescued still attached to his bike.

Throughout the years there were many drownings of infants and those working on boats in the Camber and alcohol played a major role with many persons falling in and drowning when drunk. The following local newspaper articles were typical of published drowning reports in the nineteenth century:

> In 1825 an infant child of Mr Moore, master mariner residing in East Street, Point, fell into the Camber on Saturday last and drowned.
> On January 28th 1860 an inquest was held at the *Orange Tree* public house on the body of Robert Ball, master of the lugger, *Godine of Lydd*. The deceased had been drinking at the *King*

William beer house, East Street, on Sunday night, the 15th inst. and left that house at eleven o'clock. He was not seen alive afterwards. His widow offered £5 reward for his recovery and a diver was employed in searching the Camber, but could not succeed in finding the body. Two days later a man named Beale, a fisherman, was grappling in the Camber when he succeeded in bringing up the body from almost the same spot as the body of a seaman was found a fortnight previously. Verdict – Accidentally drowned.

On October 7th 1871 William F Gordon, 6 years of age, the son of William Gordon, keeper of the *Camber* beer house, East Street, Point, left his home to go to school and as he did not return home at the usual hour his parents became alarmed and commenced a search for him, circulating handbills and giving information to the police at the various police stations, but nothing could be ascertained about him until 5 days later when a police constable found the body quite dead in the outer Camber where it had evidently been washed in by the tide. It was removed to the parent's house where the doctor upon an examination said that the cause of death was drowning.

The following article from a reader appeared in the Hampshire Telegraph newspaper on January 9th 1864 highlighting the number and regularity of accidents of people falling into the Camber and calling for something to be done to improve the situation:-

LOSS OF LIFE IN THE CAMBER

The statement I shall lay before you, will I trust find a space in your journal and if supported by your powerful influence I have no doubt it may lead to favourable results.

On the night of Saturday 5th January last, a man named Edward Smith belonging to a collier brig discharging at the quay, when crossing a plank to the ship slipped off and was drowned. On the 1st inst. a man named Henry Lingwood belonging to one of the many fishing vessels now in the Camber, when ascending a plank to get on board fell over and was drowned. This man was of steady habits and known to be perfectly sober at the time.

Although 14 persons have fallen into the Camber within the last 12 months, fortunately they are the only deaths to swell the catalogue of the many that have occurred within a few years.

On 13th December 1859 a man belonging to the brig, *Brothers*, of Sunderland was drowned. The beginning of January 1860 two seafaring men were drowned, one of them supposed to be a Prussian, recovered on the 6th. On the night of 15th January 1860 a fisherman named Robert Ball belonging to Newhaven drowned with the body being recovered on the 24th.

On 17th December 1860 a man dressed as a railway porter was found drowned on the patent slipway. On 26th April 1861 a lad belonging to a collier picked up nearly drowned and removed to the Union House. On 9th August 1861 a child drowned near the Camber Bridge, body recovered on 25th.

These have been the fatal results of a few years which have come within my notice. With such a sacrifice of human life, does it not demand a remedy if possible?

This article really highlighted the very large number of deaths from drowning in the Camber at that time and following another accident of a man falling from a plank in 1874 the Corporation carried out some improvements. Proposed works recommended included the deployment of some life saving devices in the area, the appointment of a night watchman and improved maintenance to Corporation equipment such as the planks used by visiting vessels that had ropes and stanchions attached.

However, there was still no night watchman by 1897 and complaints were still being made about the dangerous state of the quay and its chains and stanchions. Reports between 1890 and 1895 indicate that a couple of people a year were still drowning in the Camber. Artificial lighting was also very poor in the Camber for years and even by 1895 the Camber & Docks Committee were still discussing whether to introduce electric lighting around the quays to replace the old gas lamps. It was reported that a lack of lighting still contributed to people falling into the Camber and resulted in deaths. All in all, the quays in the Camber were very dangerous places to be in the eighteenth and nineteenth centuries and the lack of safety facilities were responsible for many deaths throughout the years.

A major accident occurred in 1889 on Point when three men lost their lives when some shear legs collapsed on the Town quay while being used to unload a boat.

Due to there being no cranes on the quay, in 1886 the Corporation erected some tripod shears capable of lifting a weight of 30 tons. At the time of the accident in 1889 these shear legs were being used by the employees of Messrs Read & son who had in hand the breaking up of the vessel *Enchantress* which was berthed in the Outer Camber.

They were being used to lift the boilers, each weighing some 15 tons on to the quay and a heavy chain was slung around the first boiler and fastened to the top by a shackle and pin. The first boiler was safely hoisted on to the ground when it was thought that in order to make room for another, the first one should be tilted over on to its side.

The boiler was again raised but just as the men were pushing it over, the chain around it snapped and the sudden jerk removed the pin from the shackle. This caused the strain to be on one of the legs of the shears for a moment with the result that the upright bent and ultimately broke at the base causing the entire structure to collapse.

A shipwright named James Tubbs was caught by one of the falling columns and was crushed to death and another shipwright was knocked down by the falling gear and died on the way to hospital. Another man also died and several people had miraculous escapes.

There were many people involved in this operation and it must have affected the community badly. The shear legs were repaired in due course after a thorough investigation and later in the year a charitable concert was held locally with all proceeds being donated to the widows and children of the men who tragically lost their lives in the accident.

Living conditions on Point

In the past, living conditions on Point were well-known to be appalling for the poorer people and in the mid-nineteenth century the sanitation in East Street was still primitive as reference is made at that time to the rebuilding of cess pools in the area.

In addition, residents lived close by to premises like slaughterhouses, referred to in this auction advert from a local newspaper in 1818:

> Also for sale, a commodious and lofty SLAUGHTERHOUSE, capable of slaughtering and hanging up twenty oxen at a time with a stage communicating with the Camber of Portsmouth, whereby boats may land and unload as occasion may require, in the occupation of Mr Joseph Reeves, shipping butcher, tenant at will.

This slaughterhouse was listed as being located on the north side of East Street on the Point.

The 1851 census shows 1500 people inhabiting the Point area, excluding military personnel at Point Barracks. The figure is higher than perhaps originally thought at this time and this is due to the very dense housing in some of the Courts in the area. For example, in East Street, there were 11 Courts housing 220 people and the three Courts in Broad Street housed 91 people. The rateable value of £2 for some of these premises in East Street were the lowest in Portsmouth.

A look at a detailed map of 1867 shows East Street and adjacent area and the numerous Alleys and Courts which existed at that time. Although the current modern day street layout has changed little from the main arteries centuries ago, all the smaller Courts and Alleys have long since disappeared.

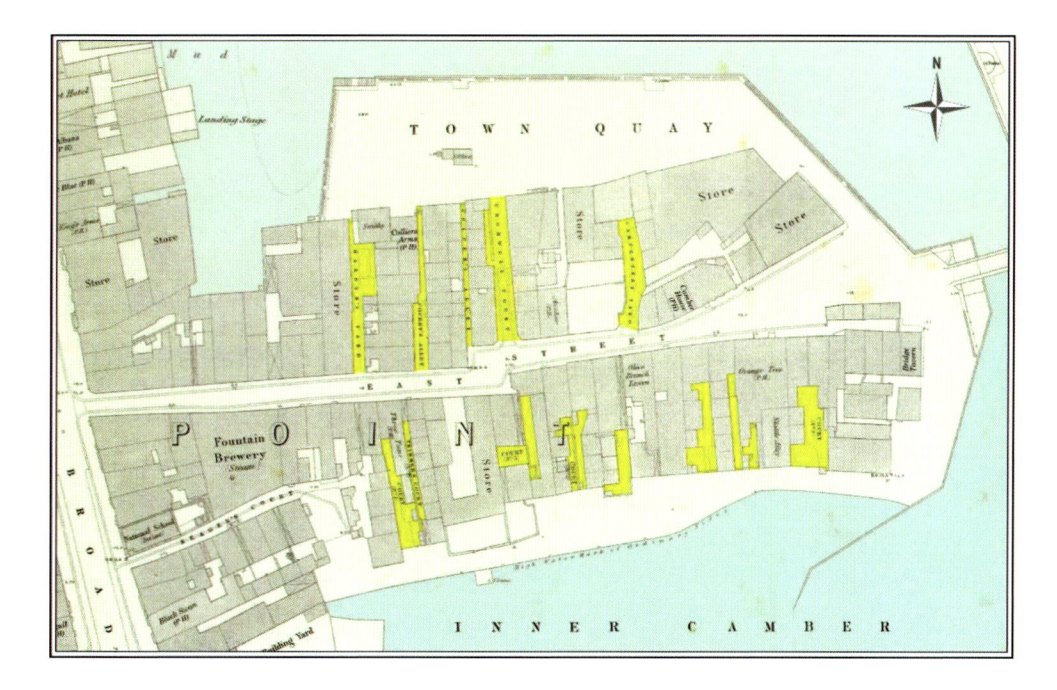

An extract from an 1867 map of Point showing the extensive number of Courts and Alleys.

Passing through Point Gate (King James's Gate) heading north there were a number of Courts on the east side of Broad Street and on turning right into Seager's Court and heading towards the Inner Camber quay there were numerous Courts, including Trimmer's Court. A walk along East Street heading east from Broad Street would find Harbin's Yard, Cockey's Alley, Piper's Alley, Cromwell Court and Carpenter's Yard on the north side of the street and others existed to the south.

It was in these Courts littered around Point, that much of the real poverty and poor living conditions existed, together with all the dense housing in the area of Tower Street which two centuries ago extended south behind 18 Gun Battery, the fortifications behind which Point Barracks were constructed.
Deaths occurred regularly in these areas of poverty where living conditions were sub-standard and sanitation almost non-existent. Diseases such as smallpox, dysentery and cholera were prevalent.

> In 1832 and thereafter for some years, cholera was a periodical epidemic in Portsmouth and in my boyhood days I have occasionally seen chains of men and women extending from the houses in Bath Square and Tower Street to the water's edge handing buckets of salt water along the line to be thrown over the fronts of the houses and squirted on the roofs to cool and purify the air on stifling hot days. The prevalent sickness made the councillors think, and moved the

doctors to action: Point wells were ordered to be repaired and steps immediately taken to hurry on the mooted scheme of drainage. You will realise the unsanitary conditions when you learn that at spring tides the Point boys could row their boats up Broad Street beyond King James gate. (Reminiscences of Old Portsmouth by F.J.Proctor)

The atrocious living conditions in Courts where there was no running water and only outside shared toilets, were reflected in the fatalities during the cholera outbreak in 1848-1849. Between July and October 1849 there were 4 deaths in Broad Street with 95 houses, but 9 deaths in East Street with 50 houses. Tower Street was even worse recording 10 deaths from 33 houses. To put all this in perspective one has to look at the High Street, a very affluent area, where they suffered 2 fatalities from 151 houses.

East Street was described by an official enquiry as "a long narrow dirty thoroughfare intersected by close and ill ventilated Alleys and Courts." There were few privies and chamber utensils were emptied into the Camber. Tower Street was densely populated with houses of the worst description. The population was mixed consisting of fishermen, prostitutes, denizens of low lodging houses and others of a similarly depraved character. Indeed there may have only been 3 properties rated at £2 in Tower Street but some 55 people were residing in two small lodging houses there in 1851.

Photograph c 1861, taken from the Harbour, shows the very dense housing near Tower Street

Certainly in those days it was not uncommon for people to live in such dreadful conditions next to professional people living in far better conditions.

In 1849 the Council debated at length how to improve the state of the mud and filth in the Camber exposed at low water and after much discussion it was proposed to clean off the surface material from the mud. It was of course realised that this would only be a temporary measure and the real problem was that much of Portsmouth's drainage ended up in the

Camber and the town's drainage system needed to be improved and extended to resolve this totally unsatisfactory situation.
At this time some drainage existed in Portsea, Old Portsmouth, Southsea, Landport and Buckland with outfalls into the sea from Landport, Portsea and Southsea. However, the only form of drainage was from ditches which gathered both surface and waste water.

In addition to the intolerable smell emitting from the Camber, the system of moats infrequently flushed and neglected by the military authorities had become an unofficial rubbish tip and common sewer and the stagnant waters was also a great offence to the inhabitants especially in the summer months.

With the appalling lack of sanitation facilities throughout the country the Sewage and Drainage of Towns Act 1845 was introduced and the following paragraph was included in its preamble:

> Whereas it has of late been made apparent that the Sewerage and Drainage of the Towns and populous Districts of the Realm, and the supply of water for the domestic use of inhabitants, and for the due cleansing of drains, are extremely defective or utterly neglected, especially in the districts chiefly inhabited by the poorer classes of Her Majesty's subjects, whereby excessive disease and great mortality have been occasioned.

The passing of this Act marked the beginning of progress in public health and sanitation in Portsmouth. Prior to the introduction of this Act, the local commissioner for Portsmouth's sanitary authority provided evidence to the General Board of Health in 1848 and some of his comments were as follows:

> The crying evil with regard to the drainage of the whole borough is the entire refuse drainage must pass over the surface, the fall of the surface gutters is but small and therefore the passage of the water is very sluggish and during the summer months the stench from these gutters is frequently intolerable. It may be difficult in underground drainage to take the run from all the sewers but there is no difficulty whatever to constructing underground drains which shall wholly prevent this intolerable nuisance.
> There is no general system of sewers laid down outside the garrison walls; one privy serves for several houses and at times for a whole row of houses. Some of these rows of houses or cottages have wells and privies so close that when the water is pumped out of the well it lowers the water in the cesspools of the privies and in these districts fever is often a regular occurrence.

In addition to the lack of sanitation, the roads, in the most part, had never had any form of pavement and in consequence the streets worked up into quagmires, almost impassable to wheeled vehicles. There was an urgent need of street pavements, drains and lights.

The specification of works required to be executed in the city included a general system of underground drainage, a full and complete water supply, constant at high pressure, proper lighting, provision of suitable paving to all courts, yards, passages and streets with some firm of artificial surface capable of being easily cleansed and resisting wear. However, it took 15 years until 1863 before the Local Government Act of 1858 was adopted by the Borough Council.

Following the appointment of a Borough Engineer, a well-constructed drainage scheme was submitted to and approved by the Council in 1864.

Construction works began in 1865 and by 1870 high and low level drainage systems existed in the south of Portsea Island extending across the island from west to east with a pumping station at Eastney and outfalls at Langstone harbour entrance and into Portsmouth harbour at the Camber and north of the Dockyard. Other lateral drains had also been built in Southsea, Landport, Buckland and Stamshaw.

Further drainage improvements were made throughout the city during the next century and it is very interesting and heartening to note the gradual annual decrease in the death rate due to poor sanitation and living conditions following the implementation of these drainage works.

In mid-Victorian times the poor houses were badly built back to back and the ground floors were very damp and Point suffered from tidal flooding in some areas.

The old properties were always in a state of filth and bad repair with their cellars, in which people often lived in soaking conditions, either with water filtering in from land soaks or springs, or worse still, from the overflow of nearby privies from which there were no drains to carry it off.

Everywhere there were Courts and many of these were closed at both ends and approached by covered passages and in them the filth flooding from the privies and the refuse thrown by the inhabitants accumulated. In some there was only a single tap and a single privy to serve 60 people. Water supply was a real problem and often people collected water in butts if they had room, or bought it from travelling water carts.

Sometimes, parents turned their children out on to the streets to fend for themselves as they couldn't look after them: during one week in 1872 no fewer than 13 children were found wandering the streets in a destitute state and this would have been typical of Point in the very poor areas. In April 1853 there was great pressure being put on the government to introduce a Public Health Act to improve the living conditions for many tenants living in appalling conditions throughout the country.

Piper's Alley (left) and Tower Street by M.Snape.

One local man, a small tenement proprietor, Mr Levy, was a very vocal opponent of this Public Health Act and the local newspaper published the following article in 1853 describing the area where he owned his property:

> The locality of Trimmer's Court in East Street was visited and it contained 8 houses. The Court was very small and narrow and there were 40 persons residing in the eight houses which had access to two privies. There was an intermittent supply of water from one tap and for this each house pays one shilling per quarter.
> On the opposite side of the street is an Alley called Cockey's Alley where a couple of houses were each paying 2 ½ d per week which was nearly three times as much as would be paid under the Public Health Act. Next to this Court was Harben's Court and it is quite impossible to describe the dirty aspect of this Court. It must be seen to be fully appreciated. The inhabitants were loud in their complaints about the dirt and filth and the absence, or rather the abominable character of the necessary convenience.
> Although Mr Levy's tenants said he was a good and kind landlord they would be far better off if the Public Health Act was introduced.
> Should this be the case, the residents of Trimmer's Court would enjoy a constant supply of water, cess pools would be filled up and proper drainage installed and the residents of both Cockey's Alley and Harben's Court would be much better off. Unfortunately, Mr Levy had assisted by every means in his power to propagate exaggerated statements regarding the working of the Act and had done more than any other man in the Borough to mislead the uneducated public mind.

In 1860 the inhabitants of East Street signed a petition complaining of the serious nuisance occasioned by the large number of cattle and sheep killed at the Commissariat slaughterhouse in East Street which threatened to seriously affect the health of the residents there. In addition the driving of so many cattle through the narrow street, the thoroughfare leading to the Floating Bridge, was highly dangerous.
Sometimes animals went astray whilst crossing the Camber Bridge to the Commissariat cattle yard and one instance refers to an ox that had sprang from the quay, a distance of 8 or 10 feet into the water and was eventually lassoed and towed to safety.

The petition was submitted to the Corporation for consideration. It was felt that an extensive slaughtering business such as this should be carried on outside the town and away from the inhabitants, particularly in such a densely populated area as this. The Council committee agreed to send a letter to the Commissariat department asking them to take steps to remove the nuisance. A year later in 1861 the following article appeared in the local newspaper:

> The slaughter houses in East Street, Point, now in use by the Government are still a continued and unabated nuisance to the inhabitants of this district. So great a source of evil in their existence in this densely populated locality that not only the inhabitants, but the Commissioners themselves also have brought the subject under the notice of the proper authorities. Medical men testify to their noxious effects in poisoning the air and breeding disease in the very centre of the garrison. We sincerely trust that the War Department will take immediate steps for the removal of these slaughter houses outside of the town. Surely some site may be found where the refuse may be easily and readily washed into the sea without polluting the air and making this Commissariat establishment so dangerous to the health of the inhabitants.

There were still health problems in East Street in 1893 and residents were again complaining of the unhealthy state of affairs here which would not be acceptable to residents elsewhere in the city. The disease referred to was that of typhoid and complaints were made about the stoppage in the drains in East Street for some while resulting in an accumulation of stagnant stinking water extending half way across the street.

In time, these properties in the Courts bordering East Street were demolished, some because they were unfit for human habitation and others to allow for the construction of the very large coal bunker belonging to Fraser & White and also for the building of the commercial sheds to store goods unloaded from commercial vessels visiting the Camber.

This photo of the Camber in the 1920s shows the very large concrete coal bunkers of Messrs Fraser & White which were constructed circa 1914 following the demolition of much poor quality housing in East Street.

Changing times on Point

By 1950, life on Point had changed significantly following the loss of many buildings by bombing raids in World War 2. There were numerous bomb sites in the area and there were very few commercial properties remaining. There were only 5 pubs left on Point: the *Still & West* and *Coal Exchange* in Bath Square, the *Union* and the *Seagull* in Broad Street and the *Bridge Tavern* in East Street.

There was Grogan's café and other dining rooms sited opposite each other in Broad Street, together with a newsagent. The other commercial enterprises were W.G.Lucas & Son, sailmakers, together with the smaller boat builders, Clemens and G. Feltham in Broad Street and H. Feltham in Bath Square. Vospers, ship builders were a major force in the Camber, together with Fraser & White, the coal merchants with their very large coal bunker and overhead gantries for unloading the colliers that berthed nearby.

Times were changing fast and during the next ten years the Floating Bridge to Gosport had ceased operations and a large area of the land at the northern end of Broad Street on the east side had been cleared to enable a new Isle of Wight car ferry terminal and slipway to be built. As a result, Broad Street became far less crowded with little or no traffic queuing for the ferries. Coasters and colliers were still trading in the Camber, which continued to be a busy place, but the future of this trade was in doubt and would gradually cease in the coming years as all this commercial traffic would move north in Portsmouth Harbour to the Commercial port at Flathouse.

Point, with its charm and wonderful waterside views, has always been a magnet for tourists and continues to be so today. Its attraction has been recently enhanced by the project to open up and decorate the arches of Point Barracks to allow different handicraft artists to operate there.
In addition, the construction of the very large Land Rover Bar America's Cup building has also proved a big draw, particularly when their fast looking multi-hulled boats are being launched or retrieved from the Camber, or when political heavyweights or members of the Royal family are paying a visit.

Today, the Point and Camber is a very different place compared to yesteryear when it was a very working class area with streets filled by men working on the many marine related jobs of the day, be they stevedores, shipwrights, watermen, ship chandlers, sailmakers etc. In addition, of course, Point was a very popular place with the crews of both merchant ships and the Royal navy.

Living conditions on much of Point were appalling and flooding was a regular occurrence suffered by many, but today modern flood defences have been installed significantly reducing the risk of flooding. Most of the properties today are relatively modern, very expensive and local characters are in short supply.

The loss of shipping from the Camber, together with overland coach travel and ferries, removed much of the heart and soul from the area, but one of the greatest losses was the gradual disappearance of the long established family names. A number of working class families used to be very numerous on Point, with names such as Butcher, Feltham, Taw, Coote, Cotterill, Hooper and many others, all being associated with the sea and they are now lost for ever.

These families and many more were the life blood of Point for generations with their children growing up on Point and they formed a significant part of its fabric. In past times those children raised on Point often married into other local families and remained on Point during their lives and the men probably entered a marine trade of some description.

As the twentieth century progressed, more opportunities arose for people to live and work elsewhere and this situation, coupled with the loss of available housing in the area and rising house prices, contributed to members of well-established families moving away from the area.

Today, there is much new blood on Point and the area still continues to be a busy vibrant place, but in a much different way to the past. Hopefully, it will continue to be a desirable place for both its residents and visitors for years to come and will add to its colourful history throughout the twenty first century and beyond.

Chapter 2

Fraser & White

One organisation that was associated with Spice Island – and particularly the Camber - for more than 100 years was Fraser & White. They were well-known coal merchants that had their own vessels and a very large coal bunker and overhead gantries that unloaded coal from colliers berthed alongside the quay in the Inner Camber.
The company had a very visible presence on Point and affected the lives of its residents for many years with their importation and distribution of coal.

Fraser & White limited was founded in 1846 at a time when coal was brought by sea to Portsmouth in sailing ships and discharged in baskets by hand. These methods soon became inadequate and increasing demands caused by the development of Portsmouth and its district led to improvements being implemented. By the middle of the century Fraser & White had established the importation of sea borne coal on an organised basis.

In 1859 they were recorded as being coal merchants on Portsmouth quay and in 1865 listed as being coal factor and merchants, agents for Western Fire, Life and Annuity office at the Quay and at King Street Southsea. It is interesting to note in the advert below, taken from a local newspaper in 1871, that Fraser & White also had stores in Broad Street together with premises in the Camber and at the Green, Gosport.

```
PORT OF PORTSMOUTH.
DAMAGED GOODS ex DUTCH S. S. WILLEM III.
    FOR THE BENEFIT OF ALL CONCERNED.
KING & KING are instructed by Capt. Oort, of the
    above ship, to SELL by AUCTION, at Messrs.
Fraser & White's Stores, Broad-street, and the New Dock,
Camber, on Friday next, 23rd June, 1871, at Twelve
o'clock precisely,—
      THE FIRST PORTION OF THE SALVAGE,
                   consisting of
                MANCHESTER GOODS,
in calicos, prints, &c., small quantity of beef, pork, and
preserved provisions, sails, rope, &c., all more or less
damaged by fire and water.
      Further particulars may meanwhile be had of
            MESSRS. VANDENBERGH & SON,
                        Dutch Consuls, Portsmouth,
   or of the Auctioneers, 180, Queen-street, Portsea.
```

In 1867 it was reported that the Fraser & White brig *Elizabeth Ray* was launched, having had extensive alterations carried out at White's slipway in the Camber. The vessel was originally built for "Ray & Sons", and was registered in London. Initially 160 tons and 84ft in length, she was then lengthened by Whites to 100 ft. with an increased tonnage of 199 tons. She was used to carry coal and although later sold on by Fraser & White, she was lost near Middlesbrough in 1894 whilst sailing between Hartlepool and Portsmouth with a cargo of coal under her new ownership.

One problem that Fraser & White frequently suffered from was that of people trying to steal coal from the company and numerous prosecutions were undertaken over the years. For example, in 1873 a man was sentenced to 21 days in prison with hard labour for stealing 1 cwt of coals from the company and this sort of theft was regularly reported in the local newspapers.

In circa 1881 the company had property in East Street, being registered as coal merchants, with their premises being at 56 East Street near the *Bridge Tavern* Public House.

Shortly after this in 1896 they still had these premises together with a coal store at 23 East Street adjacent to the *Blue Anchor* Public House.

In 1887 the local newspaper published a report that Messrs Fraser & White are importing the celebrated Caradoc Wallsend Coals from Durham, the same as those being used by Her Majesty the Queen at Osborne. The coals were advertised as being available at Portsmouth, Fareham, Gosport and in the surrounding district.

An interesting article appeared in the local newspaper in December 1889 referring to a new Portsmouth industry producing a cheap fuel at that time:

> Messrs Fraser & White, coal merchants of The Portsmouth Town Quay have just introduced a new industry into the Borough, which besides employing a number of work people will enable the poorer classes to obtain really excellent fuel in small quantities and at a very reasonable rate.
>
> It is a well-known fact that the waste on coal from the time it reaches the store of the merchant until it gets into the cellar of the consumer is 10%. That is to say, on every thousand tons delivered from the ship there is a residue of small dust coal to the extent of 100 tons. In an extensive business such as that carried out by Messrs Fraser & White, the accumulation of this small and dust coal after screening and the loss is proportionally heavy and to date the firm have been content to sell it to gas companies at any price the latter have chosen to offer.
>
> For a long time past the problem as to how this waste coal could be utilised has puzzled coal merchants all over the country, until recently a Dover coal merchant, Mr Mowil, has together with a marine engineer, Mr Messenger of Chatham, succeeded in perfecting a briquette making machine.
> Fraser & White have just secured the rights for Portsmouth and the surrounding district and Isle of Wight from the Universal Patent Fuel Machine and Manufacturing Company Limited who have the patent rights to the machine.
>
> They have erected a machine in their East street store which is driven by a powerful engine capable of driving other machines as the necessity for erecting them arises.
>
> The machine occupies a space 8 feet in length by 4 feet in breadth and almost 6 feet in height. The fine coal is received on the floor of a loft above the machine. There is a small mortar mill in which pitch is ground to a fine powder; this is mixed with the coal in the proportion of one of pitch to nine of coal.

> The mixture is well turned over then fed down a hopper and is stirred by revolving blades and then a steam jet is percolating the mass of coal and pitch to attain the right plasticity.
> The mixture is then forced into a mould and the ejector following up the operation pushes the fully formed briquette out of the machine.
>
> The briquettes are taken away to dry and to be stacked in piles and measure 4 ½ ins long by 2 ½ ins square which is a more convenient size for ordinary domestic use than that of the old style of briquettes to which we have been accustomed.
>
> They give off a beautiful bright flame, burning indeed better than the blocks of coals themselves and the embers remain in full glow for such a long time that fresh blocks put on will quickly light up and a good fire can be renewed.
>
> The machine is capable of turning out 1500 briquettes per hour, but it has been impossible to satisfy the great demand for them by hawkers and others who have readily sold them at five for a penny.
>
> The blocks are just as suitable for consumption in the mansion as in the cottage and there is no doubt that when Messrs Fraser & White open up the household trade with them, further means of production will be found imperatively necessary.

In 1894 Fraser & White complained to the Corporation about the inadequate accommodation for shipping at the Town Quay. They quoted a steamer named the *Danebill* that had arrived in the port with 1050 tons of coal aboard and they also had the steamer *Perseverance* carrying 1250 tons due, so requested notification as to where to berth her.

The problem was that, because of insufficient depth of water in the Inner Camber at low water, all operations would have to cease when loading barges between two ships. The only response they received from the Corporation was that there would be no berth available until a berth in the Outer Camber was vacated. This was obviously not an ideal situation and was a problem that was to cause the Corporation much concern throughout the years, until improvement works, including dredging were carried out in the Inner Camber.

In the second half of the nineteenth century the company owned numerous vessels, including coal hulks, brigs and ketches and other sailing craft and later screw colliers, as engines became more acceptable and cost efficient for the transportation of coal. The company also chartered vessels from other companies.

In 1889 it was reported that the screw collier, the *Bruges,* chartered to Messrs Fraser & White had unfortunately collided with the plates of the Camber bridge. This resulted from her running aground whilst trying to manoeuvre as she left her berth but as the tide rose she heeled over and caused the damage. The vessel suffered some minor damage but after she had floated off and got clear she proceeded on her passage.

One sad story relating to a chartered vessel occurred in 1890. In that year a mysterious wreck was discovered off the Nab lightship and it turned out to be that of the *Anna Helena,* a schooner on its way to Portsmouth with a cargo of coal for Messrs Fraser & White. She had a crew of seven hands and three bodies were discovered floating in the vicinity. Divers' reports suggested she had been in a collision.

Advert posted in 1897 Local Commercial Directory.

The following newspaper article published in May 1906 in the Evening News about an incident involving a barge confirms that Fraser & White had their own vessels trading coal locally at that time:

WRECK OF A BARGE

PORTSMOUTH VESSEL OVERWHELMED
NARROW ESCAPE OF TWO MEN

The barge *Hope,* belonging to Messrs. Fraser and White of Portsmouth and bound for Nutbourne with a cargo of coal was overwhelmed in the surf at the entrance to Chichester Harbour on Monday night. The loss of the *Hope* was very similar to the wreck of the *Edith* and several other vessels at the same spot.
In fine weather without a breath of wind, but slightly inclined to fog, the boat arrived off the mouth of the harbour shortly before 9 o'clock. Almost without warning a heavy ground swell got up. The first of the seas threw her on the banks and the next swept her deck cargo overboard.
The two men who constituted the crew, Alfred Clarke from the Camber and Edward Dunn of Derby Road, Stamshaw immediately got into their boat which capsized in the surf. Two young men who were fortunately on the beach at the time rushed into the sea to their rescue, Meredith Twine of East Stoke Hayling and William Clements, nephew of Mr George Miller, coxswain of the Hayling lifeboat. Clarke, who was caught under the boat was rescued by Twine, but his companion had been thrown out into the surf with several turns of the boat's painter around his legs and in this position he was being carried off the beach by the back set when Clements pulled him out of the water.
The *Hope* is now on the beach, but being an old vessel, she will not be refloated, although some of her cargo may be saved.

This article certainly demonstrates what a dangerous place the entrance to Chichester Harbour could be in certain unfavourable weather conditions. By 1909 the company owned offices in East Street, together with 4 cottages, Ash's store (former coal merchants), other land nearby, stables in Warblington Street, cottages in Cockey's Alley off East Street and had also purchased the *Sir Charles Napier*, formerly a beer house, in East Street.

At Gosport they owned offices, stables and four houses adjoining a store in Mount Street and on the water they had 8 open barges, the hulk *Alarm* and their horses were stabled at Portsmouth, Fareham and Gosport. The company also owned a Briquette works.

Some of the typical expenses paid out for running the company included costs for wharfage, towage, meterage, carter's wages, fodder, labour, stable expenses and other normal business costs.

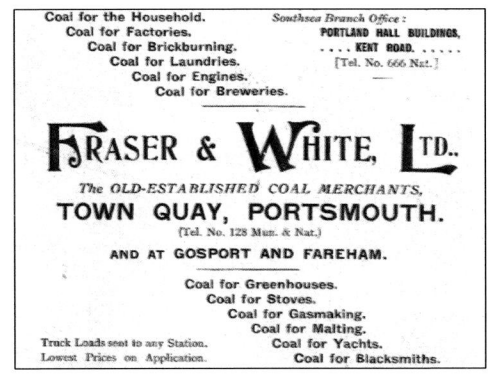

Advert posted in 1910

At the annual meeting of the Company in 1914 the Chairman referred to the necessity for introducing up–to–date methods for the handling of coal and stated that a scheme for the rapid discharging of steamers by electrical transporters was in the process of being carried out. In the same year their premises were recorded as being located at 26 – 52 East Street as coal stores, together with an office at 23 East Street on the opposite side of the road.

It was about this time that the large coal bunkers were constructed and overhead gantries and cranes installed to unload from the colliers that berthed alongside the wharf in the Inner Camber.

The concrete coal bunker near the quay with the overhead gantries.

When the coal bunker was in operation there was a weighbridge and its operating office was built into the wall of the silo.

Early in the twentieth century the company continued to develop, introducing the appropriate equipment for handling coal with large steerage space at the Camber. In 1916 retail coal sales for the company at Portsmouth totalled £24,000, Gosport £3,300 and Fareham £2,650 and there were at least 5 sailing barges and sea going lighters on their books.

At this time they were also trading to the Isle of Wight with offices in East Cowes, Whitwell, Newport and Yarmouth.

After World War One the plant was modernised and further expanded to cope with increased business, both wholesale and retail. Wharves were opened at Fareham, Gosport and the Isle of Wight and a rail borne depot was also established at Fratton Station.

This photo taken in East Street circa 1920 shows Fraser & White coal carts and those of other local companies queuing up to load coal from their depot. The building on the right with the man leaning against it may well be the *Anchor* Public House.

In 1921 Fraser & White purchased a three-masted double topsail schooner named the *Belmont*. She was re-registered as the *Camber* and was later stripped down to become a coal hulk. After long service with the company she was broken up and disposed of in 1944.

By 1922 their plant included Foden steam wagons, Sentinel wagons and Dennis wagons and at that time retail coal sales at Portsmouth totalled £38,000, Gosport £4,300 and Fareham £4,500. They had also expanded, taking over the well-established firm of J. T. Crampton and Co, coal merchants at the Town Quay, who were one of the forefathers of the coal trade in Portsmouth, being already established when Fraser & White opened their business in 1846.

Prior to this date the two companies had worked side by side in friendly rivalry until up-to-date methods of handling and distribution triumphed and the newer firm absorbed its rival.

The overhead plant of Fraser & White at this time was capable of discharging 1000 tons of coal during a tide instead of in two to three days.

By 1923 the company had sold its Isle of Wight assets to a company called Jolliffe Bros Ltd and these assets were at Brading, East Cowes, Newport, Ryde, Shanklin, Ventnor and Yarmouth.
In 1924 it was listed in their accounts that branches existed in Lymington and Cosham in addition to Gosport and Fareham and trading was still very buoyant to the Isle of Wight.
Retail coal sales at Portsmouth totalled £29,500, Gosport £10,200 and Fareham £9,200.

It was reported at that time that although there was little difference in the ultimate price of waterborne coal in comparison to that brought by rail, a far greater proportion of the money paid in handling and discharging was circulated locally, thus benefitting the local area more directly.

In the 1920s, 1930s and 1940s Fraser & White were one of the largest suppliers of fuel on the south coast with coal arriving at the Camber from the coal fields of South Wales, the North East and elsewhere and the Camber coal bunkers were capable of storing 15000 tons of coal.

In 1934 Fareham wharf was modernised and in 1938 the new head office building at Quay House in Broad Street Portsmouth was opened.
During World War Two the shipping department was busily engaged as agents for the Ministry of War Transport and was responsible for arranging supplies, organising repairs and bunkering for the many merchant ships using the port.

As Lloyd's agents this department still had busy demands upon its services and handled the ships of all the principle owners using the port. Quay house was badly damaged during the Blitz and whilst the rebuilding of the main structure was carried out in 1942, it was not until after the war that the interior of the building was reinstated.

Conveyor truck

Steam truck circa 1930 used to deliver coal to areas outside the immediate Portsmouth area.

Coal merchants inside the Fraser & White coal bunker loading up for local deliveries.

The former pictures show the activity and some of the plant used to handle the coal which would be unloaded from the colliers. There were different grades of seaborne coal, including house, slack etc. and coal dust was supplied to local hospitals for use in their furnaces.

By 1942 the company's assets included Quay House, their headquarters at 62-70 Broad Street, workshops at 52-54 Broad Street and general stores at 82-84 Broad Street, with an oil store at Seager's Court and garage, tyre store and stables in Lombard Street.

Quay House was the embarkation area HQ for the Portsmouth Sector during the D Day operation planning in the Second World War. It had the role of co-ordinating the loading of troops on to the ships at the four main Portsmouth embarkation sites, one of which was the nearby Camber quay.

This operation named "Operation Neptune" was part of "Operation Overlord" and was the first phase of the amphibious invasion and establishment of a secure foothold for Allied troops in France.

Due to the number of Allied troops involved on D-Day, it took several days to load them on to the ships and landing craft that would take them to Normandy. This was done according to a detailed timetable which was the result of a huge amount of planning. To prevent congestion and delays, troops were held at camps to the north of Portsmouth, only moving down to the embarkation points at the appointed time.

During the war the company also had offices at Westbourne, a retail office at Fratton Station and coal order outlets at London Road, Southsea, Havant and Littlehampton.
Extensive holdings existed at Fareham, Gosport and Lymington where there were wharfage facilities, weighbridges, offices and stables.

However, as more mechanisation was adopted the number of horses reduced and by 1942 there were only 4 heavy draught horses based at Lombard Street with the names, *Turpin, Duke, Punch and Blossom*. At Fareham there was only one horse and none recorded at the other branches.

Plant at Portsmouth totalled 20 vehicles (2 - 4 tonne) including Dodge tipping vehicles (hand and engine operated) Bedford steel sided lorries, Scammel mechanical horse and trailer, Dodges and Fordson 4 yd. shingle tippers. The equipment at the other branches was much less with smaller capacity plant.

In 1940 Fraser & White Limited which had its interests at that time mainly in the Portsmouth area, joined with JR Wood and company Ltd which was based in Southampton to form a coal distributing unit covering the area of Portsmouth, Southampton, Bournemouth and the Isle of Wight.

As part of this initiative the company acquired the use of a further wharf at Rudmore and a rail borne depot was established at Fratton Station.

The Company's shop located in Broad Street near West Street circa 1953.

During the next few years other major coal distributing companies, particularly in Sussex and Kent, joined the new group. The new organisation was called Associated Coal & Wharf Companies (ACW Group), but all these old established companies formed by families continued to trade until 1962 under their individual company names.

The main interest for all these companies has been the shipping of coal mainly from Northumberland and Yorkshire but also from South Wales to ports along the south coast and the discharging, preparation and resale of this coal to other members of the coal trade and also to the public.

During the 1950s the group became the sole distributor for Mobil fuel oils to this area and this oil trading business became an increasingly important part of the group's activities.

Advert for new coal fires in 1952

In 1954 the company started selling fuel oil to a supply terminal that was built at Tipner and this was followed in 1959 by a larger marine terminal at Twyford wharf.

As individual companies joined the family, it was obvious that this new organisation would have to introduce their own particular approach to the problem of fuel distribution as time went by and eventually it was made clear to the public the link between the various individual companies which has in fact existed for many years.

In 1962 a fleet of 700 coal lorries and fuel oil tankers were introduced at over 100 different trading points displaying a new name, Corralls. It was under this name that Fraser & White Ltd of Quay House Portsmouth commenced trading in October 1962.

The reason for the change was the general streamlining of the ACW Group, which was one of the country's largest fuel distribution organisations whose operations covered six of the southern counties of England and the Isle of Wight. In order to improve the efficiency of the group a reorganisation was proposed to divide the newly formed company Corralls Ltd into two main divisions, one for wholesale, industrial coal and the oil fuel business and one for retail.

The most able directors were put in charge of these divisions, each of whom had a specialist knowledge in his own particular field.

Corralls Ltd undertook all the coal and fuel oil trading and fuel discharging which had until that time been carried out by 10 existing ACW subsidiaries under separate names.

Quay House, Corralls Company headquarters in Broad Street.

During the 1950s and 1960s Fraser & White owned a fleet of 17 vessels consisting of the ex-Admiralty tugs *Industrious* and *Zealous*, the crane dredger *Lypta* and 14 barges that worked in the Solent area and Portsmouth harbour.

The tug *Industrious* berthed in the Inner Camber alongside a barge fully laden with coal ready for transportation.

The tug *Zealous* alongside a barge being loaded in the winter of 1963 when the Camber froze over.

The *Industrious* in the Outer Camber with what looks like the *Lypta* ahead moored in Dirty Corner.

The *Industrious* with the *Zealous* alongside.

The two photos above appear to show a company day out with staff and families on board.

The *Lypta*, whilst undertaking dredging operations, would find an amazing assortment of items whilst dredging silt or shingle, including cannon balls, automatic pistols, ancient and extinct sea shells, old clay pipes, trees from primeval forests, wreckage from sunken ships, bits of bomb casings and occasional live lobsters. She was built in 1891 for the Manchester Ship Canal Company and later purchased by Vectis Transport, Newport, Isle of Wight, before being bought by Fraser & White in 1953.

The two tugs carried out all sorts of tasks in addition to towing the barges and their normal cargos of coal or shingle, including off beat jobs such as towing Admiralty surplus vessels to Pound's yard at Tipner for eventual re-sale and also undertaking the ritual of burial at sea.

The bread and butter job of the two tugs was to tow coal barges to the shallow water wharves at Fareham and Gosport from the trans-shipment point in the Camber. Both these wharves relied entirely on the barges for the supply of house coal and deliveries could only be made at high water.
They also towed barges containing bunker coal for the Isle of Wight steamers.

The *Lypta's* prime role was to keep these two wharves, together with the two deep water wharves at the Camber and Rudmore, free of siltation. Coal deliveries were made by barge to Newport in the heart of the Isle of Wight and other cargoes were also transported from Portsmouth to Newport.

Lypta working at anchor

Raising the grab

Cargo of pipes for the Isle of Wight

Barges at Upper wharf, Fareham

Barge under tow

Dredging underway

Typical maritime operations carried out by the Company.

When transporting coal to Fareham the route ran past the Dockyard, through the Reserve fleet and up the Wallington River. In such confined waters the barges were lashed alongside and not towed.

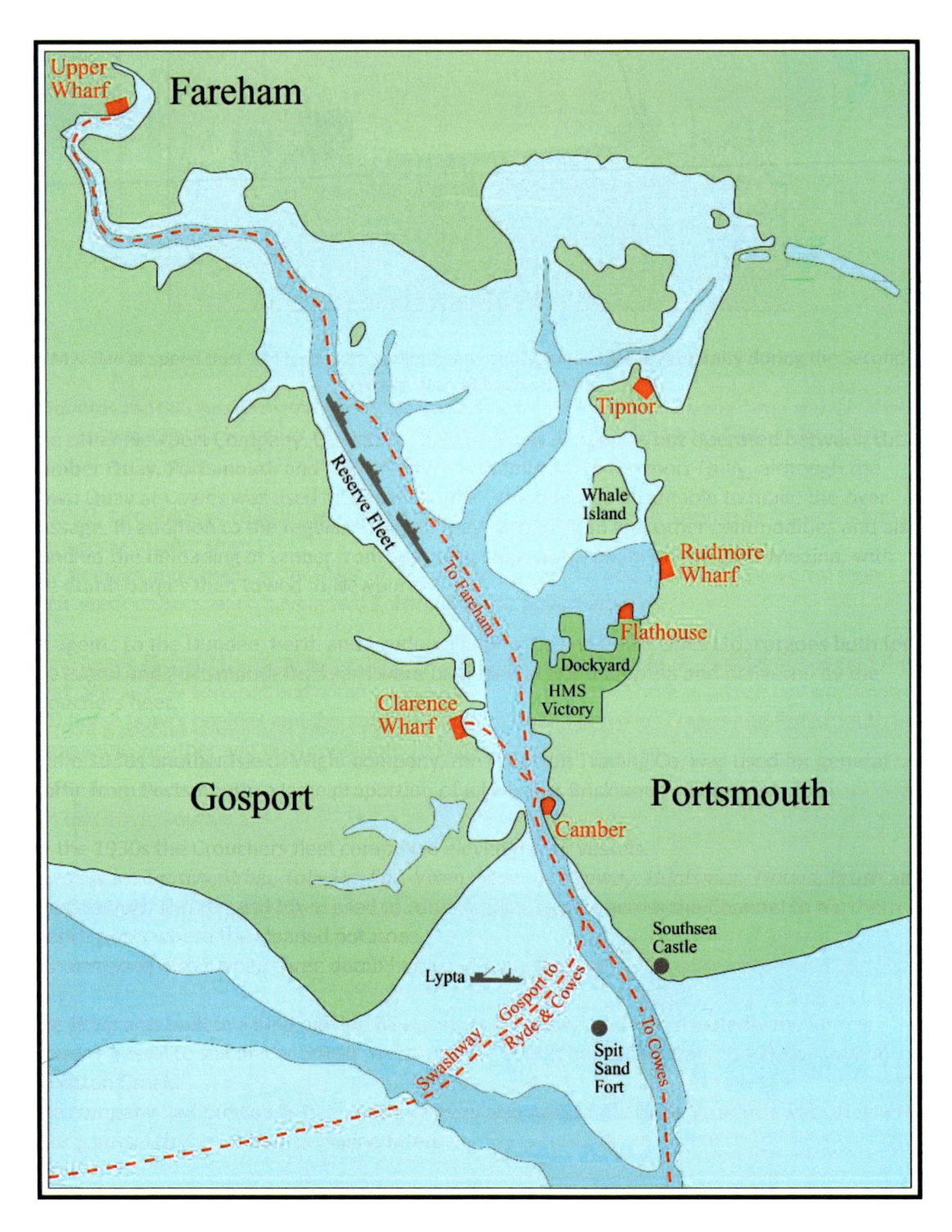

Wharf locations in Portsmouth Harbour where the Company traded

The *Lypta* was also frequently employed on shingle dredging at Spithead and other tasks included mud dredging for Portsmouth Corporation, lightening colliers at buoys and even bunkering colliers at buoys.

The *Lypta* dredging in the Outer Camber as part of the construction works for the new East Street Isle of Wight Car Ferry terminal circa 1960.

Sometime during the 1960s the *Lypta* sank in the Inner Camber as the photo below shows.

The sunken *Lypta* in the Camber. The large baulk of timber held by the crane at the bows was being lowered into position on the bed of the harbour at the time of the accident. Unknown to the crew there were the stumps of two other timber piles protruding from The mud and these pierced her bottom plates. As she was an old ship it was not thought worthwhile to repair her

Following the creation of Corralls, the demand for coal gradually began to reduce and with the Camber shipping trade gradually being transferred north to Flathouse Quay, Fraser & White eventually closed down their coaling operation in the Camber. The massive coal bunkers and overhead gantries were demolished, bringing an end to this long-established trade carried out by numerous firms in the Camber throughout the centuries.

Throughout their life the Fraser & White silos were a major visible sight in the Camber and in the twentieth century some of the residents of Spice Island used to remove the slack (small coal) in buckets: this was assumed to be acceptable because the company never seemed bothered at that time, even though in the late nineteenth century they were regularly prosecuting people for theft of small quantities of coal.

Many former residents and those who worked in the Camber probably recall that the colliers that berthed at the quay opposite Fraser & White's silos were too large to be able to manoeuvre into the berth without assistance and they used to be pulled round the corner of the quay using the ships winches and wire cables.

Although the Company created many regular jobs in the area, it also brought dust and pollution and since many houses had sliding sash windows or ill-fitting casements, this allowed the dust easy access into people's homes. Washing hung out to dry would also attract soot so cleaning was never a straight forward battle.

However, Fraser & White and its coal trade will be remembered by many for years to come, as it had such an influence on life on Spice Island and the Camber and during its existence certainly contributed to the history of Point.

Chapter 3

Pickford & Co

Another company that had a very long association with Point was Pickford & Co, setting up in Bath Square in 1862 and running their operation transporting goods to and from the Isle of Wight by water from Point Wharf (known locally as Pickfords wharf). Prior to setting up their business in Bath Square they are recorded as having premises in the High Street in 1859.

The inland carrying trade was a very important industry before the advent of the railways and the greatest of the national concerns was the firm of Pickford & Co. Founded in the mid-eighteenth century, it alone of its contemporaries on the roads and later competitors on the canals, survived for many years.
Pickfords business was that of the common carrier, the transportation of all manner of traffic, including passengers in the early days, initially between London and Lancashire but eventually, after the advent of the railways, over the whole country.

The clearance of goods for shipping and payment of duty on bonded goods were included among Pickfords advertised service in 1881. By this time Pickfords had ceased to act in Scotland but operated in Bristol, Portsmouth and West Hartlepool instead.
Pickfords was by then agent for the East and West India Dock companies and also forwarded goods daily to the Continent.
Apart from shipping interests in London, Pickfords shipping interests also included a service of sailing boats carrying general cargoes from Portsmouth and Southampton to the Isle of Wight.

In September 1862 a notice was issued by the company which read:

> Pickford & Co, Railway Agents and General Carriers have removed their Portsmouth establishment to the premises known as the Old *Quebec Hotel*, whence their steam and sailing boats start daily with goods for Ryde, Cowes and all parts of the Isle of Wight. From 1st October next they will add their general trade the Cartage Agency of the London, Brighton and South Coast Railway in Portsmouth and the Isle of Wight.

The *Quebec Hotel*, formerly called the *Quebec Tavern* was built circa. 1780 and was a very well-known hostelry for many years. By 1840 it was a point of departure for Ryde's steam packets to the Isle of Wight.
The hotel was also a staging post for coaches to and from London with the timings of coaches arranged so that passengers could make connections to continue their journey by water.
The hotel was last listed as a hotel in the following advert from 1859, which declares it for sale or to be let.

> TO be SOLD OR LET, with immediate possession,—the QUEBEC HOTEL and TAVERN, situate in Bath-square, Portsmouth, for many years occupied by the late Mr. Hale, but now occupied by his Widow, who, from failing health, desires to quit business. The house stands on the shore at the entrance of the harbour, commanding an uninterrupted sea view, and from its situation is admirably adapted for carrying on an extensive business in connexion with passengers by packets and other ships, besides being attractive to visitors. The Quebec Hotel is an old established house, in which for many years a good trade has been maintained.
>
> The premises may be viewed by leave of Mrs. Hale, the tenant, and other particulars, may be ascertained on application to
>
> Mr. C. B. HELLARD,
> Solicitor, Portsmouth.

An article published in a local newspaper around 1863 detailing Portsmouth Council minutes referred to the *Quebec Tavern* being sold to Pickford and Company for the sum of £1,100 several months previous.

In the early days of trading, vessels moored alongside Point wharf to unload and load goods, taking the ground at low water and unloading goods by hand across a form of gangplank.

A very early photograph, circa 1862, showing a sailing vessel alongside the new Pickfords premises at low water.

After setting up in Bath Square, goods were moved around by horse and cart and it is likely there were stables somewhere nearby on Point to accommodate the horses. Horses would have been a regular sight on Point at that time, as local coal merchants would have used them to collect the coal that was delivered by ships to the Camber wharves and then deliver to customers locally on their carts. Horses were also used to pull the first trams that visited Point. The following article, originally written by Charles Dickens and published in a local newspaper in the 1860s, describes the horses used by Pickfords:

Employing more than 900 horses in London, 300 are kept at Camden town. Going into these stables we are at once struck with an air of substantiality in connection with Pickfords. There is special potentiality in their stables with their asphalt pavements and their large swinging oaken bars, in their big horses, in their strong men, in their enormous vans. Most of the horses are splendid animals, many of them standing over 16 hands high and all are in excellent condition.

They are all bought by one man, the recognised buyer for the establishment who attends the principal fairs throughout the country; the average cost of each is £45. They are fed on a mixture of bruised oats, crushed Indian corn and peas which is found to be capital forage. Each horse, when bought, is branded with a number on the front of his fore feet hoofs and is named; the name and number are entered in the horse book and by them the horse's career, where he may be working and anything special relating to him is checked off until he dies or is sold. Pickfords horses last on average seven or eight years and then they are killed, but in many instances when no longer fit for roughing it over the stones they will be bought by some farmer for plough work and after a hard London life will peacefully end their days in some secluded village.

W.F. Smith, General carrier's horse drawn trailer outside Quebec House in 1906. The container of settler's effects refers to British Columbia, Canada.

A favourite story of the 1850s concerns a horse called *Toby,* who, after doing his day's work in Gosport, had to cross the half mile wide Portsmouth harbour by floating bridge to reach his stables in Portsmouth.

After waiting some time for the bridge, the horse became impatient with the slowness of these new-fangled mechanical contrivances, entered the water, swam across to the other side and made his way home to his stables.

The horse keeper commented: "An all wise horse this and worthy of promotion".
Horses continued to be used by Pickfords into the twentieth century.

On July 19th 1880 the following article appeared in the local newspaper:

> NEWPORT, JULY 10.
> NEW STEAMERS FOR ISLE OF WIGHT GOODS TRAFFIC. Two screw steamers were launched on Saturday last from the shipyard of Messrs. R. and H. Green, Blackwall, to the order of Messrs. Pickford and Co., the well-known carriers. The vessels are named the Glowworm and the Firefly, and will run exclusively between Portsmouth and the Isle of Wight. The dimensions are :— Length over all, 75ft.; beam, 14ft.; depth, moulded, 7ft. 7in.; draught of water loaded, 5ft. 6in. We mention this as these are the first steamvessels of Messrs. Pickford's fleet employed on our Island goods' traffic.

Initially, all the ships in their fleet were sailing vessels until four steam vessels were introduced in the 1880s for its Solent operations.

In 1893 the following advert was placed in the local newspaper:

> The Steamer *Blanche* is running between Portsmouth and Fareham with goods at moderate rates of freight. Goods will be received and despatched by Messrs Pickford & Co, carriers, Bath Square Portsmouth and Mr Walter A Ayres, Lower Quay, Fareham. For particulars as to rates etc., apply on board or at 93 Queens Road, Gosport.

In the early days their ships were allowed to ground on Ryde sands and their cargoes were unloaded on to high wheeled horse drawn carts and distributed in the district. At Cowes a more conventional method of discharge was in operation.

In 1906 Pickfords took delivery of the motor vessel *M.V. Wasp* which was claimed to be the first motor cargo vessel ever built and traded regularly between Portsmouth and Cowes for more than twenty years.

Late nineteenth century painting by H Caish showing a Pickfords steam powered vessel unloading at Point Wharf.

52

Sometimes, adverse weather caused problems trying to unload cargoes at Ryde, as the following newspaper article in 1893 reported:

> The heavy gale on Friday last was severely felt in the Solent and considerably impeded navigation. One of the Pickfords boats, after she got over to Ryde, could not land her cargo and had to return to Portsmouth harbour. Messrs Chaplins' *Advance* and another of the Pickfords boats got to the west of the pier where they rolled about in rather an alarming manner, but fortunately neither sustained any serious damage.

In 1920, the company was sold to Hays Wharf Limited, on the back of a burgeoning post-World War I home removals business.

Pickfords still continued to operate under its original name and in turn Hays Wharf was taken over by the four main British railway companies in 1933.
However, the advent of this acquisition appeared to change things very little and as far as the vehicle fleet it was business as usual with no policy change in that direction.

Before Pickfords started their business transporting goods to and from the Isle of Wight, two Newport companies, Crouchers and Shepard Brothers were already operating a freight business which they had started in the early 1800s. They had a service from Southampton Town Quay to Newport.

Shepard Bros eventually used both Newport Quay and Medina Commercial Wharf (later known as Shepard's Wharf) Cowes, as their Island base. In addition to other traffic carried, they held the Railway Agency for the Newport and Freshwater areas and worked from Southampton Town Quay. Handling the rail traffic was eased by the fact the trucks could be shunted on to the quay and unloaded directly into the ship.

At Portsmouth there was always cartage involved between the station and the wharf.
By the 1920s Shephard Brothers had acquired a varied fleet comprising two steamboats, *Foam* and *Spray*, the motor vessels *Wave, Bee* and *SLB6* together with the sailing vessels *Arrow* and *Iona*.
It is interesting to note that the *Bee* had at least two predecessors of the same name since Bills of Sale to Mr Shepard dated 1849 and 1860 show that two different sailing ships of the same name were purchased by him at those times.

In fact the original *Bee,* purchased by Shepard Brothers in 1849, was built in 1801. She was a 41 ton sailing ketch and continued working as a freighter until 1927 when she was deliberately run aground in the River Medina opposite the Folly. Such was the quality of her build that many years after her running aground her timbers was said to still be in good condition despite her age, since she was constructed before the battle of Trafalgar.

The new *Bee* was a motor barge built by James Pollack & Sons shipyard, Faversham, in 1928 and arrived in Newport on 31st January 1928 with a cargo of cement as ballast and was later to be requisitioned by the Admiralty, together with other vessels, to rescue servicemen from the beaches of Dunkirk in the Second World War.

M.V.*Bee* at speed post 1947, she had earlier been requisitioned by the Admiralty during the Second World War. © Michael Wills

The other Newport Company, Crouchers, held no Railway Agency, but operated between the Camber Quay, Portsmouth and Town Quay, Southampton, to Newport Quay, although the Town Quay at Cowes was used on occasion when the tide was unsuitable to make the river passage. In addition to the regular services, they carried grain and other commodities and also handled the unloading of timber from sea going ships at Medham on the river Medina, with the dumb barges then towed to Newport.

As agents to the Dundee, Perth and London Shipping Co and Coast Lines Ltd, cargoes both for the Island and Portsmouth Dockyard were unloaded at Southampton and delivered by the Crouchers fleet.

In the 1930s another Isle of Wight company, the Wootton Trading Co, was used for general traffic from Portsmouth, a large proportion of which was Brickwood's beer.

By the 1930s the Crouchers fleet comprised eleven motor vessels.
These were *Tantivy, Whip, Tally Ho, Fox, Vixen, Mask, Harkaway, Huntsman, Hound, Brush* and the *Chamois*. The *Fox* and *Vixen* used to run a regular service across the Channel to northern French ports where they loaded potatoes.
The company also owned three dumb barges – *Hunt, Cub* and *FEP*.

The *Whip* was built in a field outside Newport on the Island and was reputedly the largest wooden vessel to sail on the Solent route and she ended her sailing days as a house boat in Wootton Creek.
The company had previously had another vessel also named the *Tally Ho* which was originally a sailing vessel that later had an engine fitted.

Chaplins was a fourth company engaged in the cross Solent trade and they operated four sailing vessels before 1898. They later purchased a steam boat *Excelsior*, built in 1898, and she was designed with a very shallow draught for unloading at Ryde, of sufficient length in the hatchway to accommodate two furniture vans which could be lifted by the boat's own gear. Motor vessels gradually replaced the sailing ships and steam boats. The M.V.*Wild Swan* was purchased in 1913 and continued in the service for more than 40 years and together with M.V.*Wilbernia,* acquired in 1923, traded regularly between Portsmouth and St Helens.

M.V. *Bat,* an original part of Pickfords' fleet alongside Point Wharf pre 1920.

In 1936, Pickfords Ltd acquired the businesses of the other three companies and this produced a combined fleet of some 21 ships, ranging from the *S.L.B.6* of 22 tons to the *Wild Swan*, *Bat* and *Krom* all of 51 tons and the dumb barges *Cub* and *Hunt*. Later that year the *Gainsborough Trader* of 48 tons was purchased and renamed *M.F.H.*

By the acquisition of Chaplins, Crouchers Ltd and Shepard Brothers Ltd, Pickfords was able to obtain a virtual monopoly of traffic to and from the Isle of Wight.

Pickfords advert 1910

The Isle of Wight end of the operation became more concentrated on Cowes, saving time in navigating the tidal River Medina. Newport Quay and its waterside warehouses was still used for the discharge and storage of bulk cargo such as sugar, flour and animal foods, but the general cargo and traffic requiring cranage was routed via Cowes.

The Wootton depot was also used for about two years after the amalgamation, mainly for discharging beer. One factor that helped the concentration of traffic in Cowes was the completion of the harbour breakwater, which sheltered the harbour from all but the occasional severe north-west gale, which could still make the berths at Thetis and Shepards wharves untenable. Furthermore, the berths could be used at any state of tide.

During 1936, a six ton electric crane was installed at Point Wharf, Portsmouth and the following year two similar cranes were erected at Cowes, one at Thetis Wharf and the other on the south Pier at Shepards Wharf. Two 30 cwt. cranes were also positioned on the unloading bank at Thetis Wharf so that they could be used simultaneously to discharge small general cargo on to the quayside in front of the store.

The general pattern of operations at this time was that three ships were engaged in regular services between Point Wharf, Portsmouth and Cowes.
One ship was on a daily run from Southampton Quay, principally for the movement of fruit and other perishable traffic requiring same day delivery, with the remainder of the fleet handling flour from Solent Mills to Newport Quay, Whitbread's beer from Camber Quay to Newport and the varied consignments which were shipped direct from Railway Company's trucks at Southampton Town Quay to Cowes or Newport.

Point wharf with other Pickfords property clearly visible to the south.

In the late 1930s the pattern of cargoes began to change with the growth of container traffic. These had previously been used mainly for furniture removal, or, like the Southern Railway, for insulated types of fresh meat.

Now, other direct consignments were being handled this way and lift vans owned by Pickfords and other companies were passing regularly.

The existing fleet was far from ideal for this work since only two containers could be stowed below, even in the larger ships. Two more were usually carried on deck when conditions permitted, but this could be dangerous if the weather worsened during the passage across the Solent. On one occasion soon after the war, the crew of the *M.V.Bat* had to jettison her deck cargo of containers in mid-Solent to prevent the ship from foundering.

To meet these changes, Pickfords commissioned the *M.V.Mount* from the yard of Humphrey and Grey of East Greenwich. She joined the fleet in 1938 and at 68 tons net (210 deadweight tons) was considerably larger than her predecessors, particularly in the beam, and could carry up to eight standard Pickfords containers of either furniture or meat according to demand, four of which stowed in the hold. Also, from the same yard the dumb barge *Remount* of 72 tons was launched and joined the older *Cub* and *Hunt* in the lighterage trade undertaken at the time.

Throughout the war years the service was maintained. The cargoes carried were probably even more varied than at any time previously and included the long steel tubes which were to carry the "Operation PLUTO"(Pipeline Under The Ocean) pipe line from Shanklin Chine to Cherbourg. This oil supply pipeline was built from the Isle of Wight to supply the troops on the D Day beaches in Normandy. A ship that played a large part in this operation was the 50 ton *Wave*. This vessel, which was about 100 years old and had started life as a dumb barge on the Thames, had a 50 ft. hatchway and was ideally suited to the traffic.

Operation PLUTO was one of the great successes of the war and was the idea of Lord Mountbatten. During the Normandy invasion the pipelines carried petrol under the English Channel. The pipelines delivered 56,000 gallons a day until the Allies advanced so far that the line was transferred to Dungeness in Kent.

Tantivy and *Whip,* along with their crews were requisitioned by the Admiralty in the Second World War and were based at Portsmouth.
Tantivy served as a supply ship ferrying ammunition from Marchwood near Southampton to Navy ships in the Solent, although she was renamed *Tantivy2*, since there was already a submarine called *Tantivy*. The wooden built *Whip* was used as a de-gaussing vessel.
The men who worked on the boats, usually four on each vessel, were merchant seamen and were not called up to do other military service as their jobs were seen to be vital to the war effort.

Five of the Pickfords motor vessels, *Bee, M.F.H. Bat, Chamois* and *Hound* with their volunteer crews, took part in the evacuation of Dunkirk during the Second World War, together with the *Murius*, a boat owned by Vectis shipping, an Isle of Wight company. Combined, these six ships saved almost 1000 soldiers.

The *Bat* was a 26 metre vessel of 51 tons with a crew of four and she was the only boat of the six to have a crew from Portsmouth, whereas the others had a crew of Island men. They left Portsmouth on 30th May 1940 and rescued 15 survivors from the French destroyer, Bourrasque and landed them at Ramsgate before returning to Dunkirk on 31st May and rescued another 100 men. By now the crew had had no sleep for three days and the engine of the ship had been running continuously for 92 hours.

The *Hound* arrived at Dunkirk late on 31st May and sent a crew of two ashore in a small boat and rescued 12 men. The ship then went to a small pier and rescued 100 French and Belgian soldiers.

The *M.F.H.*, a vessel of 48 tons with a crew of four arrived at Dunkirk on 31st May during a bombing raid. She ferried troops to larger vessels offshore before returning to Ramsgate with 140 men.

The *Chamois* had been involved with air attacks initially hampering her efforts to pick up survivors, but later 130 men were rescued from other damaged ships. This was a huge achievement, since she only had a crew of two including the captain!

The *Bee* with a crew of four rescued 375 men on their first trip ashore and more later. Eventually, she had to return home on one engine since a wire had got caught around a propeller while close to the beach. As she only had a draft of 2 metres when loaded this was a real advantage at Dunkirk, as she was able to get very close to the shore to pick up troops.

The local newspaper published the following story by Mr Fred Reynard of Newport, engineer on the *Bee*, giving a thrilling account of the gallant way in which they successfully carried through the task allotted to them:

> "Last Wednesday we were at a mainland port discharging a cargo, when a naval officer said the ship would be required and we volunteered to go with her.
> There were four of us on board, the skipper, Mr C.W.Trowbridge, the mate, Mr H. Downer, Mr M. Hocking and myself, all Island men.
>
> A young naval lieutenant came aboard later and after we had taken in fuel and stores we slipped out of the harbour and reached a south east coast port the following afternoon. On the trip we had been told that we were going to Dunkirk to take on board men of the B.E.F. (British Expeditionary Force) and you can imagine that we were thrilled at the news.
>
> We left the English port that evening and anchored off Dunkirk about midnight.
> We could see the flashes of guns in the distance and saw the flares dropped by German aircraft who were bombing the outskirts of the town, but they did not spot us and we were left in peace.
>
> Next morning, just as it was getting light, we moved in closer, narrowly missing being cut in two by a destroyer, which raced by and made for the quay.
>
> About 20 German planes were flying around and one dived and gave us two or three short bursts from its machine guns but the marksmanship was bad and we were not touched. We were then ordered to go with a tug to a part of the beach where an isolated party of our troops were waiting.
> Apparently, they could not get to the quay where the larger ships were embarking thousands of men.
>
> As we neared the beach we could see the soldiers lined up waiting for us. With a stout hawser from us to the tug, we ran in and beached our vessel bow on. There was between four and five feet of water where we grounded and immediately the men came down the beach and waded out to us. Some of the shorter ones were up to their necks by the time they reached the ladders which we had placed over the side and we had a busy time hauling them aboard. They were very tired (some of them had been fighting and marching without sleep for four days), but they were still cheerful and there was not the slightest disorder or hurry, as they came down the beach to wade out to us. They gave a magnificent example of discipline. It was not long before

we had about 375 on board. One man had three machine gun bullets in his leg but he managed to swim out, helped by his comrades, and we made him comfortable.
Before we ran into the beach a squadron of our fighters had appeared and the German planes did not wait to try conclusions with them. They quickly sheered off and as the Hurricanes patrolled overhead, we were not interfered with. After packing in as many men as we could, below and on deck, the tug towed us out and we transferred the men to her.
Then we started to go in for another load, but the wind had freshened and the sea became so rough that we could not get close to the beach owing to the risk of being carried ashore broadside on, so we anchored.

Even then our anchor dragged at times. Then a naval motor boat came on the scene and she went and picked up 20 men and put them on our vessel, but in going in for another lot she capsized in the breakers.

All the men who manned her, with the exception of one, swam ashore but he tried to swim out to us. He could make very little progress against the tide, so we floated a lifebuoy down to him on a line and we hauled him aboard.

Just as we had decided to get away from the shore for safety we saw a small boat leave the beach so we waited for her. She had five French soldiers on board and we took them off and then put out to deeper water under orders and we were then told to go back to the East Coast port, which we reached in the early evening.

One of the party we brought back was a Ryde man. As we left the Belgian coast the Germans were shelling the beach from which we had taken the men.
Unfortunately, in going ashore we got one of our propellers fouled with a piece of wire and this so handicapped us that we were ordered to return to our home port.
We did so on one engine and reached home safely on Sunday evening.

As we were returning to the East Coast port from Dunkirk we saw four other local vessels, the *Hound, M.F.H, Bat* and *Murius* on their way across to do their job at Dunkirk.

When the naval officer left us he said "Thank you for your co-operation and help. We set out to do a job and we have done it. The navy always does its job. If I have another job like this to do I shall ask for you and your ship. We must have a day together at Portsmouth when we have finished with Hitler"

The *Murius*-a wooden barge built in 1888, reported that all the ships were being bombed and machine gunned while his ship was taking part in the rescue but that, despite being outnumbered the RAF did a fine job. Remarkably, all of these vessels survived the ferocious enemy attacks and a few days later they were back in the Solent doing their usual job - an amazing story!

In view of the wartime dangers locally, it was fortunate that none of Pickfords ships were lost during the war, since there was always a possibility that an enemy plane could have attacked any of the ships whilst they were crossing the Solent.

There were other dangers in the local waters too, as the Portsmouth to Ryde passenger ferry, a paddle steamer named the "*SS Portsdown*"', discovered when she was struck by a mine in September 1941, sinking with the loss of twenty passengers and crew.

During the Second World War, Pickfords also helped transport sections of the Mulberry harbours from throughout the UK to the south coast in advance of D-Day.

Pickfords became involved in aircraft haulage after the war and the success of the operation led to a contract to move a Saunders Roe flying boat from Cowes to Portsmouth in the late 1940s and convey it by road to Preston for the fitting of engines, thence to sea.
These flying boats had the distinction of being the largest all-metal flying boats to have ever been constructed, although only the prototype, G-ALUN, of the three constructed, ever flew.

The return to peacetime conditions caused a further reappraisal of the fleet, since at least five of the ships had been built before the First World War and needed to be replaced. Furthermore, the container traffic was growing rapidly, not only in volume, but also in the actual size of the containers which had generally been of about 550 cubic feet, but now were 200 cubic feet larger, meaning that the *Mount* was no longer adequate. The replacement programme was in hand when a change of ownership occurred.

Under the 1947 Transport Act the railways were given virtual control of the competing road transport industry. The Act provided sweeping powers for the newly constituted British Transport Commission (BTC) to compulsorily acquire and nationalise any road haulage company whose operations fell largely within the sphere of long distance operations. Pickfords was therefore nationalised since it was already controlled by the four main line railways and thereby helped to give the new BTC setup a great chunk of the heavy transport fleet in the UK under the company name of British Road Services (BRS).

On the face of it nearly all their operations made them exempt from nationalization, but as they had been voluntarily acquired they were kept as the ninth Division of BRS handling removals, meat haulage (soon to be separated), bulk liquid, giant/indivisible 'out of gauge' loads, explosive and inflammable loads and new furniture, as well as several of their old contracts and their travel agencies. This nationalisation meant that all the Pickfords boats had the new name of BRS painted on all the vessels from 1947.

Along with its road and rail interests the BTC also had an executive concerned with docks and inland waterways. From various sources (mainly railways) it had inherited all sorts of coastal and inland waterway vessels and in 1954 the fleet stood at 116 ships of 66,491 net tons plus a further 20 jointly owned or operated. Many of these ships were transporting rail cargo and passengers to Ireland or the Continent but not until the importance of 'roll-on, roll-off' ferries for lorries became evident was BRS directly involved.

By the 1960s BRS was made up of four main operating areas: British Road Services Ltd, BRS Parcels Ltd, Pickfords and Containerway and Roadferry. In 1969 it was renamed the National Freight Corporation (NFC).

In late 1949 and early 1950, the motor vessels *Field, Crop* and *Covert* were built for the company at J. Bolson and Sons yard at Poole, Dorset. These were sister ships, each of 89 tons and powered by two Kelvin 66 horse power diesel engines. Each ship could carry ten containers and took over the daily service from Point Wharf to Cowes.

The *Crop*.

At first the service with these three new ships was done in the manner of previous years, with two of the ships carrying thousands of small packages, but this was very time consuming, both in loading and discharging. This led to the containerising of most small general traffic and the three ships sailed daily across the Solent to a timetable.

Even so, during the summer months when tourists swell the Island population, the demand for ice cream, frozen food and meat was almost double the normal requirements, so it was necessary on three days of the week to run a double trip with one ship. This meant that the crew of that particular vessel worked a 14 or 15 hour day.

In 1950 the *Norris Castle* was brought into service on the Southampton to East Cowes route. She was an ex-tank landing craft which permitted cars to drive on and off the ferry for the first time. Previously they had been lifted on and off by crane. This marked the beginning of the end for the river freighter service.

The service operated by BRS was a vital one to traders on the Isle of Wight and goods came from as far away as Ulster and Scotland and included anything from a pens to a harvesters, telephone poles and steel girders to milk powder. The vessels carried all the bricks that were used in the construction of the massive chimneys at Kingston Gasworks on the Medina River, steel doors for Albany prison, Sydney Smith's famous boat *Nova Espero*, aeroplane wings, a Shetland pony and a plastic swimming pool. However, most cargoes were more run of the mill with goods like soap, tobacco and sugar.

Bill Stringer, who joined the company in 1957 was the crane driver at Point wharf for more than 15 years, recalled the occasion in 1960 when the battleship *HMS Vanguard*, under tow and on her way to be scrapped, suddenly veered off course and nearly collided with the wharf and his cab. He recalled, "I could have reached out and touched her bows with a broom handle, she was that close" and he also quipped that "it was a pity they brought her under control when they did as we would have had a new quay by now!"

Apparently over the years *HMS Vanguard* was not the only vessel to veer off course, since the ice patrol vessel, *HMS Protectorate*, actually rammed the *Covert* which luckily escaped with only a few cuts and bruises.

BRS boat in reverse trying to escape from the bows of HMS Vanguard in 1960

Pickfords and BRS vessels regularly used the Camber Docks for loading/unloading cargo and this photo taken in 1958 shows one of the vessels leaving the Camber. © Helen Mabel Smith (1905-1990)

In 1960, two ships were launched from the Richard Dunston yard at Thorne to replace some of the ageing smaller ships.
The *Needles* and *Cowes*, sister ships of 52 tons net, were considerably more powerful than their predecessors, each having two Kelvin 88 horse power engines.

Once again, Richard Dunston were the builders when in 1962 the *M. V. Northwood* joined the fleet. She was 97 tons net and could carry fourteen containers. She was driven by two Kelvin 120 horse power engines and this reduced the time taken between Cowes and Portsmouth in reasonable weather and tidal conditions to little more than an hour.

M.V.Northwood alongside Point Wharf circa 1965.

By using this vessel on the double trip when necessary, the daily capacity in each direction was raised to 48 containers.

Unfortunately, the traffic pattern did not remain static for very many years. Loads which had traditionally travelled by goods train were being diverted to road, often on the sender's own transport, making the final leg of the journey on the roll-on roll-off ferries.

In March 1969 the Town Quay at Southampton was closed from where the regular service to Cowes used to be based.

The fleet was reduced accordingly, until in 1971 only four ships remained in service and by 1972 only the *Northwood* and *Needles* were in regular service with one of the older ships, the *Covert*, in reserve. At this time the *Northwood* handled the flour from Southampton.

M.V.*Northwood*   M.V.*Needles*

Until the mid-1960s it was fair to say that the link Pickfords established with the mainland was absolutely vital to the Isle of Wight. In retrospect, a ship like the *S.B.L.6,* with her 40 ton carrying, capacity may seem rather futile, but in the days of the horse and cart and the three ton petrol lorry, 40 tons delivered 5 miles nearer to its ultimate destination was an important consideration.

In addition to this, she was of very shallow draft and to quote a slightly exaggerated comment by one of her previous skippers "would float in a heavy dew". In the Medina river conditions this enabled her to be away from, and back to Newport Quay well ahead of her bigger and deeper drafted rivals.

The *Northwood* was to later operate in the Thames area and several of the older ships did a worthwhile job elsewhere, but so far as the Island was concerned the ships of the BRS fleet passed into local history alongside the steam locomotive and the horse drawn parcels van.

And what of the men who manned these ships? In the main they were a hardy, independent breed and had to be when one realises that it was not until the Second World War that a number of the older ships were fitted with wheel houses.

Before that time the helmsman stood on the open deck, his only shelter from the elements being a four feet canvas dodger. Another task always unpopular with the crews was mooring the ship on the buoys at Medham in the River Medina when the berths at Cowes were untenable and then rowing ashore in the dinghy.

The skippers had invariably grown up in the business: many of them had started as boys in the position of fourth hand and progressed through the mate's job to being appointed skipper. The seamanship was of the strictly practical variety - the watch and the compass were their navigational instruments, allied to their experience. The very small number of trips missed and the few major accidents pay tribute to their skill. The seaman's old enemy, fog, was the greatest problem and ironically the invention of radar increased the hazards. In earlier days it was safe to assume that coasters, tankers and liners would heave-to in foggy conditions, but radar changed all that and even greater care had to be exacted by the Solent crews.

Despite all this, the ships provided a lifetime's occupation for many of the men. A survey taken in 1953 showed that of the 51 seamen employed, 14 of them had from 35 to 47 years' service. This was probably a fair reflection of the situation at any time during the preceding years. As in some other industries, members of the same families tended to follow one another into the cross Solent fleet. The names Knight, Woodford, Hobbs, Chiverton, Butcher and Appleton are prominent in this connection, but there must have been many more families involved during the long history of the service.

In the second half of the twentieth century, Pickfords became more isolated in an area of Portsmouth that was becoming more residential year by year as smaller businesses disappeared, being replaced by residential properties.
This resulted in conflict with some residents, particularly as a large part of the business operations in Bath Square involved the continual movement of flat-bed trucks and containers. It resulted in a very congested area with trucks parked over much of the Square when the company was open for business and even when closed, the trucks took up much of the parking area which was not popular with local residents.

The vehicles that were used in Bath Square for shunting around the goods were Austin/BMC tractor units and the flat bed trailers were Scammell couplings regularly used where trailers were being changed several times a day, which was the case here.
These combinations were referred to as articulated vehicles at that time and the most common form of containers put on these trailers were railway containers.

Furthermore, damage was sustained occasionally by vehicles colliding with properties nearby when manoeuvring in tight spaces and when the company finally closed their operations and left the area many residents heaved a sigh of relief, even though it marked the end of an era and the loss of another long-standing business from Point.

Pickfords trucks and containers often caused congestion in Bath Square

On 12th December 1975, the *M V Northwood* sailed from Point Wharf, Portsmouth, bound for Thetis Wharf, Cowes, Isle of Wight. This caused little interest on the waterfront of Old Portsmouth, as the *Northwood* and her predecessors in the fleet of small ships operated by British Services Ltd had been sailing this route daily for more than 100 years. This passage was notable only because it marked the end, not of the service which carried on via roll-on roll-off ferries, but of this long established method of providing it.

In 1982 Margaret Thatcher announced that the NFC was to be denationalised, the first privatisation of a state owned industry. Pickfords MD, Geoff Pygall, was instrumental in facilitating the purchase from the government. Employees were encouraged to invest in shares of the company and the subsequent growth fuelled by acquisition and investment, ensured that some employees became financially secure for life.

In 1999 Pickfords was acquired by Clayton, Dubillier & Rice and became part of SIRVA Inc.

The name of Pickfords still continues to be seen across the world today and it is still expanding its business into new countries.

Although the Pickfords trade between the mainland and the Isle of Wight was only a small percentage of the company's overall global business it was very important locally to the Solent area and to Point in particular, where it was based for more than 100 years.

Chapter 4

W. G. Lucas & Son Limited

Sail making and ships chandlery shops and stores were associated with Spice Island for many years and one firm that was very well established for more than 100 years on Point was W. G. Lucas & Son Limited.

When William George Lucas, an East coast sailmaker, came to Old Portsmouth in 1884 to establish his own business, he could hardly have envisaged that it would still be flourishing over a century later in Broad Street.

The Sail Loft in 1918

When he arrived, one of the competitors in Broad Street was a firm named C Groom Ltd (Sailmaker, Ship Chandler, Tent, Marquee and Flag Maker) and they were based at that time at Nos 42, 44 and 46 Broad Street.

CHARLES GROOM,
Sail Maker, Ship Chandler, Tent, Marquee, & Flag Maker,
42, 44 & 46,
BROAD ST., PORTSMOUTH.

Awnings, Waterproof Covers, Rick Cloths, and Sacks made to Order or Let on Hire.

TENTS AND MARQUEES
From 6 feet diameter, square or round, up to 300 feet long.

New and Second-Hand Ropes, Canvas, &c.,
ALWAYS IN STOCK.

SHIPPING SUPPLIED
With Paints, Oils, Pitch, Tar, Oakum, Best Hemp Manilla, Wire and Coir Rope, Engine Packing, Cotton Waste, Tallow and Sponge Cloths, Anchors, Chains and Bolts, Blocks, Hanks, and Hand Spikes, &c., &c. Coal Buckets, Shovels and Brushes.

Sole Agent for Peacock's & Buchan's Patent Composition Paint.

42, 44 & 46, Broad Street, Portsmouth.

An advert for Charles Groom in 1887.

In the early years W G Lucas was registered as living at No 29 Broad Street and later moved to No 7 Broad Street, registered as a sail and awning maker.

William George Lucas worked for over a quarter of a century in a hay loft above old horse stables on Point, in the historic maritime heart of the city. In those early days most of the work was for commercial craft, as sailing for pleasure was still something of a novelty in the 19th century, and did not really come into great prominence - and then only for the wealthy - until the dawn of the Edwardian era.
In the early years sails made of flax and cotton were made for fishing boats and trading barges.

At the end of the nineteenth century a large company named Websters based in Scotland specialised in manufacturing hemp and flax. It was all narrow 24 inch sail cloth and they had the monopoly until Egyptian cotton was introduced. Unfortunately this became very sought after and difficult to obtain after a while and people used to rely on cotton from America or from India which was inferior.

The founder died in 1912 aged 50. By this time the family traditions were already being laid as W G's eldest son, William, took over the business at 25, with his brother Reg as foreman.

W.G.Lucas & Son were by now among the biggest sail making firms in the country alongside Ratseys (the largest), Jeckells and Gowans of the East coast.
Several years later (c.1917) the company moved into the premises vacated by Messrs C Groom Ltd at 42 – 46 Broad Street which had a purpose built sail loft, water access to the Inner Camber and a workforce of 30 people.

The First World War saw them concentrating on government contracts for tent making and the production of canvas aircraft hangars for the Royal Flying Corps. They also started a hire business after the First World War renting out marquees.

Sail making came into its own between the wars as vast changes, enormous growth and considerable diversification came to the yachting scene, all serving to emphasise the Solent's position as one of the world's foremost sailing centres.

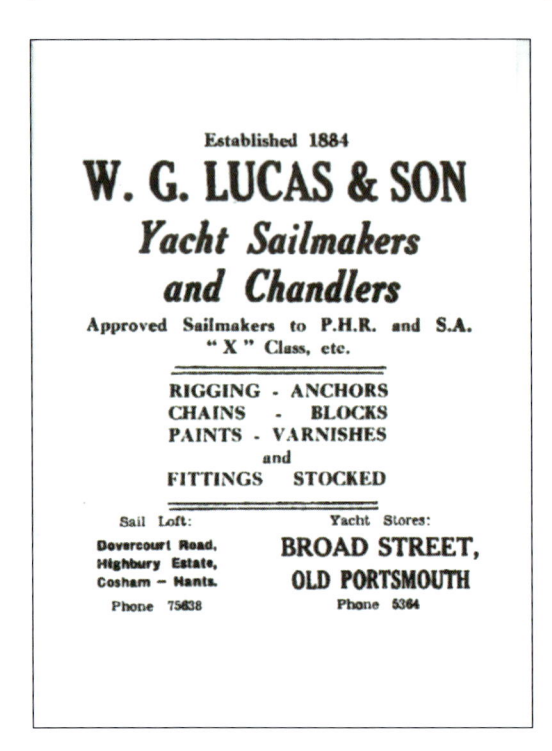

Established 1884

W. G. LUCAS & SON

Yacht Sailmakers and Chandlers

Approved Sailmakers to P.H.R. and S.A. " X " Class, etc.

RIGGING - ANCHORS
CHAINS - BLOCKS
PAINTS - VARNISHES
and
FITTINGS STOCKED

Sail Loft:
Dovercourt Road,
Highbury Estate,
Cosham – Hants.
Phone 75638

Yacht Stores:
BROAD STREET,
OLD PORTSMOUTH
Phone 5364

For many years the company erected some very large marquees in the spring and took them down in the winter at a location near Pagham harbour and then put them into storage for use again in the following year. This type of work helped the annual cash flow since sail making is a very seasonal business.
Although the Broad Street premises had water access at high tides, there wasn't a great depth of water and sails and covers etc. were either collected by or sent by road.

Big bertha in use.

The Second World War, like its predecessor, saw all the firm's production given over to government contracts until the premises were bombed in 1941 when the buildings were destroyed together with all the company records. Several sewing machines had to be dredged out of the Camber Docks, so that work could be restarted on a temporary site at Dovercourt Road, Cosham and one of these machines (named Big Bertha) was still in use until it was disposed of in 1995.

The company stayed at Cosham throughout the war and were very busy making gun covers, tank covers and other covers for the MOD.

Peter Lucas recalls moving back to Broad Street in the late 1940s and remembers there being only a Nissen hut with a chandlery and rigging service provided at that time.

The Nissen hut can be seen in this photo to the left of the three warehouses.

William Lucas, who had headed the firm for nearly 40 years, died in 1950 and his son Leonard became managing director of the company to be followed later by his brother Colin.

The loft was rebuilt after the war in the mid-1950s and at this time the company was a real family affair with family members in charge of the rigging business, undertaking the book keeping and several female family members working as machinists.

In the early 1950s nylon was replacing cotton. Peter Lucas, the current Managing Director, who when working for the company as a teenager in the 1950s, recalls a full suit of sails being made for a very large 69 ft. catamaran named "Ebb and Flow" based in Langstone harbour. The sails were very stretchy but nylon was ideal for spinnakers.

However, people were becoming aware that there was a lot of potential for using synthetic materials and terylene was developed shortly afterwards, becoming a revolutionary material in sail making.

There was a huge boom in dinghy sailing between 1955 and 1960 and one of the northern mills at Rochdale started making terylene sailcloth.

Lucas's company records indicate that between two and three thousand sails were being made annually, mainly for dinghies, following the introduction of terylene. Among the classes for which large numbers of sails were made were Albacores, Graduates, Merlin Rockets, Wayfarers and Fireballs.

The sails that took Sir Alec Rose across the Atlantic in 1964 in the second single-handed transatlantic race and around the world a few years later in 1967/68 were made by W G Lucas and Son.

A steel barge that unexpectedly smashed into the rear entrance sometime in the early 1970s.

In 1974 a second storey was added to the building, but unfortunately this work coincided with the miner's strike and the three day week. Whilst this work was underway the firm moved their sail making business to a temporary site in a gymnasium at Eastney and the Chandlery moved to Elm Grove, Southsea.

On completion, after 9 months' building work, there was a total working area of approx. 14,000 square feet, (7,000 sq. ft. on each floor) which was suitable for making all types of sails.

On the ground floor there was also a popular and comprehensive chandlery and a sail repair shop which made an assortment of covers for the Ministry of Defence, thus maintaining a link with the services which went back 70 years.

Colin Lucas died in 1984 and his son Peter, who was a very successful racing helmsman with 25 years' experience in sail making behind him, continued the longstanding family traditions by taking over as managing director, although he had been heavily involved in running the firm before this time.

On officially taking over Peter was quoted "Just as it was when my great grandfather founded the business a century ago we are first and foremost a family business".

The Sail Loft in the mid-1980s

A local man named Len Hackett, Portsmouth born and bred, started with Lucas in 1937, and in 1985, a few years before he retired, he recalled his early days:

> My apprenticeship began when I left school at 14 and lasted for seven years. At that time most of the sails were hand stitched with exactly 31 stitches to every 9 inches of cloth and a big one would take about three days to make.
> Cotton was the only material used then - it had to be treated afterwards to prevent rot - as terylene did not come into being until the late 1950s.
> There was a special art in the handwork, with far more satisfaction than using a machine, and I suppose that in my time I must have worked a few million stitches, but it has all been well worthwhile and I enjoyed my work.
> In spite of changing methods, craftsmanship is still very important, and I am pleased to see that the youngsters coming in now are just as keen and interested as when I started 48 years ago in 1937.

At that time in 1985 the skills of Len Hackett, and one or two older employees who worked part-time, enabled the loft to still offer an extensive hand stitching service for those who believed that this method is best for really hard wear. Lucas was at that time probably one of only a handful of firms in the country that could still do the job.

Sails that took the replicas of Drake's *Golden Hind* and *Nonsuch* half way around the world were hand stitched in flax at the Broad Street sail loft. The sails for the *Nonsuch* were commissioned by the Hudson Bay Company for the replica of the original vessel used 300 years before and the sails were hand stitched in 20 oz. flax in the style of 1660.

Golden Hind in Camber in the 1980s 　　　　　*Nonsuch* in Camber in early 1970s

A complete suit of sails were produced in 1984 by a combination of hand and machine work made for the freight carrier *Guinness Clipper* (later *Atlantic Clipper*)– which used to trade regularly sailing on the Plymouth - West Indies run.
A 104ft wishbone ketch, she was built in Wales and her first sailing trial was in the Round the Island Race.

The continued success over such a long period owed as much to the skill and dedication of the firm's employees as it did to the management's involvement and though Lucas's catered for most sailing requirements, the bulk of their trade lay with the average club cruising owner, rather than the exotic spectaculars or even the racing circuit.

Being based in Broad Street meant that many members of the Portsmouth Sailing Club and the Victory Class, both based in Bath Square, used their services for cutting new sails and maintaining old sails, together with the purchase of chandlery when needed.

The company always tried to keep the best of the past, such as still offering a hand stitching service, while looking towards modern developments to improve their techniques, in which computer technology began to figure very prominently.

Indeed, Lucas was one of the first sail makers to venture into this field, building up their own auto plotter in the mid-80s, developed under the direction of Peter Lucas by their consultant, David Mathias, one of the foremost computer programmers in the country.

Capable of computing luff and foot round, panel shape and size of sail, besides altering one or more of the parameters as required and changing any others at the same time, the Apple computer translated this information into instructions to the auto plotter.

The panel shapes were then drawn directly on to the bolt of cloth, so eliminating the human element and ensuring ability to reproduce repetitively and with utmost accuracy.
In the mid-1980s they also invested in the latest heavy duty wide arm sewing machine, one of the first to come from the German makers Adler and costing £10,000 at that time.
.
Working on compressed air, the wide arm allowed the machinist to sew all the modern types of sailcloth, some of which were difficult to gather and pass through a narrow arm.

This was a far cry indeed from Colin Lucas's 30 year old Singer machine dredged up from the Camber after the Second World War!

With an obvious eye to the future, many of the firm's workforce came from the younger age group and were promoted within the company, having served their four year apprenticeship.

The company expanded their export market to Scandinavia, where they secured an order for the Albin Ballad design in the mid-1970s, producing 250 mainsails and jibs a year, together with another 100 No 1s, No 2 Genoas and storm jibs. – No headsail furling at that time!

The company also ventured into a close association with Moody's in the late 1970s, enabling them to start producing many sails for the cruiser market as well as making racing sails for Illingworth and Primrose designed boats.
Many of the employees were keen on sailing and were very pleased to have the chance to work for the company. Learning the trade as an apprentice was quite hard going, but regretfully the apprenticeship scheme finished in the mid-1980s.

However, after the apprenticeship scheme finished the company still tried to take on school leavers and many became competent sailmakers after a couple of years.
In the mid-80s the company was one of the five largest lofts in the country and with the founder's great grandson, Peter, at the helm they were established sailmakers and yacht outfitters with an enviable international reputation.

At that time their familiar logo was just as likely to be seen in the United States or the Far East as on the Solent or the North Sea. Annual turnover was then £1/2 million from the sail loft with £150,000 from the chandlery, 25% of production going in exports and a well-filled order book.

Lucas's had a reputation for making very large sails as they had one of the largest sail lofts in the country and produced sails for the sail training schooners.

Among the largest jobs they undertook were the awnings for the Royal Yacht, *Britannia,* which involved a lot of handwork and stitching which the navy weren't keen to undertake themselves. They had the contract for this work for 20 years making them to the original specification. They had to pitch a wire around the edge and all this work was very time consuming.

The largest commission the company ever undertook was in the mid-1980s as a one off, were sails for the large staysail schooner *Fleurje* (187 ft. length and registered as 295 tonnes) with wishbones 140ft overall. The sails were over 100ft on the luff so to stretch the sails out diagonally in the sail loft, the doors had to be removed from the office. This was the largest sail they ever made and the total order was for 8 sails. At that time the cleared sail loft floor was 120ft x 70ft.

The staysail schooner *Fleurje.*

One side-line introduced by the company in the early 1990s was the production of woven polyethylene trolley bags for supermarkets, of which they made more than a million in the UK and another million in the Far East. They were sending container loads of 40,000 bags every month and this business continued for 4 or 5 years.

Sail making loft and chandlery in Broad Street

By the end of the 1990s the yachting industry was changing: sails were being made in China and Indonesia and margins were being squeezed.

By the mid-1990s much of Old Portsmouth, including Point, was being redeveloped for residential properties and the site was a very desirable plot, so the company decided to sell in 1999 and relocate to Wicor at Fareham, where they remained for many years. They are now based at Portchester.

They will certainly be remembered by many as a company that left their mark on Point

Chapter 5

Grogan's

"Grogan's" was a very well-known cafe/restaurant that existed for more than 50 years in Broad Street.

Grogan's restaurant was a very popular place in the twentieth century and was a widely used eating house for many locals and visitors to the area including members of the Portsmouth Sailing Club with their headquarters being located nearby in Bath Square.

The restaurant was located on the east side of Broad Street adjacent to the *Star and Garter* hotel and the building was originally the *Ship Worcester* pub which ceased trading c. 1908.

The premises were used for several years as a dining house after it was opened as the Coronation Coffee Tavern in 1911. Later in c 1918 Mrs Sophia Grogan (known as Granny Grogan) took over the premises, having already previously established a restaurant in Gosport.

Sophia Grogan in 1942.

The front window in 1935.

The property extended from its entrance in Broad Street to the back of the premises which fronted "Dirty Corner", overlooking the Camber where there was an open deck for eating outside and steps down to the beach below. The properties nearby had been built long ago and there were numerous small boats moored up on the beach, afloat at high water.

The rear of the premises (the white building) can be see fronting on to Dirty Corner.

The downstairs of the property was where one was served a cup of tea and the like and upstairs was the main dining room.

The downstairs of the property.

GROGAN'S CAFE :: RESTAURANT
PHONE 737541

OPEN ON SUNDAYS

Grogan's of Old Portsmouth

Links up with the past in this way . . . it was originally the famous old public house "Ship Worcester". In Coronation Year 1911, it was opened as the "Coronation Coffee Tavern". Through the years it has become a favourite rendezvous of sailing club members and others. In fact it is the place for an excellent meal—reasonably priced

We shall be pleased to welcome you to
BREAKFAST, LUNCH,
AFTERNOON TEA or HIGH TEA

Advert showing the main dining room upstairs in the building.

Sophia Grogan had a large family and her sons and daughters were well known on the Point. One of her daughters, Ella went on to run the *Union Tavern* on Point for many years.

After Granny Grogan passed away, the business was run by two of her daughters, Kitty and Nip MacDonald, who had both married brothers from the same family who were tragically killed whilst in the Forces.
Nip's husband was killed during the Second World War and Kitty's husband was lost in the tragic sinking of the submarine M2 that sank off Portland with the loss of all 60 hands in 1932.

The M2 submarine was the first submarine in the world to carry an aircraft on board.
This accident occurred when the submarine was on exercise: the disaster was thought to have been caused by the hangar door being opened too early when the boat was still submerged.

Like other properties in Broad Street, Grogan's suffered from tidal flooding on occasions as this photo c 1955 shows, which made for interesting times for both customers and the owners of the café.

Kitty MacDonald lived in Bath Square, but the back of her house was in Broad Street and was directly opposite the café.

Grogan's continued to flourish on Point for many years, but eventually was forced to close in 1959, along with a number of other adjacent properties, following a compulsory purchase order served by the City Council. This order was served to allow for a new terminal building, car park and slipway to be constructed to allow the Isle of Wight car ferry operating from Point to have more space.

Grogan's café photographed just prior to its demolition.

The Floating Bridge ceased its operations in 1959 and with the opening of the new car ferry terminus in 1961, life for many residents in Broad Street became much more bearable with the cessation of the queuing traffic.

However, it was a sad day to see such a large part of Broad Street and its history lost for ever, particularly as these properties had managed to survive the worst of Hitler's bombing of the city.

Following the loss of the restaurant, Grogan's then moved to new premises sited on the upper floor of the new terminal building and continued to operate there for several years until Kitty MacDonald (known as Mrs Mac) retired in 1970, later passing away in 1975.

At this location Grogan's offered a daytime view of Portsmouth's commercial harbour and a night time setting of unfussy comfort.

The restaurant set out to meet the requirements of two major customers – the traveller on his way to or from the Island, or the gourmet intent on spending a leisurely hour or two with good food and a comprehensive wine list. The restaurant was very proud of its reputation for always serving fresh caught lobsters supplied by local divers.

Although the new building provided modern facilities, the character never matched that of the original premises and it was a sad loss to Point when the building was demolished, resulting in the loss of more local history for ever.

Nevertheless, the new premises were very popular, catered for numerous wedding receptions and were missed by many when Mrs Mac finally retired. The premises are no longer used as a restaurant, but as offices for K B Boats.

Grogan's café/restaurant was well loved and used by many local residents, visitors and many of the workers in the Camber and it was a sad day when the café ceased trading. However, there are still large numbers of people in the city today and elsewhere that have vivid memories of this family business that was an integral part of Point in its day.

Chapter 6

Portsmouth Sailing Club

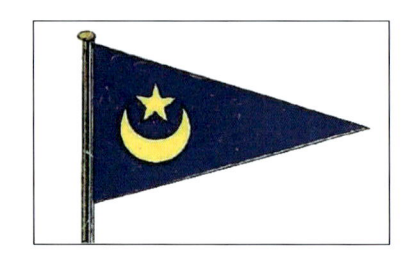

Original burgee

Existing burgee

The Headquarters in Bath Square

The early years

The Portsmouth Sailing Club has existed on Spice Island for nearly 100 years. Still very active today, it is located in its original headquarters in Bath Square.

The Club was formed on 17th March 1920 at an inaugural meeting held at the Mission Hall, Broad Street which was reported in the Portsmouth News on 18th March 1920 as follows:

PORTSMOUTH SAILING CLUB.

Promising Inaugural Meeting.

The Portsmouth Sailing Club came into existence on Wednesday evening at a meeting held in the Mission Hall, Broad-street, and presided over by Mr. W. L. Wyllie, R.A. Over 30 members were enrolled there and then, and Mr. W. L. Wyllie undertook the responsible position of Commodore, while the meeting decided unanimously to ask the Mayor (Councillor John Timpson, J.P.), and Mr. W. L. Long to become vice-commodore and rear-commodore respectively. Mr. C. Sherlock was appointed hon. secretary pro. tem., and Mr. A. J. Bowden hon. treasurer. Rules were framed, and it was decided that the entrance fee should be 2s. 6d., and the annual subscription 7s. 6d. or by payments of 9d. per month). Sea Scouts under 19 years of age will be admitted at an inclusive subscription of 5s. per annum.

It was left to a committee to frame sailing rules, to prepare the book of rules, and to carry out any other details in connection with the formation of the club; and another meeting is to be held at the Mission Hall, Broad-stret, a fortnight hence. Hearty thanks were extended to Mr. Wyllie for presiding, and to Mr. Sherlock for undertaking the secretarial work, the former remarking that if they all pulled together he could see great possibilities for the Club. He hoped it would be possible for them to have a handicap class and a one-design class.

Mr. Sherlock said he was in hopes they would have had one good club for both Portsmouth and Gosport members. Gosport had forestalled them in holding their meeting and forming their club, but he still hoped that in the near future there would be a fusion of the two.

The founder members of the Portsmouth Sailing Club (PSC) encompassed a small but broad spectrum of the local seafaring community: - boat builders, fishermen and artisans, topped up with some notable personalities from the Services, business and artistic world.

The latter included the famous W. L. Wyllie, coupled with the likes of Admiral E. Charlton and A. G. H. Macpherson, men of high standing in their respective fields. Add the infusion of the capable 1st Portsmouth Sea Scouts, and there was the effective mix that made an impact in the sailing world and on standards of seamanship in the area.

A few days after this meeting the following advert was placed in the Portsmouth News inviting new members to join the club.

PUBLIC NOTICES

PORTSMOUTH SAILING CLUB

Commodore W. L. Wyllie, R. A.

THE ABOVE CLUB HAS BEEN FORMED TO ENCOURAGE

BOAT SAILING AND RACING.

THE SECOND MEETING

Will he held at

THE MISSION HALL

BROAD STREET, PORTSMOUTH

ON WEDNESDAY MARCH 31st at 8pm.

TO ENROL MEMBERS INTERESTED IN THE SPORT

Applications by letter should be addressed to the Hon Sec, C. Sherlock, 81 Somerset Road, Southsea.

At the second meeting it was decided to invite the Lord Mayor, Councillor John Timpson J.P., to become the club's first president. It was also reported that the club had written to the Gosport Sailing Club, inviting them to join the Portsmouth Sailing Club to enable the formation of a strong club in Portsmouth Harbour: this suggestion was rejected.

A design for the club burgee was agreed and it was to be of the Borough colours: a Royal blue background with crescent and star in the centre worked in yellow or gold.

This early design was later changed to the current burgee in the 1930s, which was created by merging alternative designs drawn by Harold Wyllie and Jack Ashdown

On the sailing side a letter was written to the Royal Portsmouth Corinthian Yacht Club, formed in 1880 and later merging with the Royal Albert Yacht Club in 1946, requesting use of their boat house on Southsea beach when it might be available. At the meeting it was also agreed that initially the sailing should be confined to cruising to enable younger members to gain sailing experience.

Royal Portsmouth Corinthian Yacht Club signal station 1883.

In July 1920 The Royal Albert Yacht Club kindly held a handicap race for the PSC. There were 9 entries that raced over a course of nearly 10 miles and the race was won by one of the bigger boats named *Goodbye,* helmed by Harry Feltham, one of the local boat builders on Point. The competitors included the Commodore - Mr W.L.Wyllie sailing the *Maid of Kent;* the Vice Commodore, Mr Long in *Lapwing* (won on handicap); and the Rear Commodore, Mr Macpherson, sailing *Query*.

Since the inaugural March meeting Mr A. G. H. Macpherson had been elected to the post of Rear Commodore.

First Cruise to Ryde 22nd May 1920. © Portsmouth Sailing Club

The opening cruise of the club was to Ryde in May 1920 and entries included the Commodore, W.L.Wyllie, in the *Maid of Kent*, the Rear Commodore, Mr A. H. Macpherson, in *Pigtail* and the Sea Scouts in their ex lifeboat *Diosy*.

On arrival, most of the boat's crews were invited for tea at the Royal Pier Hotel Ryde and after tea the competitors returned to their moorings at Portsmouth.

At the end of the first season the first annual meeting of the PSC was held at the "George" Hotel, High Street. It was well attended and it was reported at the meeting that both Southsea Rowing Club and Portsmouth Swimming Club gave support to the revival of a Southsea Regatta.

A wide-ranging discussion was held about future racing and it was agreed that a one-design centreboard dinghy be designed which could be home built by members: 10ft pram dinghies were favoured. The club's balance sheet at the end of their inaugural year showed cash of £10 0s 11d in the bank.

In 1921 a new headquarters was adopted at the *Dolphin* Hotel, High Street. 70 members attended the second AGM in October 1921.

The second season was very successful, with a good attendance for the handicap races and the club's one design "prams" proving themselves to be remarkable little sea boats.

The Commodore promised to paint a picture depicting the Club's Headquarters to be hung over the hotel entrance and this was completed and hung up in May 1922. It was framed in teak and protected behind glass. The painting shows the mouth of Portsmouth Harbour with the *Victory* floating proudly in her old position and many of the club members' boats are included in the painting. This painting, shown below, still hangs in the club premises today.

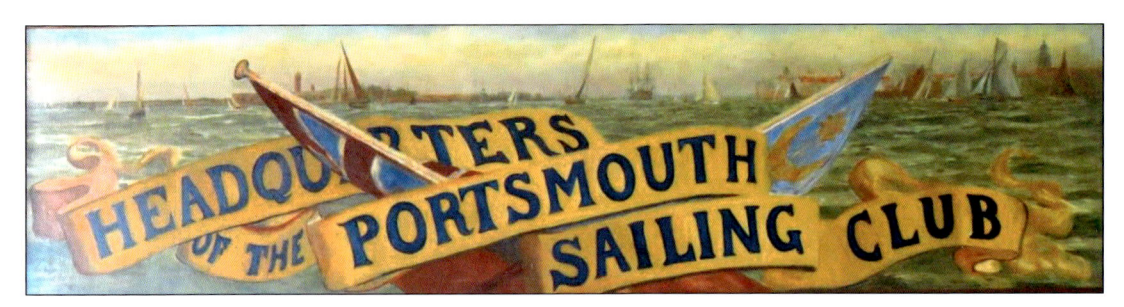

Racing continued to prosper, both in the handicap fleet and also the one-design pram class. In 1922 the club rented the Boomyard at the West Street/Tower Street junction at a nominal rent and part of the yard was sectioned off for use of the 1st Portsmouth Sea Scouts. There was a slipway extending from the Boomyard into Portsmouth Harbour entrance for launching dinghies at this time, although this unfortunately fell into disrepair towards the latter part of the twentieth century.

The Boomyard once housed an engine that was used to raise the defence boom that was deployed across Portsmouth Harbour entrance during war time.

At the 6th annual dinner in December 1925 the room was decorated with bunting, palms and other plants, together with trophies and pictures of sailing craft. The club offered its sincere thanks to the Royal Albert Yacht Club (RAYC) for allowing the PSC to start and finish their races from their signal station on the seafront. Great thanks were also accorded to the East Cowes Sailing Club with whom the club had inter club races: the clubs had formed a great relationship that would be continued, for many years.

At this meeting the Commodore mentioned that the club was in negotiation to purchase the Consulate House in Bath Square as a premises for their own clubhouse.

In addition to an excellent racing season many members had successful cruises to the West Country, Brest and other French ports and also to the Thames and East Coast. It was the Rear Commodore, Mr A. G. H. Macpherson who undertook the most extensive cruises, which was no surprise when one considers the cruises he was to undertake in future years.

Another event held in that year held in a large Southsea café was the "Annual Ladies Night", an event at which there were extensive musical performances by artists with an excellent musical programme.

Permanent headquarters

1926 was a landmark year for the club as it purchased the freehold premises of the Old Consulate in Bath Square, a building with three floors and a basement. It was refurbished and refurnished, providing a spacious billiard room with billiard table, piano etc. very suitable for whist drives, dancing and other social events. It also had room below for storing small boats and equipment.

This building had a well-known history and had for many years been the offices of Louis Arnoldus Van den bergh & Son. A listing in an 1865 Portsmouth Directory shows their business at that time to be:

> Merchants and shipping agents, Consuls and Vice-consuls for France, Austria, Turkey, Prussia, Holland, Hanover, Belgium, Lubec, Bremen, Portugal and Oldenburgh, agents for the Hamburg and Bremen Maritime Assurance Company.

Painting of P.S.C headquarters c. 1922.

The new Clubhouse was opened on 27th March 1926 by the Commodore's wife, Mrs M. A. Wyllie. The purchase was financed by members purchasing debenture shares at a minimal interest rate. Presents of pictures from the Commodore and other members helped to decorate the premises and visitors from other sailing clubs attended the opening.

It was reported at the annual meeting of that year that the season had again been very successful on the sailing side with 112 additional members, more boats than previous years and a number of racing successes.

Various social events were held throughout the year including a "Trafalgar" Smoking Concert, which boasted an extensive musical programme and included much singing by both professionals and amateurs, including club members.

In August 1927 a Harbour Regatta was held under the burgee of the PSC with 26 different events including sailing, rowing, swimming and novelty races between Clarence Pier and the Round Tower with large crowds watching the Regatta from the beach.

The Patron of the club in 1927 was recorded as being the Commander in Chief, Portsmouth, (Admiral Sir Osmond de Brock), President; the Mayor, Cllr Frank Privett, Commodore; W.L.Wyllie, Vice Commodore; Mr A. G. H. Macpherson, Rear Commodore; Admiral Sir Edward Charlton.

The racing since the club had been formed had been relatively successful during the first 10 years with the 10ft pram dinghy class proving to be a good sea boat. There was also racing in the "B" class (less than 16ft in length) and "A" class (16 ft. length and over) with some starts being from the Boomyard premises in the harbour entrance and other starts using the RAYC starting line at Southsea beach.

The club had formed very strong links with local clubs including East Cowes SC, Locks SC and Portchester SC and Inter Club competitions were introduced.

An interesting article concerning the Vice Commodore appeared in the local newspaper in 1927.

> **Yachting Officer's Narrow Escape.**
>
> RESCUED BY NAVAL PINNACE.
>
> Southsea, Monday.
>
> Mr. G. H. Macpherson Vice-Commodore of the Portsmouth Sailing Club, and a member of the Royal Albert Yacht Club, narrowly escaped being drowned at Southsea yesterday. Whilst sailing his 18 footer "Idea" single handed the boat capsized and Mr. Macpherson was thrown into the water.
>
> He seized a lifebuoy and chair which were on the boat but he was in the water an hour before he was rescued by a pinnace from H.M.S. Furious. Mr. Macpherson had been taking part in a race but had retired and was returning to Portsmouth Harbour when the mishap occurred.

This description of an unfortunate incident could have ended in tragedy but fortunately did not and Macpherson went on to accomplish great things during his life.

Newspaper article in May 1927.

There were some extensive cruises undertaken by members during this time. In 1929 A. G. H. Macpherson, the Vice Commodore, undertook two cruises in his 24 ton yawl *Myth*, the first to Havre, Cherbourg, Channel Isles and St Malo and the second to the Scillies, south and west coasts of Ireland, the Hebrides, the Clyde and Irish Sea and later sailed across Biscay to Santander via Brest and back home to France and the Channel Isles. All this cruising in a single season totalled in excess of 5000 miles, which proved to be an introduction to the extensive cruising he was to undertake later.

One class of boat that proved very popular when designed and built locally in the early 1930s was the Wyllie 10 ft. clinker One Design dinghy designed by W. L. Wyllie. These craft were quite revolutionary in their time as they carried 90 sq. ft. of working sail and a 50 sq. ft. spinnaker and took some handling in a moderate wind.

Boats on the foreshore in the 1930s. © J.Copeland.

Wyllie 10ft dinghy under sail

In April 1931 W. L. Wyllie passed away with the funeral service for this great man being held in Portsmouth Cathedral. All in all this was a very sad day for both the Nation and Portsmouth and its community.

Wyllie had led the PSC since its very beginning, being elected as Commodore from its formation and still holding that office when he died in 1931. Fortunately the club had very able members that took over his role, although in many aspects he couldn't be replaced, particularly with his extensive maritime knowledge and worldwide connections.

Wyllie performed a striking act of heroism when he was a boy of 18 in 1869. During a furious gale he was walking along the seashore at Wimereux, Boulogne, along with his brother in law, the late Lionel Smythe R.A. An English schooner, the *Wheatsheaf* was driven on the rocks and, both being good swimmers, they swam out to the wreck and set up communications with the shore, which resulted in them saving the lives of the crew of 6.

Shortly after this event an English brig named the *Harmony* ran aground at the Pointe aux Oies about 3 miles from the first wreck and again Smythe and Wyllie repeated their courageous act, swimming out a second time and saving another 11 lives.

Following W. L. Wyllie's death in 1931, A. G. H. Macpherson became Commodore and later in the year introduced a proposal to have a new German one design class, the Sharpie, adopted by the Club, one of which had already been built locally by Mr Feltham.

A dozen sharpies were ordered by members during 1931 and other clubs including East Cowes, Portchester and Upper Hamble (Bursledon) were also ordering boats.

At the end of the year A. G. H. Macpherson held the office of Commodore, Admiral Sir Edward Charlton that of Vice Commodore and Col Harold Wyllie that of Rear Commodore.

During the 1930s there were some remarkable voyages in small boats by PSC members which were reported in the newspapers of the day, such as the following:

In October 1931

> Mr C. A. P. Clover and Mr S Searle referred to their cruise from Dungeness to Hardelot in France in a 10ft dinghy in June taking 11 hours 40 minutes to cross in an easterly wind. They left at 9am in the morning, passed the Varne lightship at 2.30pm and arrived ashore at 8.45, the crossing taking 11 hours 40 mins for just under 50 miles. It had taken them 30 hours over the previous two days to reach Dungeness from Portsmouth. They tried to sail to Belgium after arriving in Hardelot but with strong winds they couldn't make it and had the boat shipped back to England from Boulogne. They later returned to Portsmouth via Belgium and Holland.

Earlier that year in March, Mr Uffa Fox of Cowes gave a talk in the club about perilous voyages across the Atlantic and English Channel in small boats that he had experienced. The last trip he described was in his National 14 ft. dinghy, *Avenger*, from Cowes to Havre and back. He was caught in heavy weather returning being driven east of the Owers in a trip that took 17 hours with his crew constantly bailing.

In this era, sometimes members capsized in their boats and it was considered quite an embarrassment as boats were designed to be sailed upright not upside down!

At the Annual meeting in 1931 cruising logs were submitted and a cup was given to the best cruise and log. This was won by A. V. Copeland in his yacht *Viking* for a cruise to Fecamp during which they experienced a Channel gale.

Harry Feltham won the prestigious Lennox-Rawson cup at Hythe in the 14ft National dinghy *Venture* in August 1932 and it was the first time this much-coveted trophy had left Southampton since 1908.

In June 1932 interclub sailing was organised with other clubs including East Cowes, Portchester, Locks and Fareham. Racing in A class, B class and Sharpie class.

In Nov 1932 the club held a social weekend: on the Saturday there was a social evening and smoking concert and on the Sunday a fishing competition, with 12 boats going to Stokes Bay. The total catch was 300 fish with the heaviest fish, a skate, weighing in at 4 ½ lbs.

The drab décor of the club and its domination by male members was recalled in the local Evening News in the 1960s, describing the writer's recollection of the club in the 1930s:

> The thing I remember about the Portsmouth Sailing Club is walking as a small boy under the vast billiards table in the clubroom. It was a high squat table, a burst of colour in the drab brown and creams all around and it was surrounded by brooding leather armchairs, like mud huts edging a cricket square. The billiards table, the ancient horsehair chairs and the upright iron stove were the epitome of what the club was. This room was the refuge, where one could relax after a hard day at sea; there was complete freedom, a bar and a bare lino floor to drip salt water on at will.

At that time women were excluded, then allowed in as guests and finally full membership was voted in during the 1960s.

During 1932 there was a North Sea drama involving six PSC members, all naval officers, including a relative of the then Commodore A. G. H. Macpherson.

They set off from Portsmouth bound for Le Havre on Wed Oct 4th in 2 boats, the half decked *Wallop*, 18ft in length, and the *Little Owl* of 16ft. They successfully reached their destination and enjoyed a week's holiday sailing in the area. They then left bound for home on the following Wednesday having got a forecast in advance which was good and set off in light airs. After 50 miles the two boats started getting stronger winds which swung around and increased, forcing them to run off under bare poles and bailing as water came on board. The boats became separated late on the Wednesday night as conditions deteriorated.

On the Thursday night the crew of the *Wallop* were rescued 13 miles from the Owers lightship by the steamer *Glen Mary,* abandoning the ship, which was lost. There was no news of the *Little Owl* until she was spotted on Friday in the North Sea by a Dutch steamer and the crew were taken off and landed ashore in Antwerp.

Macpherson's voyages

In March 1932 the Commodore's famous yacht *Driac II,* built by Harry Feltham, was launched in Bath Square and lowered down the beach on a trolley with the mast stepped and fully rigged.

Driac II, a younger sister to *Driac I,* had much of a family resemblance with her Bermudian rig and bumpkin, supporting a permanent backstay and with a very pronounced sheer and freeboard.

Driac II   A.G.H.Macpherson

She was a cutter of some 32 feet overall with a 25.5 foot waterline, beam of 8.5 ft. and draught of 5.5 feet (8 tons Thames measurement).

Macpherson's previous yacht, *Driac I*, purchased in 1930, was a new 13 ton (40ft overall) cutter built for him by Camper and Nicholson. In her he cruised the Baltic and German Coast, followed by extensive Mediterranean cruising in late 1930 and into the following season.

The distance logged on his exploits in the Baltic was 3039 miles and during the cruise to Malta and the Northern Mediterranean he logged 5539 miles.

For her shakedown cruise, Macpherson took *Driac II* for a blow across the Bay of Biscay, starting in mid-April with Colonel B. T. T. Lawrence, V.C., as his cruising companion, together with Bill Leng as paid hand.
She set off for the Channel Islands under trysail in a fresh fair wind (Macpherson did not want to stretch the new mainsail) and on arrival spent 3 days in St Peter Port.

After working her way down the Brittany coast making numerous stops, she arrived at Brest where they visited Madame Angot's, taking in a show, although Macpherson commented that the chorus girl fairies were heavy weights and must have averaged 16 stone in weight!

They then set sail for Santander, a distance of 275 miles on May 3rd and made a bad landfall, finally arriving in Santander on May 6th after suffering from bad visibility and unreliable sights.

The return voyage took in numerous ports along the French Coast including Les Sables, Belle Isle and the Morbihan, which Macpherson found "wonderfully pretty, if a little chocolate- boxy compared with the ruggedness of the Spanish coast, but could have spent a week exploring".

Further time was spent visiting many ports in south Brittany on the homeward voyage and they set off back across the Channel, arriving at Brixham, experiencing fog and head winds en route. The distance made good on the cruise was 1,359 miles.

The trip had been a good shakedown cruise, but what had turned out particularly worthwhile was the partnership that grew out of it, since Bill Leng had shipped as *Driac's* paid hand at the age of 22 and he subsequently never left her.

In 1932 they cruised to the Azores logging 3022 miles.

In 1933 they cruised to Iceland logging 2806 miles.

Driac II left Portsmouth on 6th September 1934 for the West Indies, Honduras Coast, Miami and Mexico Coast to Bermuda and then to Gibraltar, north coast of the Mediterranean, Black Sea and Dalmatian Coast to Haifa and Port Said and through the Red Sea and across the Indian Ocean, calling at various islands to Colombo.

They cruised up the Bay of Bengal to near Calcutta, then down to Singapore and through the Malay Straits to the East Indies and on to Australia (Port Darwin), back through the Timor Sea, across the Indian Ocean to Madagascar calling at the small islands and thence to Durban.

From 1932 to 1938 *Driac II* sailed 45,000 miles and during this period she had refits at

Gibraltar, Haifa, Singapore and Durban.

Mr. John Scott Hughes, who edited the record of "Macpherson's Voyages" published in 1944, states in his introduction:

> In this small yacht the series of voyages undertaken by Macpherson exceeded in scope and duration anything comparable in the annals of seafaring.
>
> With Bill Leng his devoted companion and fellow club member, Macpherson sailed his 25 foot waterline cutter across many oceans, visiting over 100 countries and states, covering in all 45,000 miles.

At the end of his last voyage from Bali to Durban he showed his appreciation by making a present of *Driac II* to Bill Leng.

After some 4 years and 9 months of almost constant sailing, *Driac II* returned to Portsmouth: during the period of 1932 – 1939 she had covered a total distance of 56,280 miles.

Despite Macpherson's sailing achievements, it must be realized what amazing foresight and mighty endeavor he possessed in amassing a superb collection of maritime art, including more than 7,500 maritime prints, rare books, atlases etc. After an examination in 1924 by Capt. H Parker F.R.G.S, F.R.His.S , a recognized art expert, the collection was stated to be "the finest and most wealthy collection of marine pictures ever gathered together and it is one that moreover can never be replaced and its value has not yet been fully recognized"

Macpherson had long realized that it was of national importance and after a visit to see the collection at an exhibition in London, King George V encouraged him to keep the collection together until help came to make it a national possession. At this time Macpherson had sunk all his money into the collection, had borrowed extensively and owed money to the trade. Fortunately, Sir James Caird, who had previously helped save HMS *Victory* from extinction, showed remarkable generosity ensuring the collection passed into the ownership of the Trustees who had been assembled for a National Museum for the Sea at that time. Six years later an Act was passed constituting a National Maritime Museum at Greenwich.

Macpherson certainly left his mark in the nation's cruising history and has left a lasting legacy with his collection of 12,000 works of art that form the basis of the National Collection at Greenwich Maritime Museum.

In August 1932 two young members of the PSC, Leslie Ayres and A. W. Griffin, crossed to Cherbourg and back in a 16ft. sharpie, the return trip taking 16 hours.

In January 1932 four members of the PSC purchased a Brixham trawler named *Iunita* and brought her to Haslar creek with a view to doing her up in readiness for a voyage later in the year to British Honduras to carry out shark fishing for the purpose of using the shark skin for making a variety of leather goods to sell.

They eventually set off in August with a crew of 5 men and a boy with A. J. Macdonald as skipper. After leaving Portsmouth they met a 6-day gale in the Channel, forcing them into Falmouth for repairs. They sailed to Vigo and then to Las Palmas and on to Trinidad for a passage of 36 days. They were becalmed in the Atlantic for 10 days but then made a record day's sailing of 224 miles in 24 hours. However, not long after reaching Barbados they decided to sell the boat.

In June 1933 another PSC member made a cross Channel trip single-handed in a 16ft boat, leaving Portsmouth on Tuesday morning and arriving at Etretat on Wednesday morning before setting off for Le Havre. The return crossing took 42 hours and the voyager got brief snatches of sleep during both crossings by putting the boat on a course, trimming the sails and lashing the tiller.

All these exploits by members in small open boats goes to show how brave these yachtsmen were when one considers the sailing equipment and lack of built in buoyancy at that time and the basic communications that were available if one got in trouble.

These two photos show how the Boomyard used to look pre-war when boats were stored on a raised platform and how vulnerable the yard was to tidal flooding.

Dinghy approaching Boomyard slipway   The Boomyard after a storm.

In the 1920s and 1930s the club held an annual dance, usually at a local Southsea venue such as Kimbells or the Mikardo club and it was always very well attended. There were also annual general meetings together with prize giving for the annual season's sailing events.

Albert (Pop) Meadows

One of the Club's larger - than- life characters in the 1930s and following years was Mr Albert Meadows, known as "Pop" Meadows, who became Rear Commodore.

This painting of "Pop" hangs in the Sailing Club and was painted by the wife of ex Commodore Harold Wyllie under her maiden name "Hilary Strain". The photo below is of his yacht *Sabrina,* a beautiful boat built by Clemens boat builders in Broad Street based on the Harrison Butler design. © Portsmouth Sailing Club.

Born circa 1891, Meadows was apprenticed on a Bristol Channel Pilot Cutter aged 14 and later was a formidable boxer. He was tall and very well built with immense physical strength as those who knew him witnessed and he created a real presence when entering a room.

On one occasion in 1937, a naval motor launch, a fast speedboat type of vessel, was involved in an accident in the harbour entrance when, due to a violent rolling action, one person fell overboard. Fortunately, Pop was in another vessel nearby with a Sea Scout in the bow. The Scout tried to get hold of the man but wasn't strong enough, at which point Pop seized the man by his collar and trousers and hauled him aboard, preventing what could have been a very serious outcome.

During the Second World war Pop laid *Sabrina* up in Newtown Creek above Shalfleet Quay on the Isle of Wight. There was a natural ditch there that he dug out further where he berthed her near some trees. He also drove in some piles and built a small landing stage and, with the trees giving protection, it was difficult to spot her from the air. This little water course was known as Sabrina Creek.

He was at one time the boatswain of the Admiralty Police in Portsmouth Dockyard before finishing his career in the Metropolitan Water Police on the Thames. He was renowned for his single handed sailing, usually along the south coast, and for many years he served as Harbour Master at Newtown Creek, being known as Captain Meadows. He lived aboard *Sabrina* into his old age continuing as a PSC member until his death in the early 1970s.

In addition to starting races from Southsea beach and the Boomyard in the harbour entrance, some racing was held in Portsmouth Harbour using the *Implacable,* the old 74 gun timber warship, as the start/finish line, particularly regattas. Fortunately, Lt. Col Harold Wyllie was in command of the *Implacable*, used as a training ship for boys and he was a PSC member.

In 1934 the "Victory class" made its debut with 14 yachts sailing in their first season, with 21 yachts available at the start of the second season. The boat rose like a phoenix from the ashes of a Bembridge Sailing Club boat first built in 1904.

Victory class Z 30 *Zena*

Alfred Westmacott is credited with her design and she started her life as a 20ft 4in part decked gaff rigged yacht with approx. 200 sq. ft. of sail and a 11 cwt iron keel, together with a board that lifted through a slot in the keel, enabling her to sail over banks and shoals near Bembridge. The "new" Victory class boat was 20ft 9 ins overall with a draft of 2ft 6ins and carried 195 sq. ft. of sail with half ton ballast in the keel. The original lifting keel had been replaced with 2 cwt of trimming ballast inboard and roller reefing gear for the main and foresail.

The class went from strength to strength and many Victory class members have continued to play a significant role in the history of the PSC. The boats are still regularly racing today, with races on weekday evenings and weekends and they still compete as a class at Cowes week.

With regards dinghy racing in the 1930s, there was Class racing for the Wyllie 10ft dinghy and the Sharpies. In 1936 it was reported that the Wyllie 10 ft. dinghies were still getting at least 10 boats competing in some of their races. However, as the decade came to an end with war on the horizon the numbers turning out in these fleets were reducing, although the fast and slow handicap fleets were still popular.

Members hauling up a boat from the Boomyard slipway.

By 1937 the sailing club had 300 members. Many of these sailed and owned boats and the percentage of active sailing members was very high and far in excess of the norm.

Cruiser racing in the club was still very popular and there were passage races to Wootton, Cowes, Portchester, Newtown, Lymington and sometimes to Poole. At Whitsun in 1937 the race to Poole had 13 entrants in a fresh northerly wind. Some very fast times were posted with the first boat "Pallas" completing the 37 mile course in 4 hours.

Many members went on annual cruises and there was a trophy awarded to the yacht with the best cruising log at the end of the season.

Another race introduced for cruisers was the annual PSC "Round the Isle of Wight" race which usually proved to be very popular. Unfortunately, during the 1937 event tragedy struck with a crew member being drowned. The incident was reported thus:

> In the Annual PSC round the Island Race in August there were 11 starters. A crew member of the 6 ton cutter *Nepenthe* fell overboard off St Catherine's. The crew launched the dinghy and took down the sail and someone went overboard with a rope but he had to be pulled back on board. Eventually the boat came alongside the casualty, Mr de Winton, a 33 year old bank accountant, not a PSC member, and got him aboard now unconscious but he sadly died.

With regards moorings in the harbour, there were insufficient available to cope with demand and pre-war discussions with the Admiralty concerning a proposal to use parts of Haslar Creek and Cold Harbour were rejected for operational reasons. In later years, after the end of the war, moorings were laid by some club members in Cold Harbour but the main mooring area was in Weevil Creek, where the club still retains moorings today, together with a few moorings laid to the north of Haslar marina and some further north in the harbour near Pile 103.

During the war, unlike most clubs, the PSC did not close down, although activities decreased as more and more members joined the Forces. Many of the club nights were spent fire watching and fighting fires on Point as it was a very "hot" area with regular enemy sorties. Immediately after the war the club underwent a rebirth that from the start directed it on a new course. In October 1942 the Commodore, Macpherson died in Scotland and his remains were scattered at sea off Southsea.

Club members outside the club headquarters during the war. The Wyllie painting is clearly visible above the entrance with the word PORTSMOUTH covered up.

Once restrictions were lifted after the war, racing grew rapidly with a strong "B" class fleet consisting of boats from numerous pre-war classes, most built by either George Feltham or his brother Harry Feltham. Timber was in short supply, making it very difficult to have a boat built during this period. After the war, Lt. Col. Harold Wyllie, O.B.E was elected Commodore.

However, when wood became more easily available the Stormalong class was designed, a 12ft 6in overall length clinker dinghy with a cruising and racing rig. The first boat, appropriately named *Stormalong* (S1), was built by George Feltham in 1946. A total of 14 boats were constructed over several years and they raced as a class at the PSC for many years. Safe, pretty and not slow, they dominated the scene until the mid-1950s.

Stormalong *Scorpion* S2

After the war interclub sailing regattas were held: racing was very keen and close links were maintained with other local sailing clubs including, East Cowes, Portchester, Stokes Bay, Locks and Hardway. By 1950 the club had 100 boats and 430 members and had purchased the old Royal Albert Signal Station at Southsea. It had also formed a cadet section and encouraged more young members to join.

Boats racing post war in the harbour entrance

A racing fleet with H M S Dolphin behind.

PSC Signal Station on Southsea beach.

In 1950 Lt Col Harold Wyllie, O.B.E., the PSC Commodore, was now in command of the *Foudroyant* in Portsmouth Harbour, used for training young boys and girls, following the deliberate sinking of his previous old ship the *Implacable* in the English Channel in 1949.

The *Implacable* being towed out of Portsmouth Harbour in 1949

The club continued to hold Annual Regattas and classes competing in the mid-1950s included Yachting World Cadets, Fireflies, National 12s, Victories, Stormalongs, Whalers and Stars.

In December 1953 a member of the PSC, Mr Bernard Needle, invented a speedometer suitable for small craft. The speedometer was tried in a Stormalong dinghy with "Farmer" Needle as crew. This new invention was taken up by Mr Ian Proctor of Hamble to undertake further tests to consider its suitability for further design as a potential commercial venture.

Popular dinghy classes in the club in the early 1950s were the 12ft Nationals and Fireflies and small fleets built up fairly rapidly and usually raced as joint classes. However, they dwindled away and by 1955 the Albacore class was beginning to emerge with the first home built boat constructed in 1955.

At this time one problem with dinghy sailing in Portsmouth Harbour was that it was very difficult to participate in class racing in a modern boat as there were too many different classes in each club and people had to move to clubs like Hayling Island Sailing Club or Itchenor to get good class racing.

What was needed was a cheap boat, such as the Albacore, which had reasonable stability and good sailing qualities and following the building of a boat by an amateur, this first home built boat encouraged others to follow suit. Furthermore, the cost to build this boat was approx. £90, about half the works price with sails from an established boat builder.

The Albacores established themselves in the club for a number of years and there were 14 boats registered in 1963.

Dinghies on the foreshore at Fishbourne, Isle of Wight in the 1950s.

At the 1960 A.G.M, Howard White was re-elected Commodore, Vice Commodore was Peter Stewart, Rear Commodore Albert Meadows. The finances were reported as being in a healthy state and membership was just below 400 members.

In August 1962 the Albacore National Championships were hosted by Portsmouth Area Sailing Clubs and racing was held off the Royal Marine Barracks at Eastney, with boats stored ashore and launched from the beach.

Headquarters for the regatta were at the PSC and there were over 100 entries, including 10 boats from the PSC. The racing was held in very rough weather with some races having to relocate to Langstone harbour and there were many broken masts throughout the week. The leading PSC helmsman was Les Waters, who was placed 5th overall.

Albacore National Championships at Eastney 1962.

In the subsequent years after these championships, the Albacore fleet numbers gradually started to dwindle and the class that now began to dominate the club's dinghy racing was the Cherub dinghy.

The Cherub was 12 ft. in length and a high performance two man planing dinghy designed in 1951 in New Zealand by John Spencer.

Cherub *Tachyon*. Courtesy Chris Forman

The first two Cherubs were home built by club members in 1959 and by 1963 there were 10 boats with the fleet growing. Chris Hornsey, a club member, became the National Cherub Champion in 1962.

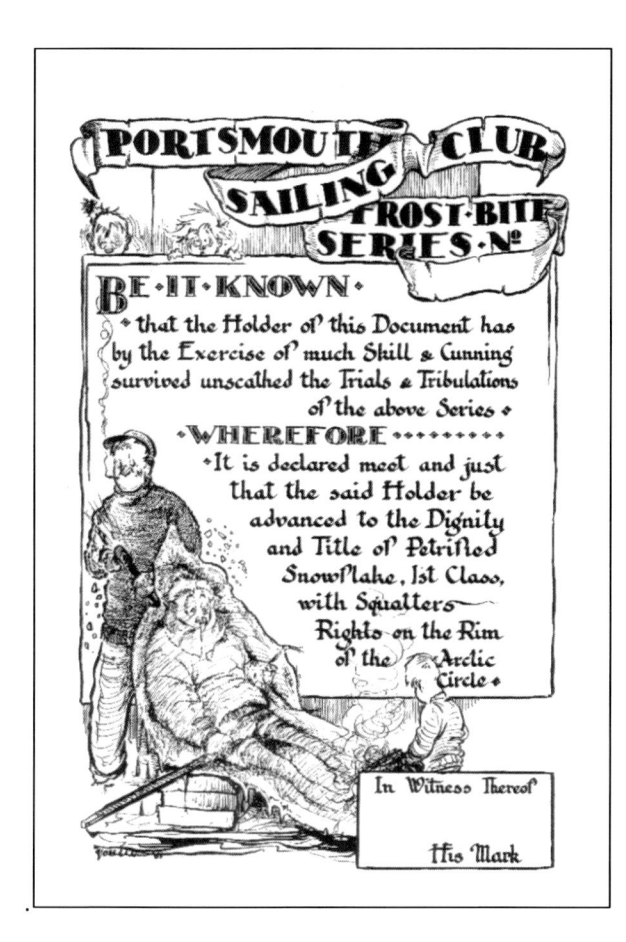

In 1963 there was an ever expanding Cadet section and the Frostbite series had become very popular since its introduction in 1959. The series comprised racing on Sunday mornings from early October up to Christmas and the series is still an annual event today.

This certificate, originally designed by Jack Ashdown is presented to competitors who compete in the Frostbite Series.

The club introduced a scheme to help youngsters purchase boats when they did not have the capital needed. Two boats, *Idea* and *Wallop II* were presented to the PSC many years ago by the late A. G. H. Macpherson, but were sold after difficulty with their upkeep. The money was put in a fund, called the Macpherson fund and any youngster who wanted to buy a boat could draw an interest free loan from this fund if the Committee agreed. Numerous cadet members used this fund to purchase their first boats.

Cruiser racing was still popular with members and the club had an active racing and social programme. Dinner/dances were held annually and there were regular talks given by members and other speakers on numerous subjects of interest. In October 1960 the annual prize giving was held at the Rock Gardens at a cost per ticket of 5 shillings.

In 1961 the regular seasonal racing programme included cups for Stormalongs, Albacores, Cherubs, B class, Nat 12 & Firefly class, together with all the passage races and fishing competition.

During the 1960s and the first half of the 1970s the Victory class continued to have regular racing and although there was handicap racing for dinghies, the Cherub was the dominant dinghy class. The club was fortunate in having Chris Forman as a member, as he produced several different Cherub designs over the years and drew up plans for easy construction for those wishing to build their own boat. This really helped the class numbers to swell and the fleet had a real boost in 1971 when five Cherubs were built in the sailing club loft by members.

Two of the Cherubs under construction in the Sailing Club loft.

It was a fun project for one and all and really boosted the Cherub fleet numbers at the club. Those members that built boats later discovered that the fire authorities who carried out the annual fire inspection at the club were less than impressed when they saw all the wood shavings in the loft. It proved to be the final curtain for building any boats on the premises due to the fire risk.

The zenith for Cherub racing at the club occurred in 1974 when the World Championships were held at Torquay. Among the 45 boat entry there were 8 PSC boats. It was a real eye-opener for many competitors from the UK since the racing was totally dominated by the visiting Cherubs from Australia and New Zealand, where the boat was originally conceived. Following on from these championships the Club numbers declined over the next few years from their peak of more than 20 boats and racing became more fragmented with general handicap racing dominating.

The regular evening dinghy racing programme became less popular over the following years and had stopped by 1977, although the Winter Frostbite series held in Portsmouth Harbour was a real success with a good competitive sized fleets of up to 40 boats with visitors entering from other local clubs. There was also a Boxing Day race to help blow away the Christmas cobwebs.

In circa 1970, the Sailing Club set up close links with the Portsmouth Polytechnic Sailing Club, resulting in them becoming affiliated to the PSC and being able to store their sailing dinghies in one of the boat compounds. This enabled Polytechnic's sailing club members to use the Portsmouth Sailing Club's clubhouse and facilities.

Many of these members stayed in Portsmouth after completing their education and some joined the PSC as full members, serving the club well over the years.

One sailing event that caught the World's attention was the Fastnet Race disaster of 1979 when 15 competitors lost their lives, 24 yachts were abandoned and several boats were sunk during a severe storm that blew up during the race whilst the fleet was in the Irish Sea.

One of the boats that sailed in that race, named *Camargue,* a 34ft sloop, had a number of PSC members on board as crew. Some famous photos were taken of her by a cameraman on the Wessex helicopter that rescued the crew.

All the crew had to abandon ship following the loss of her steering gear, broken by a huge wave. Crew members had to jump off the stern of the fast moving yacht, one by one, to be picked up by helicopter, which must have been a terrifying experience.

Fortunately, the operation was successful for all 8 crew members who were safely landed at Culdrose.

Camargue in heavy seas trailing warps

The Club continued its activities throughout the 70s and 80s, although dealing with the club's finances was challenging at times. The social events in the club continued and there were very successful inter club social events held home and away with local clubs for many years.

The cruisers in the club continued to visit the Solent ports at weekends and venture further afield on their holidays, but the cruiser racing came to an end through a lack of interest, apart from the odd boat that raced in the Junior Offshore Group (J.O.G) series and/or Cowes week.

There was little interest in cruiser racing, although some members purchased South Coast One Designs in the 1980s and some participated in Cowes Week and in the South Coast One Design (S.C.O.D) sailing programme in the Solent and English Channel.

Dinghy racing in the summer was briefly revived in the early 80s for a five year period and Cherub numbers swelled to 8 or 9 boats, but racing then stopped due to a lack of interest, resulting in those keener racing members moving to other clubs in order to fulfil their racing ambitions.

The only seasonal racing that continued to flourish was that of the Victory class, although the winter Frostbite continued to be popular.

One PSC event that proved to be very successful for many years was the *Pompey Perisher* dinghy winter race, first introduced in 1970 - to celebrate the club's 50th anniversary as a handicap race, initially for monohulls, but later as two separate races, one for monohulls and one for multihulls.

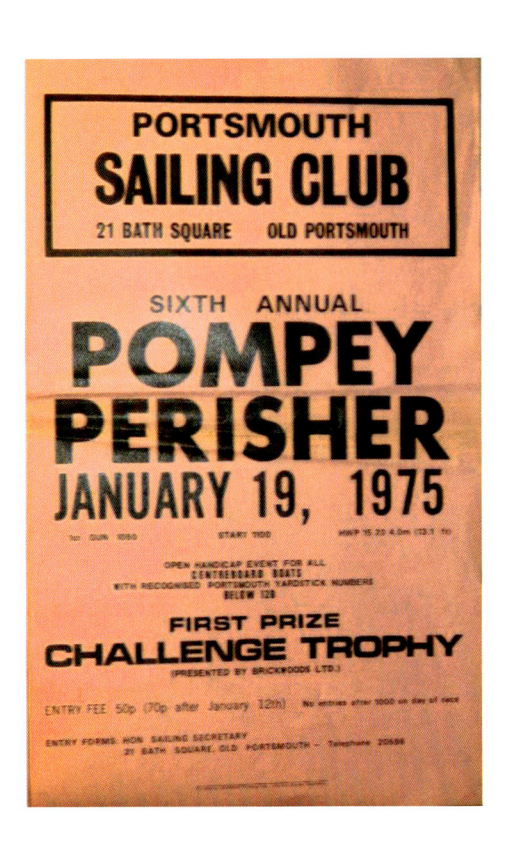

Held in January, it became an annual event with many classes of boats entering from all around the country. Racing was usually held off Southsea, but on a few occasions it had to be held in Portsmouth Harbour due to adverse weather. Prior to the race starting, the Point was amazingly busy with dinghies rigging in the roads near the launching sites at the northern end of Broad Street, the old East Street car ferry slipway and the old slipway in Bath Square directly into the harbour entrance.

In the early 1990s the race was so popular that entries had to be restricted to 150 monohulls and 50 multihulls for safety reasons. In 1994 there were boats entered from 80 different Sailing Clubs throughout the UK with more than 40 different classes competing. The largest fleets were the Fireballs, Laser 5000s and the 505 class. The race continued to be hosted by the PSC until 2002 when the last (33rd Pompey Perisher) was held.

Dinghies rigging on Point before a Pompey Perisher race.

In 1995 the club held a 75th Anniversary regatta which included racing in the Solent over a weekend for a number of classes.

With the demise of seasonal racing at the club in the summer, this affected the winter Frostbite series and numbers fell away in the late 80s and 90s, although the Victory class started to enter the series circa 1992. In 1996 the race fleets were boosted by the amalgamation of the series with Royal Navy Sailing Centre's series and the Portsmouth University boats, resulting in fleets of more than 20 boats. In the past twenty years the number of entries varied but never matched the high numbers of the 1970s and 1980s.

However, in 2015 and 2016, boat numbers began to increase when a number of club members bought Squibs (a small one design racing keelboat, 5.79m in length). Their numbers were further boosted by the Portsmouth Sail Training Trust, which became affiliated to the club and also purchased a number of Squibs which are moored in the harbour. The Trust was set up in Portsmouth to raise the aspirations of young people through their teenage years and provide boats and training for local schools. The pupils also built rowing skiffs at Boathouse 4 in the Naval Base and studied for RYA qualifications.

Hopefully, this affiliation with the PSC will help to increase boat numbers in racing events and in years to come some of the children will become full time members of the club.

In the 2016 Frostbite there were 10 Squibs, 5 Tempest and 6 Victories competing, together with some Firefly dinghies from Portsmouth University along with other boats.

In the last decade the club has become very successful with a swelling membership and a very full Social and Sailing programme. Social events are very popular, sometimes being oversubscribed and there is a full cruiser rally programme throughout the sailing season. On the racing front there is both a spring and autumn series organised for racing keel boats off Southsea known as the "Parhelion" and this has been successfully running for approximately 15 years, having replaced the earlier RAYC series.

Yachts racing in the Parhelion series © Portsmouth Sailing Club

The Victory Class still operates its summer racing programme on some weekday evenings and on Saturdays and competes during Cowes Week.

The club's current annual sailing programme culminates with the Christmas Day "Hot Turkey" race for both cruisers and dinghies, starting from the Boomyard in the harbour entrance over a short course, either inside or outside the harbour, depending on the weather.

Start of Cold Turkey race 2014.

The club was given permission to start the race in the harbour entrance several years ago by the Queen's Harbour Master, since most shipping movements cease on Christmas Day. It is advertised as an opportunity to get out on the water and blow away the cobwebs but still have time to have a drink at the club bar and return home before the Queen's speech.

The Portsmouth Sailing club has had a very successful history to date as it approaches its centenary in 2020. It has been very fortunate with its beginnings in that some of the founder members and others that joined in the first couple of decades of its existence were "men above par" and their personal achievements have left a lasting legacy for both Portsmouth and the nation.

The club was fortunate to have a founder member like W. L. Wyllie, who, apart from being one of the greatest British marine artists, also provided great support to the armed forces during his life, formed the 1st Portsmouth Sea Scout troop and was instrumental in the club's formation. He also painted the "Battle of Trafalgar Panorama" in the Dockyard together with his daughter Aileen and was hugely involved in the restoration and moving of H.M.S *Victory* to her berth in the Dockyard, along with his son Lt. Col Harold Wyllie, also a well- known artist and past Commodore of the club for a period of 6 years.

Another member of the Club trained by W.L. Wyllie was Jack Ashdown, associated with the Club for more than 60 years until his death in 1979. He was Troop leader of the 1st Portsmouth Sea Scouts for decades and, together with his Sea Scouts, was heavily involved with the Club, always helping other members and assisting in Club activities. His influence on the Club was immense and many of his Scouts became active members of the Club and remain so today.

In addition to the above should be added the name of the club's second Commodore, A. G. H. Macpherson, (1931-1942), who sailed some 45,000 miles across the oceans of the world during the 1930s in his 32 ft. yacht *Driac II,* built locally by Harry Feltham (also a founding PSC member). When one discovers that his maritime art collection formed the basis of the Greenwich National Maritime Museum's initial collection, it soon becomes apparent what a special heritage current PSC members have and should be proud of.

The current and former members and officers of the PSC have helped to guide the Club very successfully into the twenty-first century and can look forward to celebrating the Club's centenary events in 2020 with much enthusiasm and optimism for the future.

Chapter 7

The 1ˢᵗ Portsmouth Sea Scouts

W. L. Wyllie helping to launch one of the Sea Scout's boats with a housemaid looking on.

Scouting began in the United Kingdom following the first experimental camp, which was set up on Brownsea Island in Poole harbour in the summer of 1907.

Boys were invited from different social backgrounds and it proved such a success that Lieut. General Robert Baden-Powell C.B. later published "Scouting for Boys" in 1908, based on his experience with the Mafeking Cadet Corps during the Second Boer War at the Siege of Mafeking and his camp on Brownsea Island. It was really this publication that resulted in the formation of the first troops of Scouts and Scouting soon spread throughout Great Britain & Ireland, the British Empire and then throughout the world.

Prior to this time numerous groups of boys and youths had been in existence carrying out what are today regarded as Scouting activities, but there had been no collective umbrella organisation for them to be a part of.

The Scout Association was formed in 1910 and incorporated in 1912 by Royal Charter under its previous name "The Boy Scouts Association"

The first camp for Sea Scouts was held in 1909 on the T.S. Mercury and was an experimental camp like Brownsea was before in 1907.

In official Scouting terms the name "Sea Scouts" first appears in committee minutes in 1910 as a separate branch of Scouting.

Robert Baden-Powell's brother, Henry Warrington Smyth Baden-Powell, is recognised as the founder of Sea Scouting. In 1911 a booklet was published by Robert Baden-Powell entitled "Sea Scouting for Boys" which gives details of what Sea Scouting was and how the training scheme could be carried out.

W.L.Wyllie, the famous marine artist who moved to Old Portsmouth in 1906, was somebody that had a passion for Scouting type activities, but in his particular case due to his lifelong fascination with the sea, the activities were marine related.

His house, Tower House, located in Tower Street, was in a wonderful location and-prior to its purchase-consisted of bachelor's quarters, stores with big posts supporting beams, which in turn had boats slung up to them.

Anecdotal evidence exists that W. L. Wyllie first established a group of young local youths interested in maritime activities on the beach in Old Portsmouth circa 1907.

Wyllie knew Baden Powell well and he asked Wyllie if he would set up a troop of Sea Scouts, so he subsequently organised a group of youths that met regularly in Tower House, sited in the entrance to Portsmouth harbour, and this group involved themselves in nautical activities.

Tower House

Although the 1st Portsmouth are the oldest Sea Scout group in the Portsmouth District the exact date they were formed is not known for certain. However, it is thought that the first year that a group of boys was set up to participate in maritime activities was in 1907 so the troop celebrated their centenary in 2007.

2010 is the centenary of the registration of the City of Portsmouth Scout District, being officially formed on 6th March 1910. However the Local Association was in fact formed a year earlier on 6th March 1909.

The 1st Portsmouth troop was first registered with the Portsmouth District Boy Scouts Association in 1919 although it was stated on the form that the date of the original registration by the Local association was listed as 1912. However, it is very difficult to know when the original registration took place as no records exist but it is certainly earlier than this date.
In May 2010 the following report was published about the 1st Portsmouth Troop in the Headquarters Gazette:-

> Under command of Scoutmaster G Hinton the above troop held a good camp. On one day the troops marched from their camp at Portchester Castle, and messages were signalled between the top of the Keep and the Scouts in the meadows below, announcing the results of those Scouts passing their tests.
> Special commendation must be made of the smartness of the Scout B.Aylott who commissioned as the bearer of some important plans, had to deliver them at the *George* Inn and return to camp uncaptured. On approaching the *George* Inn he was somewhat disconcerted to notice that several of the troops were standing about outside, but waiting for a favourable opportunity

he slipped in unobserved, delivered his dispatch and with equal success slipped out and returned to camp, evading the whole of the troop, who were endeavouring to capture him. On a night alarm, the smartness with which the Scouts turned out was very creditable, Scout "Bury" being the first, in spite of having one foot in bandages.

W. L. Wyllie, R.A. was listed with rank of Commissioner on the original registration form and W. A. Hearn was listed as Assistant Scoutmaster. At that time there were 9 Sea Scouts and 7 Rovers in the troop. The age range for Sea Scouts was 11 to 18 in 1919 and Rover Scouts - which started in 1919 - were required to be at least 17 years old with no upper age limit at that time.

Not long after the official founding of the troop, W.L. Wyllie posted the following advert in the Portsmouth Evening News on 21st February 1914:-

> TO BOLD STURDY BOYS WHO ARE ABLE TO SWIM.—There are vacancies in the 1st Portsmouth Sea Scouts. You can have the best of times rowing and sailing. Muster every Saturday 2.15, Club night Wednesday, 8 p.m. Join now and you will be fit to take part in the enjoyable week-end cruises and camps when the summer comes. Don't put it off. Parents may be assured that their boys will be well looked after.—W. L. WYLLIE, Tower House, Portsmouth.

W.L threw himself heart and soul into the work of training the boys and the one store left in Tower House was used for years as their meeting place and working headquarters. The store was located beneath his bedroom and must have been very noisy on occasions!

The boys under his supervision were very lucky, since apart from his reputation as being very good with the boys, he had an extremely wide range of friends and acquaintances in the Royal Navy and other distinguished people so his influence was great, which must have helped immensely in being able to acquire equipment and boats for the troop.

Wyllie made numerous visits to the boat pond in the Dockyard, seeking out suitable boats and managed to find a big strong cutter that the troop christened *Lord Charles*. The boat was named after Lord Charles Beresford, a great friend of Wyllie who was a British Admiral and had been elected as Member of Parliament for Portsmouth in 1910. He had a reputation for championing the navy in the House of Commons.

After acquiring and naming the boat, Lord Charles was taken on board for a row up the harbour.

W.L.Wyllie with his Scouts afloat in the Inner Camber.

Another very significant boat which was acquired by the troop was reported in December 1913 in an article published in the Luton Times & Advertiser:

> Lieutenant Colonel Kenneth R Campbell has given his yacht *Vendetta*, a ketch of 76 tons for the use of the 1st Portsmouth Sea Scouts. The vessel was 66 feet in length, 17 ft. beam and draft of 9ft 6 ins. She was also equipped with a 40 Horsepower auxiliary engine.

His wife Marion wrote the following about the Scouts:

> Most evenings in the summer after work, the boys would congregate on the terrace, to swim, row or sail and on Saturday afternoons long expeditions took place, often lasting over Sunday evening. I always thought as I watched them all, that the youth around Bill kept him young and I am sure that he deserved a vote of thanks from the mothers of the boys for the safe and happy times they passed on the terrace.

Wyllie managed to obtain various privileges for his Scouts, such as receiving permission for them to have their big parades on the Victory Barracks Square, but the greatest honour was theirs when H.M.S. *Victory* was made their flagship. Coupled with this was the permission that allowed the troop to have a parade on board once a year on the quarter deck where each boy in turn renewed his promise. This must have been an unforgettable experience for youngsters clambering aboard such an historic old timber warship

Another privilege bestowed upon the troop and one that was greatly prized, was that the boats of the Sea Scouts were the only ones allowed to sail or manoeuvre in the harbour and Solent during the period of the War.

The smaller boats acquired by the troop were kept on the beach adjacent to Tower House known as "Wyllie's beach".

This beach had a very narrow entrance with a short breakwater on the southern side and it could be very difficult launching and beaching boats in bad weather when there was a sea running. It taught the boys good seamanship since one had to be aware of exactly what to do when making an approach so as not to hit the concrete wall of the Boomyard or the breakwater to the south. Often it was a case of entering at speed with oars stowed and a Scout jumping off the bow with painter in hand followed by others to control the boat before hauling her up the beach with all hands. Circular timber "skids" were used, being placed in front of the boat to help drag her up the beach on an even keel.

The boats were always well stowed after use and the equipment was also carefully stowed away for future use.

On one occasion the whole performance was being watched by a local boat builder (probably Harry Feltham) who remarked that it was a pleasure to see a gentleman who knows how to keep a boat, since he built them with a lot of hard work and care and more often than not saw them left lying on a beach or rubbing against a wall. In his opinion Mr Wyllie was a gentleman and a pleasure to work for.

The Sea Scouts became more and more active now that they had some boats and went away to camp to places like the Isle of Wight which was where they were with Wyllie the day that war was declared in 1914.

The 1st Portsmouth troop, with their excellent reputation for boat handling skills were very highly thought of by Uffa Fox who ran the Sea Scouts troop at Cowes. He once wrote:

The only rivals we feared on the water were the 1st Portsmouth Sea Scouts with W.L.Wyllie in charge; it was never decided which was the better team of the two for war broke out and camp was struck.

Members of the troop in 1914.

Wyllie's beach was always exposed to heavy weather and on one occasion during World War 1 when Wyllie happened to be at home in Tower House there was a mighty gale and two Scout boats together with a boat belonging to his son, Harold, were carried out to sea and broken up as the tide ebbed.

There were occasions when trying to look after the boats on Wyllie's beach that Wyllie was injured, breaking ribs. His wife Marion describes him being a real Spartan where pain was concerned and recalls twice seeing his fingers drawn into the big mainsheet block on board the barge when the mainsail gybed making no sound, only going below quietly to have the crushed fingers bound!

One of the best-known boats of the troop was its "old lady", the ketch *Royal Arthur,* known to yachtsmen for miles around and reputed to be the fastest Scout craft in the Solent. With her blue hull and tan sails she was very distinctive and when there was no wind the Scouts rowed her with immense style.

She was one of the oldest craft around, for when she was acquired by the Group in 1921 Mr Wyllie traced her history back 40 years, but she was certainly older than that. Jack Ashdown, who was associated with the troop for more than sixty years, thought she was built in Italy and was used as a work boat aboard the old warship, the Cruiser *H. M. S. Royal Arthur,* built in 1893. She used to be rigged as a 30ft cutter but was later rigged as a ketch. Built of double diagonal planking, she sailed very well and could be rowed if necessary. The *Royal Arthur* became the flag ship of the troop for many years and could often be seen sailing on the Solent.

Royal Arthur underway in a good breeze.

Her mooring used to be in the "pool "at HMS Dolphin, the submarine base in Gosport. She was very heavy, weighing in at two tons which Jack Ashdown, who later became Scoutmaster of the troop, found out when the troop sailed her to France.

In July 1923 the following article was published in a local newspaper almost certainly referring to that voyage to France of the *Royal Arthur:*

> Probably quite oblivious of the mild controversy that followed the cruise of a 30ft cutter to the Channel Islands with a biscuit tin lid and pipe stems as navigating instruments, a party of the 1st Portsmouth Sea Scouts with Scoutmaster G Newton in charge crossed to Boulogne some days ago and after having had an enjoyable time are about to return by easy stages. They are in a 30ft cutter and have navigating instruments.

During one voyage the crossing to France went well but there was no wind for the return voyage so the crew had to row back across the Channel and on another occasion they encountered a severe storm and had to beach her at Newhaven.

In August 1924 Major Charles A. J. Younger presented his magnificent 100-ton barge the *Cawana* to Mr W L Wyllie, RA, Commissioner for Sea Scouts in order to complete the education of the boys. She was one of the finest barge yachts in existence and was well adapted for the purpose for which she had been presented. The gift was regarded as a very handsome one indeed. This resulted from prior discussions with Major Charles Younger and he was also kind enough to assist in rigging the yacht, bending on sails and sorting the gear.

Prior to handover he arranged for the yacht to be hauled up on Camper & Nicholson's slipway at Gosport to be scraped and cleaned before being launched for her new role.

The beautiful barge yacht *Cawana*, built on the lines of a Thames barge was 85 ft. in length, 22 ft. beam and gross registered tonnage of 100. She had a draft of 4ft and was ketch rigged and had all new standing and running rigging, together with a 30 horse power Kelvin engine to push her along at 5 knots. She was built in Rochester in 1904.

Below she was fitted with every possible luxury. All her cabins were warmed by hot water and lighted by a dynamo and the bathroom and galley were paved with marble. The saloon was panelled in carved oak with tables and lockers to match. The cabins would sleep 20 comfortably and indeed it would be impossible to find a more perfect craft for the training of Portsmouth lads.

She had recently sailed around the Isle of Wight in 11 hours prior to her being donated to the Sea Scouts.

Following receipt of this good news, Robert Baden-Powell wrote the following letter to Wyllie:

> My Dear Wyllie, this is good news indeed that you have sent me regarding the acquisition of the yacht for your Sea Scouts. I congratulate you most cordially upon it, as it points to the recognition of the good work done on your part by Major Younger. Yours sincerely.

Her first voyage with the Sea Scouts occurred in September 1924 and was recorded as follows:

> The ship's company comprised the following:- Captain, W. L. Wyllie, R.A; Cook, Miss A. Wyllie; Bo 'sun, Sea Rover Ashdown; Deck Hands, Sea Rovers Thompson, Cause, Peel; Cook's mates part of the time, Sea Scouts Cyril and J. Wyllie; Engineer, Sea Rover E. Wyllie.

> Before we started, two naval officers, Capt. Wilson and Commander Bampton kindly offered their services for the first day, which we gratefully accepted.

> We slipped our moorings on Saturday afternoon and came out of Haslar Creek under power, a very tricky proceeding with an ebb tide, and made sail off Fort Blockhouse. At first it was rather a job, as none of us, except the Captain and the Naval Officers had handled anything so large before and we had to think carefully "which was what" when the command "up on the peak" was given.

The Bo'sun did yeoman work up aloft, easing the peak brails etc. while the naval officers ably directed us in getting everything more or less shipshape. The rest of the afternoon consisted of beating to windward against a foul tide, and to our joy the *Cawana* handled perfectly under sail.

As it was getting late we were off Lee-on-the-Solent and reluctantly had to bid adieu to our naval friends, so we put them ashore in the four oared boat, while the *Cawana* was hove to under the enviable glances of a troop of Land Scouts on the pier head.

Then we stood for Cowes and anchored off Old Castle Point at dusk.

After stowing the canvas and hoisting the riding light, we fed – and the cook "did us proud" and sang for the rest of the evening, until we turned in and slept very comfortably.

The next morning, Sunday, we weighed anchor – phew! Warm work – and sailed through Cowes Roads where we saw the *Royal Yacht*, the *Sunbeam*, Guinness's yacht and many others and *HMS Warspite.*

Then we bore up and went to Calshot and anchored the Southampton side of Calshot Castle. When she swung we noticed she was too close to the Fairway to be comfortable, so after we lunched we weighed anchor and made for the mouth of the Hamble river during which an amusing incident occurred.

To come about, we put the helm over and backed the staysail and on the command "let draw" we let go and rove in on the leeward sheet well. There were three Rovers and one small Scout backing the staysail and the command "let draw" was given.

The Rovers let go but the Scout hung on and he was carried right from starboard to port (about 22 feet) in a giant stride amid shouts of "let go". Luckily he hung on or he would have been clean overboard.

We then anchored off the Hamble and as it was raining the Captain held a short service and for the rest of the day we amused ourselves in various ways, one Rover doing sketches of incidents which occurred, the others playing with a Meccano set and singing, and last but not least, feeding. Then we turned in and slept like the dead.

The next morning, Monday, we weighed anchor narrowly missing the Hamble buoy, sailed past Cowes and saw the *Britannia, White Heather* and *Shamrock* racing. We then headed for the "Kicker" and had lunch on deck.

When we got round the "Kicker" we furled the sails and the Engineer started the engine and to his annoyance she started missing one cylinder so he changed a plug underway.

At the time there was a junior Sea Scout looking on and when the last thread of the sparking plug became free, naturally there was a bang and he ran up the companion ladder like greased lightning.

We then steamed up to our moorings and made all snug and so ended the cruise, which everyone concerned agreed was a great success.

Every weekend a fresh party of Scouts was taken out and trained in all the duties of a seaman. It was hoped that a nucleus of Rovers fit to take command would be formed before the end of the following year with more than 100 younger boys sufficiently expert to carry out their orders.

It was thought at that time that Portsmouth ought now to become the chief centre for Sea Scouting.

The troop sailed the boat extensively, sailing her to France, Poole, Weymouth, the Isle of Wight and Dartmouth.

Cawana underway.

Often they had a substantial crew aboard, including 20 boys together with their Scout masters. W.L was the skipper and in 1925 Harold, his son, was first officer. Bert Copeland, Mr Jones and Jack Ashdown were his 1st and 2nd troop masters.

Swabbing the decks on *Cawana*.

Sometimes on these voyages W.L would sail off in a dinghy to paint alone, often spending a long time absorbed in his work and returning cold and damp.

Marion Wyllie, in her book "We were one: a life of W.L.Wyllie" describes the idyllic scene on board *Cawana* after dropping anchor off Ryde on one occasion

> The anchor let go and the sails snugly brailed, all hands made a dive down the hatchways and companion-way to the saloon which looked delightful. The electric lights with their little Chinese shades twinkling all-round the cabin lighting up the long tables laden with big plates of bread and butter, cheese, cake and whatever good thing our caterer had thought fit to provide, together with big jugs of cocoa. The boys sat happily, sun burned, riotous souls. Quiet reigned for once, whilst they attacked the food with healthy appetites: the three Scoutmasters at their own table talking among themselves, with every now and then a burst of laughter at the irrepressible wit of Mr Ashdown, one of their number, and our table in the opposite corner, where I controlled my sideboard, cupboard and locker stocked with good things and kept a dainty table with flowers on it.
>
> It would have been a pleasant sight for anyone peeping in at the moment: Bill leaning back on the cushions satisfied and happy with the young life around him.

W.L still had a great interest in dinghy racing in his later years and raced at Cowes in his International 14 ft. dinghy *Venture* and often the *Cawana* stayed at Cowes during Cowes week.

Cawana anchored off Cowes in 1926.

In 1926 Sir Robert Baden Powell, the Chief Scout, appointed Lt. Col. Harold. Wyllie to the office of Assistant District Commissioner for the Portsmouth Sea Scouts. He had done much for the local Sea Scouts on board the yacht *Cawana* and his new appointment was met with public enthusiasm.

In October 1926 a registration form was submitted for the formation of a cub pack within the 1st Portsmouth Group. At that time there were 14 cubs listed as members. Aileen Wyllie, W. L. Wyllie's daughter, was the assistant Cub Master and Mrs Spencer was listed as the Cub Master. The meeting headquarters for the cubs was the Mission Room in Broad Street. In this year Jack Ashdown became Assistant Scoutmaster for the troop.

Wyllie with his Scouts on Southsea Common. Image by S.Cribb.

It should be noted that although W. L. Wyllie had set up the troop and was actively involved when he was able, much of his time must have been taken up with his painting work and other important maritime matters throughout the country.

In the late 1920s the Sea Scouts were sailing in three of Wyllie's old racers, the *Maid of Kent, Pensee Fugitive*, and the *Venture,* which were all moored in the lee of the old 74 gun ship *Implacable* which was in later years commanded by Harold Wyllie.

The *Pensee Fugitive* was a Kittiwake class dinghy with a good racing record and the *Maid of Kent* had a real pedigree, having been owned and raced by the Wyllie family for many years.

In 1898 an Australian named Mr Mark Foy sent out a challenge to any yacht club in England to meet his crack Sydney harbour boat, *Irex*, to race against any English boat of the same size.

W.L.Wyllie took up the challenge as Commodore of the Medway Yacht Club at that time and a boat was designed and built called the *Maid of Kent*. The *Maid of Kent* was built as a skimming dish having 17ins freeboard, being 24ft in length, 22 ft. waterline length and 7ft 7ins beam and a 7ft centreboard.

This boat subsequently raced against the Australian yacht with Mrs Wyllie helming and resoundingly beat the Australians 3-0 winning the Challenge Shield for England.

The Sea scouts were very fortunate to have these wonderful yachts at their disposal and must have been the envy of other Sea Scout troops throughout the country.

In September 1927 Bert Copeland was promoted to Scout Master of the troop with Aileen Wyllie as Cub Master: in 1928 there were 24 Sea Scouts and 12 Wolf Cubs in the troop.

The dry point etching above drawn by W.L.Wyllie in 1916 was given to Jack Ashdown in 1927 and shows the boats of the troop together with Sea Scouts, both on the beach and afloat. The boats seen are the *Imp, Lord Charles, Jolly Miller, Diosy, Pensee Fugitive, Maid of Kent* and the *Vendetta* (40-rater) in the distance. *HMS Victory* can be seen afloat, on board which the Sea Scouts made their "promise".

In December 1929 the *Cawana* was reported as having been sold. The Scouting Association had reluctantly come to the conclusion that the boat was too big for the practical purposes of the Sea Scout training and that her upkeep was too great an item for the income of the Association. However, with typical generosity Major Younger who had originally donated the boat, consented to the sale of the *Cawana* and the application of the proceeds to general Scout purposes.

Thanks were given to Mr W. L. Wyllie, R.A, Assistant Commissioner for Sea Scouts, who had generously met sundry expenses, and for the sale of the boat which had resulted in the sum of £1,108 19s. That excellent state of affairs had been increased by an anonymous donation of £5 and by a gift from Mr Wyllie of a number of his etchings which will be sold.

There was, however, another side to the financial question. Income from their subscriptions, although larger than last year, had barely covered their needs.

The *Cawana* was later renamed the *Mamgu,* eventually becoming the club headquarters of the Marconi Sailing Club on the east coast. She was later broken up and her remains still lie on the foreshore in the area. During her demolition some parts of the hull were salvaged and incorporated in the modern Marconi Sailing Club clubhouse.

The troop had many different boats over the years and the standard of oarsmanship and seamanship was high, a reputation of which they were proud. They had pulling and sailing gigs and smaller dinghies, some of which were kept on Wyllie's beach in Tower Street.

The troop launching one of their boats from Wyllie's beach where they were stored.

By 1930 Bert Copeland was listed as Group Scout Master and J.O.H Ashdown was listed as Scout Master.

W. L. Wyllie sadly passed away as a result of a heart attack in 1931. The funeral was planned by the Navy, Scouts and the Sailing Club and the service was held in the Cathedral. The coffin was then transported to Point beach where thousands of people witnessed it being placed in the stern of *H.M.S.Nelson's* cutter, manned by his own Sea Scouts, now grown men, with heads bent in distress over the looms of their oars.

The coffin of W.L.Wyllie in the cutter alongside at Point.

The weather was calm and as the cutter drew abreast of *HMS Nelson* the bugles sounded the "Still" with crew standing to attention lining the deck as the ensign fluttered down. The cutter passed the *Victory* and then the battleship *Warspite.*

The cutter passing H.M.S *Warspite*

A procession of launches, steamboats and many others followed behind, showing their respect for the man who lived for the sea and his art. As the upper reaches of the harbour were reached the Admiral's launch took the cutter in tow to the final destination of Portchester Castle where huge crowds lined the shore.

Wyllie's coffin was then transported on a trek cart by a party of Land Scouts to the church beyond, with cortege behind. On reaching the church gate his Scouts bore his coffin shoulder high to his resting place alongside where his little daughter Eva was buried.

After Wyllie passed away in 1931, Tower House ceased to be the meeting place for the troop. Establishing a headquarters was a problem for the troop for many years, but they never strayed beyond the bounds of Old Portsmouth and the group soon recovered and activities were back in full swing.

The troop used the Portsmouth Sailing Club as a meeting place since they were always welcomed in the club and the boys were thought of as members; indeed, many went on to become full members in adulthood.

Camping in the 1930s. © J.Copeland

Aboard the *Royal Arthur*

In the 1930s the troop had a number of Rover Scouts, as can be seen in the above pictures. They used to set off in cruises in the *Royal Arthur* and several had air rifles which they took with them using them to hunt rabbits and for target practice on occasions – not the sort of thing you would see today.

Bert Copeland and Jack Ashdown continued to run the troop up to the outbreak of World War 2, although Jack Ashdown was more heavily involved, particularly when he was stationed locally in the Royal Navy and not posted overseas. Bert Copeland used to sail his own boat, *Viking*, regularly throughout the sailing season, often setting off on cruises with senior Scouts.

The *Viking* was moored in the "Pool" at HMS Dolphin along with the *Royal Arthur*.

Viking under sail.

In 1939 many of the Rovers went into the Service and the Scouts were evacuated, but the troop managed to keep going due to the dedication of a few stalwart Rovers, such as men like George Dubber.

During the war the *Royal Arthur* was laid up in Fareham creek and it was practically a miracle that she was not lost completely or even severely damaged as all around her in the mud were gaping bomb craters. At that time the troop had a small building in the Boom Defence yard alongside Tower House which was always inhabited with at least one lad sleeping there every night.

After the war things got underway again under the stewardship of Jack Ashdown and the troop was soon flourishing. They were still attending the Victory celebrations on Trafalgar Day but now the service was of course held in the Naval Base where H.M.S *Victory* was berthed.

Trafalgar Day parade in the Naval Base 1950.

At this time the Sea Scouts' fleet consisted of much smaller boats than when the troop was first formed as they were very fortunate to have been donated two very large yachts at that time and had a fleet that was the envy of other troops throughout the country. The fleet now consisted of the *Royal Arthur* and numerous clinker sailing and pulling boats.

Sea Scout's boats on Pickfords beach in the 1950s

The troop were able to use the concrete building in the PSC Boomyard, known as the "Cave" to boys in the troop, for storing some of their day to day gear, including oars, that could easily be taken out and lowered onto Wyllie's beach below where the pulling boats were berthed. The smaller boats were always kept on Wyllie's beach adjacent to Tower House.

The troop met for many years in an old building in Grand Parade on the landward side of Ten Gun Battery, but in circa 1960 they had to vacate the premises. For a short while the troop were using Portsmouth Sailing Club as its meeting place and stored gear in the loft of the building. Often gear maintenance was carried out there including rope work and wire splicing.

In 1961 the group's headquarters had transferred to the ground floor of the Square Tower which wasn't ideal as it was quite damp inside the building and hadn't been used for years.

The pilots were based above and it was rumoured to be haunted. However, the troop made the best of it and stayed there for many years before having to move on again in the late 1970s.

For a short time they were allocated storage in one of the brick bunkers near Long Curtain moat which was totally inappropriate as it was very damp and could not be used for regular meetings.

At this time the troop used to meet in the loft of the Portsmouth Sailing Club.

Headquarters in Grand Parade

Clearing out the building in Grand Parade.

Square Tower with entrance on the left.

The brick bunkers near Longcurtain moat.

The troop was dependent on the City Council for accommodation as they did not have their own building, but in the early 1990s they were allocated their current headquarters in Bath Square in the newly restored timber storehouse sited opposite the Portsmouth Sailing Club, previously used by a local rowing club for storing rowing skiffs.

The boat store in Bath Square, the current headquarters.

Jack Ashdown aboard *Foudroyant* in the 1960s

Throughout the 1950s, 1960s and 1970s the troop were very fortunate to be able to spend their summer camp at Cobnor Point, Chidham, where the camp was set up every year with the two patrols, the *Hawks* and *Lions,* in competition with each other.

Great times were had on those camps with all mucking in and eating in the large mess tent, and in the evening all were sat around the campfire, drinking hot cocoa and listening to the fascinating tales told by Jack Ashdown (skip).

Scout songs and shanties were learned and these songs became etched in the memory of many Scouts who later became full members of the Portsmouth Sailing Club and were often to be heard being sung by members on a Friday night in the clubhouse.

Cooking underway at Chidham camp

The author (4th from left) at camp c 1961

Tents in the field at Chidham.

Loading up the gear in Tower Street.

Another very popular camping location was at "the Folly" on the banks of the river Medina on the Isle of Wight. Tents were erected in a field nearby to the *Folly Inn* and it was a great waterside location for the Scouts to enjoy themselves.

Inspection and gathered around a camp fire at "the Folly"

Swimming in the river Medina off a walkway at "the Folly" and a photo of the *Folly Inn* nearby.

Probably the last Solent cruise of the *Royal Arthur* was made by a number of Senior Scouts in the early 1970s to numerous ports in the western Solent including Lymington, Keyhaven and Yarmouth.

Royal Arthur in cruising mode laying alongside the quay at Yarmouth during her last cruise.

The *Royal Arthur* under full sail.

The troop continued to sail in the Royal Arthur during the summer. She was so distinctive with her blue hull and tan sails and regular visits were made to Priory Bay, Wootton creek and Stokes Bay.
Many local yachtsman would know her well and on calm days the Scouts would row her whilst standing up in a style in keeping with the high standards of oarsmanship that were drilled into the troop from the first time they held an oar. Feathering oars and strict boat handling skills were all part of the standard procedure and high standards demanded.

The *Royal Arthur* with her distinctive tan sails and blue hull being rowed on a windless day.

In addition to the annual camp held at Cobnor, another regular camp was held in a garden near to the old Mill at St Helen's on the Isle of Wight.

Sadly Jack Ashdown passed away in 1979, having been with the troop since 1915. He was a remarkable person with many talents who was associated with Point throughout his life and a separate chapter has been written about him in this book. For his sterling service to the troop he was awarded two long service medals.

The years were beginning to catch up on the *Royal Arthur* and her condition deteriorated as she was now more than 100 years old. She was eventually handed over to the Portsmouth Naval Base Property Trust with the intention of restoring her in the future when funds became available. She was stored in the Naval Base adjacent to the Mast Pond for a while but unfortunately was damaged beyond repair whilst being moved in the Base – a very sad day for all those persons who had sailed on her, including myself.

The *Royal Arthur* being moved in the Naval Base.

After Jack Ashdown's death the troop continued to meet, initially under the leadership of longstanding members of the troop, George Horner and Colin Thackray.

However, it soon became apparent that the troop had financial problems and it was evident that Jack Ashdown had been subsidising the running of the troop heavily from his own finances.

Ex-scouts and other senior local members of the Portsmouth Sailing Club were instrumental in saving the troop from extinction and it continued under the new leadership of Derek Lee. During this time Cubs and Beavers were introduced. Colin Thackray later moved away from Portsmouth due to work commitments and George Horner died c. 1995.

Before George Horner passed away he asked an ex-Sea Scout, Bob Stewart, to become involved in the troop, particularly with water activities as little was being done in this area at that time. Bob kindly obliged and later took over the troop in 1997 and successfully ran it until 2016. For a number of years after taking over the troop he was very ably assisted by James Clapham who was knowledgeable in modern day Scouting.

One has to understand that Jack Ashdown ran the troop in his own style for decades, often not in accordance with official Scouting procedures and of course those that followed were ex members of the troop so were trained in Jack's way of Scouting. James provided an insight into current Scouting methods and techniques which were then incorporated into the troop.

In 1997 the number of Scouts in the troop aged between 10½ to 14 years of age varied from 3 or 4 to 12 with numbers being greater in the summer. In addition there were approximately 18 Cubs who were supervised by a Cub mistress at Cathedral house some distance away. She retired in 2005 and was replaced at that time by another lady, Jenny Cox, who continued to supervise the group at Cathedral house until moving away in 2011/12 and being replaced by Phil Jones.

Explorer Scouts (aged 14 to 18) were introduced into the troop in 2003/4 and there were approximately six in the troop at this time.

With regards to boats, after Jack's passing and the subsequent donation of the *Royal Arthur* to the Maritime trust in the Naval base, a fund raising exercise was set up to purchase a new grp boat, a "Home Counties" gig. Named the *Jack Ashdown*, she was launched by W .L. Wyllie's daughter, Aileen Wyllie in 1982.

The launching of the *Jack Ashdown* on the East Street Car Ferry slipway.

Other boats owned by the troop in the years following Jack's death included the remaining clinker pulling and sailing gigs from Jack's era, together with a number of more modern sailing dinghies.

After Bob Stewart took over the stewardship of the troop he realised that the troop had dwindling funds and managed to source numerous grants and lottery funding to enable the troop to invest in some new boats.

During his time in control of the troop he acquired funds to purchase a number of rigid inflatable boats (RIBS), together with *Pico* sailing dinghies and a large 26 ft. *Drascombe* sailing gig for use by the troop. In addition, some *Coypu* dinghies and canoes were obtained after the 38th Portsmouth Sea Scout troop ceased operations.

The *Drascombe* under sail

Picos in Portsmouth harbour.

The troop continues to lease the old boathouse in Bath Square from Portsmouth City Council as their headquarters and also Wyllie's beach for the storage of boats.

In 2007 a Special Centenary plaque and certificate were presented to the troop in recognition to mark the outstanding achievement of providing 100 years of Scouting to the local community. Under Bob Stewart's stewardship, the troop met once a week on a Friday when, amongst other activities, knots and rope-work was taught to the Scouts together with many other nautical skills. During the summer, troop members were taken out on the water for sailing lessons which is still the case today. Bob Stewart relinquished his stewardship in 2016 but the troop continues to flourish today under new leadership and will hopefully do so for many years to come.

Although the troop's main activities revolve around Point, they also travel to other places to allow the youngsters to experience new activities. In 2017 the summer camp was held in the West Country where activities including caving, abseiling and sailing were enjoyed.

After caving activities

Gathered on Dartmoor

Ever since its formation, the troop has been known as one of the leading junior sailing groups in Portsmouth, being renowned for its proficiency in Sea Scouting. Both the Royal and Merchant Navy have much to be grateful for from the 1st Portsmouth troop having supplied many Captains in both services throughout the years, a lasting legacy of the troop.

The troop was so lucky in having such a man as the founder of the troop, W.L. Wyllie with his love of the sea and connections throughout the maritime world and to have had such wonderful Scout leaders throughout the years, particularly Jack Ashdown, who dedicated his life to the troop and was associated with it for more than 60 years.

Chapter 8

John Patrick O'Halloran Ashdown
(1ˢᵗ October 1905 – 12ᵗʰ March 1979)

John Patrick O'Halloran Ashdown, known as Jack or "Skip" to his Sea Scouts, was involved with the 1st Portsmouth Sea Scouts for more than 60 years, joining in 1915 aged 10 and with the Portsmouth Sailing Club from not long after its formation in 1920 until his death in 1979.

During much of this period he was a very familiar face on Point and was greatly admired by the locals.

He was a very talented man who dedicated his life to the Sea Scout troop based on Point and ensured that the troop was always on hand to help both sailing Club members when necessary and, on occasions, the local people on Point.

It was a well-known fact that residents on Point were very keen to encourage their sons to join the troop to obtain a first class education in seamanship that they would carry with them throughout their lives, often into professional seafaring careers. Jack established a reputation in the troop that was second to none and passed on his skills and knowledge to hundreds of boys over the years. It was deemed a real achievement to belong to this band of brothers, thought by some to have been set up in 1907 by the great marine artist W.L.Wyllie.

As Scout Master of the 1st Portsmouth Sea Scouts everyone locally knew him and always spoke of him with affection and respect.

This chapter seeks to portray what an amazingly talented character he was, the very full life he led and the lasting legacy he left in his wake. Since the 1st Portsmouth Sea Scouts formed a large part of his life, much is also written about him in Chapter 7, which chronicles the history of the troop.

Jack was born in Whitegate, County Cork, on 1st October 1905. His father, Harry George Ashdown, was born in Brighton in 1869 and met Jack's mother whilst serving in Ireland in the Royal Navy as an ERA (Engine Room Artificer).

Jack was the youngest of four brothers and was brought up in Portsmouth, living in Hewitt Road North End. He was a keen athlete and was educated in Portsmouth, prior to joining the Naval Dockyard Apprentice scheme in 1921. On his 18th birthday he signed on for 12 years with the Royal Navy and qualified as a Shipwright 5th Class in 1926 and finally obtained the rank of Chief Shipwright in 1941. In 1942 he was promoted to Temporary Acting Warrant Shipwright and in 1943 he was promoted to Temporary Commissioned Shipwright, Officer Status.

During his time in the Royal Navy he served on the *Iron Duke, Benbow, Peterel, Ladybird, Diomede, Argus* and on the 3 stacker cruiser *Emerald* during WW2.

He would have gained a vast amount of experience on such different types of ships that included Dreadnought class battleships, Cruisers, River gun boats and an Aircraft carrier.

A few years prior to World War 2 he served several commissions abroad including:

(a) Anti slave patrols in the Persian Gulf

(b) More than 2 years on Gunboats, with most time served on H.M.S. *Ladybird* on the Yangtze River, penetrating some 2000 miles inland into China.

H.M.S. *Benbow*    H.M.S. *Argus*

H.M.S. *Emerald*    H.M.S. *Peterel*

H.M.S. *Iron Duke*    H.M.S. *Diomede*

Some of the ships that Jack served aboard

HMS *Ladybird* was an "Insect" Class River Gunboat. She was launched in 1916, first deployed in the Mediterranean, and later in 1919 began service at the China Station and joined the Yangtze flotilla to protect British Shipping and British Nationals in an emergency. Jack served aboard her for a couple of years from 1935 to 1937.

H.M.S. *Ladybird* on which Jack served on the Yangtze river in China.

During the war Jack served at HMS Hannibal (Algiers) and HMS Angelo (Malta) and it was during this time that he became seriously ill with malaria. Whilst on one of these postings in 1944 he was sent to La Maddelena in Italy to supervise Prisoners of War.

He was extremely gifted and very creative and this talent was put to great effect in his woodcarving, sketching, water/oil painting and photography. This ability was no doubt stimulated through his early days' connection with W.L.Wyllie of whom he used to say "The greatest thing that happened to me was to rub shoulders with the Old Man".

He simply idolised W.L.Wyllie, who had realised Jack's potential and encouraged him to take up art. There had been occasions when Jack Ashdown, as one of his most able Sea Scouts, had sailed in W.L's famous *Maid of Kent* to various sectors of the Solent to enable the artist to capture certain subject matter that he would later include in major painting.

Jack was fascinated by the way W.L operated.

In 1972 an exhibition and sale of W.L.Wyllie's paintings, drawings, water colours and etchings was held in the Malcolm Henderson Gallery in London and Jack was asked to contribute some comments on his time with W.L.Wyllie.

Jack recalled two of his many reminiscences in the exhibition catalogue as follows:-

> The Old Man could sketch and paint under any conditions that be thrown at him. I remember that one day we had sailed round to the Hamble to look at *Dulcibella*, of the "Riddle of the Sands", and he followed us in the *Maid of Kent*.
>
> He wanted to sketch the sunset on the way home, and I was shanghaied aboard to take the helm. There was a stiff south westerly breeze and some sea, and The *Maid of Kent* roared off with her lee rail awash and plenty of spray flying with the Old Man sitting below on the centreboard trunk, with paper in one hand and brush in the other, getting what light there was through the open cabin door and perfectly happy.
>
> I was hanging on to the helm and she was doing her best to round up. Well, eventually she did just that, and before I could do anything about it there was the Old Man in the bilge with his gear all around him, canvas slatting, block hammering and considerable tumult, but no shouting. I squared away again and he sat down on the centreboard trunk and carried on as though nothing had happened, and by the time we had rounded Gilkicker, the sketch was finished and the sun had set.

To Wyllie discomfort was just one of those things of no real account, as shown in this account of Jack's:-

> On another occasion we had sailed to Lane End on a bitter winter day, so he could make sketches of the lifeboat. Our gig was four oared and carried a dipping lug.
>
> Wind and tide were right, but it was a real freezer. When we lowered the lug it came down in slabs, it was frozen hard, and when we laid out the oars we shook them free of snow. It was alright for us – we were young and tough enough, but he was upwards of 73.
>
> He went about his sketching and we ran around the lifeboat slip keeping warm. We might have thought we were tough but he was far far tougher.
>
> One last impression that has never left me is that we were always ready to duck for cover if we had perpetrated a particularly bad piece of seamanship under his eye, but when a real emergency occurred, as it must sometimes to all who follow the sea, he was quiet, contained and master of the situation, in fact "The Old Man."

During the periods that Jack served abroad in the Persian Gulf and in China on the Yangtze River, he observed and recorded everyday life which fascinated him immensely.

He made sketches of things that interested him and also took photographs which was uncommon in the 1930s.

Throughout his time in China and Persia he became very knowledgeable about the local boats, the Junks and the Dhows and their methods of construction and sailing techniques.
Upwards of 5000 different types of Junks and Sampans operated on the mighty Yangtze and being a First Class Shipwright he was very interested in the building techniques used and their methods of sailing these interesting looking vessels, so different to the craft familiar to him at home.

He experienced the very wild and challenging Yangtze that was such an unforgiving river with its fearsome currents, sandbanks and tricky terrain that claimed many victims including vessels that either struck rocks or were marooned on sand banks.

Navigation would have been extremely difficult and hazardous, particularly when passing through the gorges to Chunking where fast flowing water was the norm. Jack would have seen the Chinese battling their way up river in their craft against these flows, with no engines, using techniques developed over the centuries.

He joined the Portsmouth Sailing club in circa 1921 and remained a member until his death in 1979.

He was a very good natural speaker and regularly gave wonderful talks in the sailing club about his experiences in places like the Persian Gulf and the Yangtze. He captivated the audience with his humour and illustrated by his collection of glass slides shown on his magic lantern or by his sketches and cartoons he described life in these faraway places.

When these talks were being held, the club was always packed out as he described the gorges on the river, the sailing craft and the Chinese way of life or the slave trade in Persia.

I recall one occasion during a talk about China when he described in great detail what such an important material bamboo was to the Chinese people and the many hundreds of different uses it had in their day to day life.

Although the Chinese live under a Communist regime, Jack always described them as natural capitalists, very hard working, earning little money, but striving to own their own boat and this has been borne out today with the way China has become a leading world power manufacturing and selling goods throughout the world.

Whilst serving in China he would head off inland to explore the area and learned to ride horses whilst there and many of the people he met and the places he visited gave him inspiration for drawing sketches and cartoons.

During his time in China, Jack became something of an expert in the local craft and recorded much information about them including photographs.

So much so, that in 1936 Frank Carr, the author of the original "Yachtmaster's guide and Coastal Companion 1940", who was secretary of The Society of Nautical Research made contact with Jack seeking information on Chinese craft.

Frank Carr probably did more than anyone since World War 2 for the world's ship restoration and preservation scene. At the top of the list of his many achievements in this field are the roles he played in saving the *Cutty Sark* and *Gypsy Moth IV*.

Carr wrote several books in the 1930s on craft around the British Isles to compile records before they disappeared for ever including "Sailing barges" in 1931 and "Vanishing craft" in 1934. He later became Director of the National Maritime Museum (1947-1966).

When he wrote to Jack in 1936, he observed how valuable Jack's research on Chinese craft would be, as he wanted to ensure that records of old sailing craft across the globe were preserved and exchanged. He mentioned at that time that the National Maritime Museum of Greenwich had a key role in this task and sent Jack a questionnaire to complete on his research in China, and it is highly likely that Jack forwarded him information that ultimately found its way to the Maritime Museum.

Jack always had a natural talent for drawing cartoons, but while he was in China he became more prolific with the ideas and new subject matter that was on view and it was at this stage of his life that he produced some excellent, highly professional work.

During his time on the Yangtze, Jack had established himself as a cartoonist on the *North China Daily News* and subsequently on the *Daily Sketch* in the UK. He also contributed regularly to the *Yachting World* Magazine and illustrated many books.

In July 1937 Jack received word from Mr E. T. Lee, writing on behalf of the *Daily Sketch* newspaper, congratulating him on the cartoons he had submitted to that newspaper and informed him that 26 were to be sent for publication and that his future could expect worldwide recognition of his work.

Whilst serving in China, Jack corresponded with G.Sapojnikoff (Sapajou), a cartoonist on the staff of the *North China Daily News*. He was a White Russian who became a Lieutenant in the Russian Imperial Army and had fought in the First World War and been gravely wounded, ending up in Shanghai in 1925 working as a cartoonist for the newspaper.

His cartoons were published over an unbroken 15 year period and he was well known internationally. Several albums of his sketches were published and his illustrations appeared in a number of contemporary books on Chinese subjects.

It is amazing to realise that Jack knew Sapajou and one could reasonably assume that from the number of cartoons of his that had already been published in the newspaper, an exciting future in that field lay open to him.

The *North China Daily News* (1850 – 1951) was the first English Language paper in Shanghai. The paper's 101 year life span ranked the newspaper as the most influential foreign newspaper of the time in Shanghai, and even in all China. Letters from this newspaper to Jack confirmed how highly they regarded his work and one of his cartoons was sold at this time for 30 shillings.

Cartoon published in the North China Daily News

Another literary friend who was very impressed with his sketches, compared some of them with those of Frank Reynolds, cartoonist of "Punch magazine," and suggested that some of Jack's work was superior. Jack's cartoon above depicts how the Chinese would cultivate any available space and Jack comments that every square inch of soil on the Upper Yangtze's perpendicular cliffs bears its crop of grain and most of it is farmed by steeplejacks!

With Jack enjoying so much success with the publication of his cartoons in numerous newspapers and journals, it is highly likely that he could have transferred into a very successful career in illustrating, be it cartoons or sketches, should he have wished.

However, during this successful publishing period in his life it must be remembered that he was still serving in the Royal Navy in China and with Japan invading Manchuria and later World War 2 breaking out in 1939, any potential change of career was put on hold.

When things finally settled down at the end of the war in 1945 at least 10 years had passed and for whatever reason Jack did not move into a new career as a professional cartoonist.

Another of Jack's cartoons published in the *North China Daily News* together with the following description: - "The ring around the cormorant's neck allows only the smallest of his catch to reach its destination – in the cormorant the larger fish are disgorged for another destination – the market place. The cormorant's ambition in life is to rid itself from the ring."

Jack also produced many sketches and cartoons socially and was a regular sketcher/cartoonist for the Portsmouth Sailing Club magazine. He produced the cartoon certificate for the PSC Frostbite sailing series, the cartoon/certificate for the Scout Charge Certificate Grade 1 which he himself was awarded, together with other prominent yachtsmen including the then leader of the 38th Portsmouth Scout troop, Lieut. Commander A. Matthews, and the legendary Uffa Fox, who was at that time associated with the Cowes Sea Scouts.

The list on the certificate, drawn as part of the cartoon, shows all the topics which the candidates had to be examined on which is a very comprehensive list and confirms why the examination and qualification was of a very high standard.

The list of topics included: Cloud formation; sailing rigs; weather information; dead reckoning; whipping; bearings; notices to mariners; buoyage; cross bearings; boat maintenance; gale warnings; boat stowing; chart work; sailing directions; life-saving; compass work; experience; Beaufort scale; harbour byelaws; log keeping; semaphore; rule of the road; morse; lights; canvas work; bends; hitches; rigging; boat management; splicing; swimming; distress signals; anchor work; serving; boat orders and seamanship.

Whenever there was an opportunity to produce a cartoon or funny sketch then Jack was always willing to draw something that would be very special and memorable. Whilst serving aboard HMS *Emerald* during World War 2 he sketched a delightful coloured certificate/cartoon to Neptune for "Crossing the line" as they crossed the Equator.

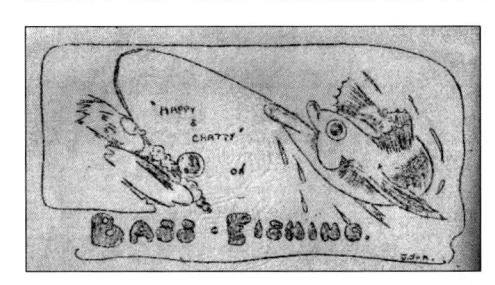

Some of Jacks's cartoons from the 1933 Portsmouth Sailing Club Journal.

Jack also turned his hand to painting and in the 1950s he produced two paintings, one in oils and the other a water colour of a well-known colourful character who was a member of the Portsmouth Sailing Club. His name was Alfred Meadows and known to all as "Pop" Meadows. One can see from the portrait below what a fine artist Jack was – another special talent!

Sir Francis Drake-Meadows by Rembrandt via Ashdown.© C.Dight.

Jack was extremely talented and skilled when working with timber and carved the head of the griffin which is today in the Portsmouth Sailing Club bar. This was done at the United Services Officers Club ground at Burnaby Road where he worked on a part time basis and had access to the workshop. The carving is thought to be of teak and was intended to be durable as it acted for many years as the figurehead of the *Norseman*, a six oared double ended gig used by the Sea Scouts.

The figurehead was brought into the PSC when the local brewery architect, Ken Hornsey, redesigned the club bar and Jack Ashdown kindly donated this magnificent carving to the club.

The *Norseman* with her Griffin figurehead on the stem.

He would readily produce a tiller for a fellow club member – often produced as an unexpected gift. Dan Lloyd had a sloop called *Morwennol*-Welsh for seagull or sea hawk - and Jack borrowed the tiller one day and soon returned it, complete with a carved bird's head.

Another very well-known club member, John Surbey, was fond of sea shanties and named a 5 ton boat he'd built *Shantyman* on which he lived aboard throughout the year. Jack carved a beautiful head to his tiller depicting him as a 70 year old with a beard roaring out in full song.

He also helped replace the stern mouldings on the *Foudroyant*, when she was moored in Portsmouth Harbour, and, following an appeal for the restoration of war damage to the altar of Tubby Clayton's (TOC "H" fame) "All Hallows" church by Tower Bridge in London, made a substantial contribution there in the late 1940s.

This lovely wooden carving above right was sculpted by Jack when he worked at the United Services Ground, Burnaby Road and was later modified and presented to the Portsmouth Sailing Club and now hangs proudly above the Club entrance in Bath Square, having been restored.

During his apprenticeship in the Royal Navy whilst stationed at HMS Victory Portsmouth, he was assigned to help with the creation of a superb model of the Naval Base.

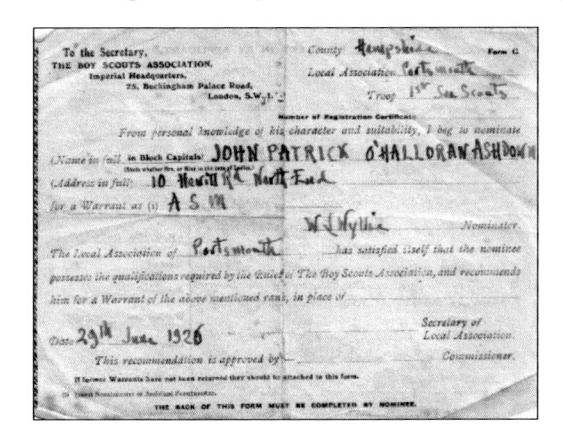

After being an active member of the 1st Portsmouth Sea Scouts troop for many years Jack made an application to become Assistant Scoutmaster which was recommended by W. L. Wyllie in June 1926. This was approved by the Boy Scouts Association in London

Jack was an avid reader and collector of books and had an extensive private library, much of which he purchased from Seaford's the antiquarian bookshop that used to be located at the lower end of Commercial Road, Portsmouth.

He used to purchase all the books he wanted and often ordered first editions from all around the world, mainly on nautical subjects. The owner of the shop once said that Jack had the finest private collection of nautical books in Portsmouth.

Jack was very well read and his subject matter went way beyond nautical books. Unfortunately, after he died his collection of books was broken up and sold and some of the proceeds went to his old Scout troop, the 1st Portsmouth Sea Scouts. Unknown to those selling the books many were first editions and quite a few of rare classification. As a collection, they would have been quite valuable and should really have been retained together, as I'm sure Jack would have preferred.

Following his posting to China in the 1930s, Jack had acquired much information about the Chinese culture and way of life which not many westerners had experienced. With this knowledge he used to lecture at Southampton University to Humanities students in the 1950s after he had retired from the Royal Navy, passing on his knowledge of 1930s China to the students

Whilst in China he would contact all the Scout groups-particularly in the Hankow district- and would invariably carve totems for Scout, Cubs and Brownie packs.

After the war Jack used to entertain PSC members with many sea shanties that he had collected from all around the world. Many of these shanties were taught to the lads in the troop, together with traditional Scout songs sung around the campfire or whilst out sailing. He had a fine singing voice and an extensive knowledge of old shanties and folk songs.

The spontaneous evenings enjoyed by so many fortunate PSC members were unforgettable and the atmosphere was really memorable. It became something of a regular feature on Friday nights in the Sailing Club when the rafters rang with the enthusiasm of the makeshift choirs under his lead. Those enjoyable evenings created a feeling of comradeship that always made the beer taste better and cemented club members together.

Jack was also a regular member of his local church choir-Corpus Christi in North End- and supported this church all his adult life.

In 1931 W.L.Wyllie passed away, severely affecting the troop, but Bert Copeland with Jack Ashdown as his assistant Scoutmaster, soon had activities back on track.

At W.L.'s funeral Jack was one of the rowing crew (stroke oar) of the cutter provided by HMS Nelson which took the coffin to the church at Portchester Castle where he is buried.

Sometime in the late 1930s Jack drew a series of 10 cartoons for his great friend and fellow Scout leader, Bert Copeland, depicting the Scout promise and these can be seen on the following pages.

The quality of the artwork is superb and Jack had an amazing natural ability to create a scene and capture wonderful facial expressions in his cartoons, which were paired with very witty captions. There is no doubt in my mind that he could have made a career as a professional cartoonist.

Copyright permission to use the following ten cartoons in this book was kindly given by Jonathan Copeland.

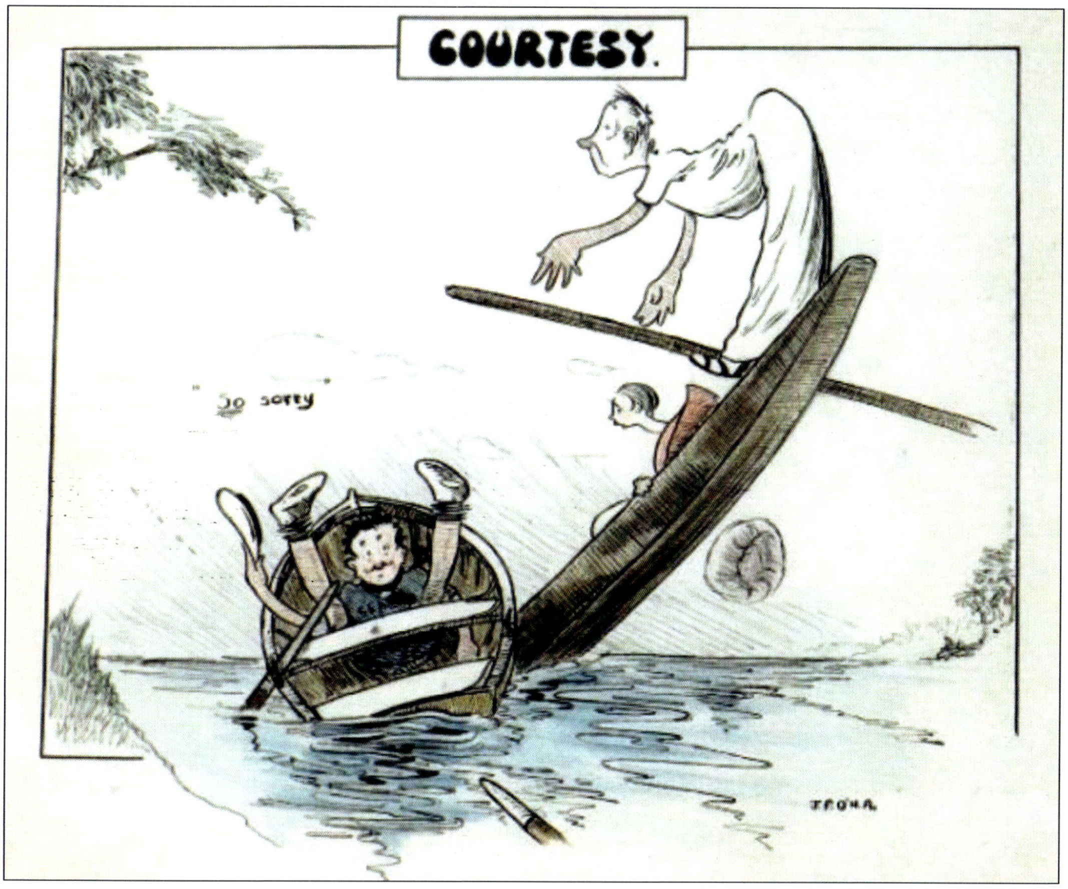
COURTESY.
"So sorry"
J.P.O.H.R.

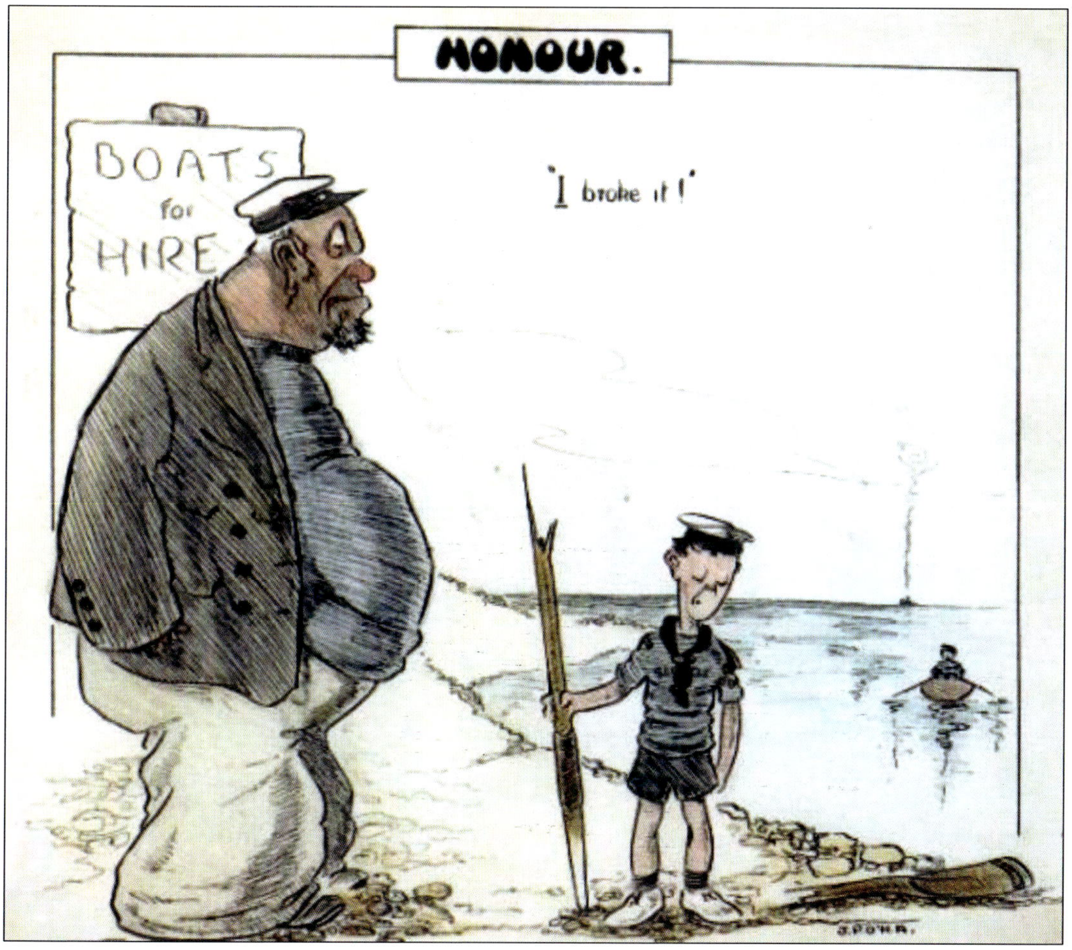
HONOUR.
BOATS for HIRE
"I broke it!"

USEFULNESS.

"Hoi! You forgot this!!"

CLEANLINESS.

OBEDIENCE.

"Hold her, for'ard!!"

THRIFT.

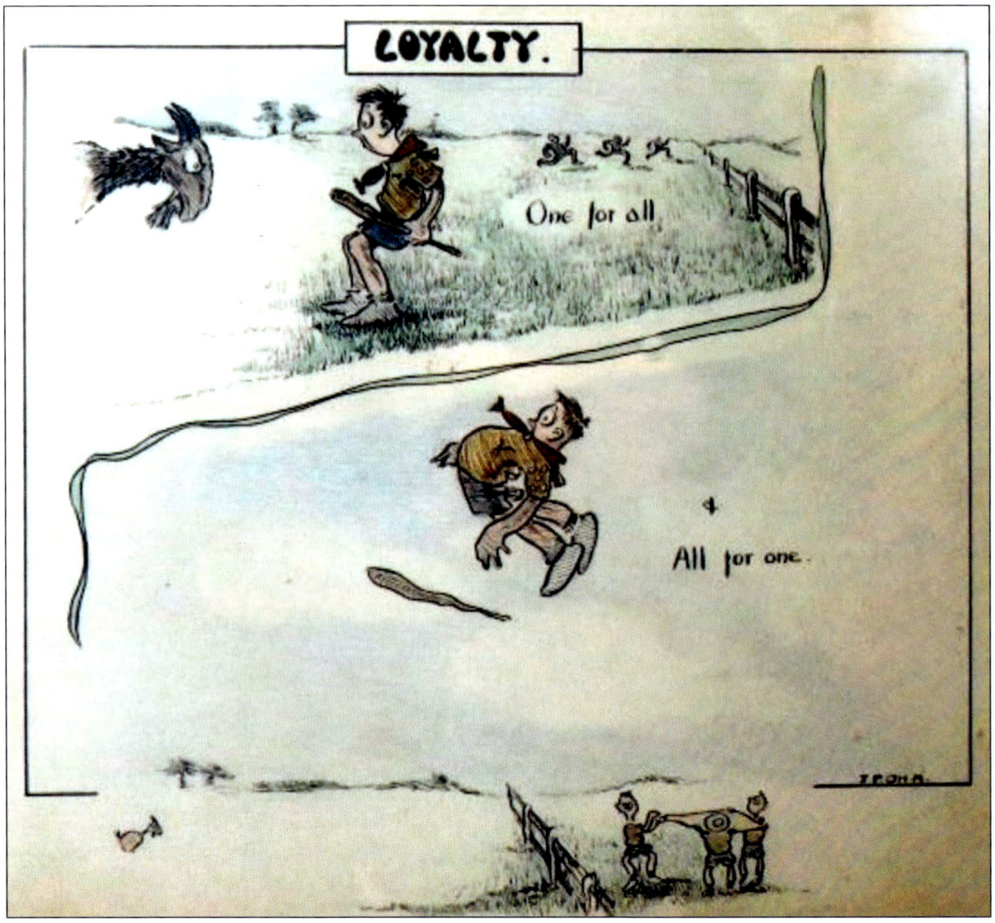
LOYALTY.
One for all
&
All for one.

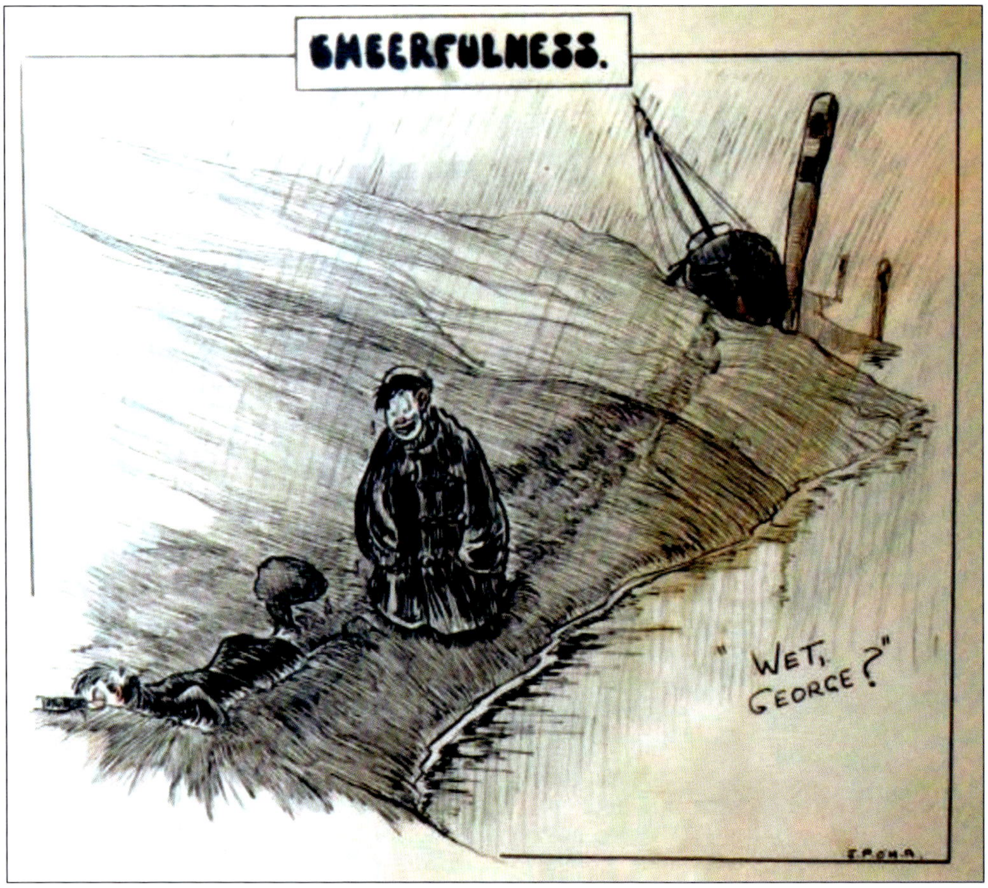
CHEERFULNESS.
"WET, GEORGE?"

Jack in his younger days underway at sea.

He took full control of the troop prior to World War 2 and was instrumental in reforming the Rover crew, which had lapsed through lack of members. He spent much of his time on Point, and was well-known by all the long-established residents. He gave as much as anyone in the city to the education and development of local boys.

Under his guidance and tremendous enthusiasm he formed a band of about a dozen Rover Scouts whose activities and esprit de corps was of high standing. They learned boat handling, maintenance and general assurance – above all things they learned to be worthy citizens under his guidance.

Rover Scouts aboard the *Royal Arthur*.

Jack's excellent reputation was acknowledged by all the other local Scout troops and he took a leading role in the organisation of the combined Scouts' regatta that was held annually in the torpedo pool at Horsea Island where there were some very competitive races.

In addition to this he used to organise the Sea Rangers' annual regatta based on the *Foudroyant* when she used to be moored in Portsmouth Harbour and the Sea Scouts would ferry some of the girls to and from Gosport. The Sea Rangers also used to be guests aboard the *Royal Arthur* once a year to go sailing, with the final destination often ending up being Priory Bay on the Isle of Wight.

These pictures show the keen racing held at Horsea Island with numerous local Sea Scout troops competing with each other in lots of different races for trophies and pennants.

In the photo on the left Jack can be seen on the right hand side of the picture, pipe in hand.

Priory Bay, Isle of Wight.   Newtown creek, Isle of Wight.

Jack always insisted on Scouts being available and willing to help pull PSC members' boats up the Boomyard slip whatever the conditions - no skiving was ever permitted! Jack would be the centre of control showing the hallmarks of the Chief Shipwright he once was in the Naval Base.

Sea Scouts helping a Sailing Club member with his boat in the Victory Class yard, Bath Square.

In October 1952 an article appeared in the Portsmouth News stating that Mr J.O.H.Ashdown of the 1st Portsmouth Sea Scouts has been awarded a Scouting Medal of Merit together with the Long Service green ribbon for his long association with the troop.

Later, the "Silver acorn", awarded for particularly dedicated service for a period of not less than 20 years was presented to him on 23rd April 1973.

These two long service medals were awarded to Jack for his dedication to the troop and Scouting in general. Both these awards were so fully justified when one bears in mind that he was associated with the 1st Portsmouth Sea Scouts troop for 64 years.

In the early 1960s I recall being on duty with other Sea Scouts at the Royal Albert Yacht Club starting line on Southsea beach near the War Memorial with a small dinghy. Jack often used to row crew members out to several of the Ocean Racing yachts that were preparing to start one of their Channel races: no mean task in strong winds and a lee shore.

Jack, with the assistance of the lads in the troop, used to maintain the PSC signal station mast that was sited to the east of Clarence Pier where club races were started. On one occasion when aged over 70 and being at the top of the mast he was seen by his own doctor who was less than impressed with him undertaking such strenuous work at his age.

On numerous occasions he used to climb the mast and occasionally he organised the lowering and raising of this mast.

He would allow no sloppiness in boat handling and all manoeuvres had to be executed properly and in a seamanlike manner. His standards were high and he accepted nothing less from his troop of Sea Scouts.

Jack was his own man with high moral standards and strong convictions about how the troop should be run. This he managed with great success and it reflected in the bearing, pride and standards of seamanship in his Scouts, and their readiness at all times to help members of the PSC.

His ace card in this connection was the fact that he personally provided most of the money to carry the financial burden which emphasises his dedication to the worthy task he had set himself.

It is of note that after the war Point, having suffered badly in the blitz, contained relatively few residential properties, but of those families who remained, nearly all made every effort to get their boys to serve with Skip, such was his impact locally. As a tribute to his largely unsung work, many of these lads in later life joined the Royal Navy and Merchant Navy, some to command their own ships.

Jack estimated that nearly half of the boys who passed through the troop entered either the Royal or Merchant Navy.

Unfortunately, Jack Ashdown passed away in 1979 leaving a great void to fill, having been associated with the troop for more than 60 years, much of that time as leader. He dedicated his life to the 1st Portsmouth Sea Scouts and many of the boys who passed through the troop remain grateful for the wonderful seamanship skills acquired during their time under Jack's leadership.

Following his death in 1979, the PSC created the Jack Ashdown memorial fund In recognition of his sterling qualities, part of which was donated to the Scout Troop for a replacement boat named the *Jack Ashdown*, duly launched by Aileen Wyllie (W.L's daughter), who was at that time the President of the troop.

Jack sailed on Arab dhows in the Red Sea, Junks on the Yangtze and collected sea shanties from foreign lands teaching many of the old ones to PSC members.

He was a man of strong character and physique, completely without malice or envy and without an enemy in the world. Scouts who served under his command consider it a great privilege to have been members of the 1st Portsmouth Sea Scouts and are grateful for their association with him.

Jack in typical pose with a pair of oars at the ready.

Chapter 9
A. R. (Sam) Loader (1897 – 1985)

Sam standing on Point beach with the polished brass bust of the "Duchess of Point".

Sam Loader was a local character who grew up and lived on Point for much of his life and was well liked by all that knew him. He was a member of the Portsmouth Sailing Club and I recall his house well, having visited it on many occasions over the years.

The building was the old *Fortitude* Inn at No 53 Broad Street where he kept a small dinghy on the ground floor in his boat-store. He also lived on the ground floor, letting out the upper half of the building to tenants that lived there for many years.

He also had a boatyard at 31 Broad Street near Bathing Lane where he kept his Folkboat, *Edith*, when she was laid up each winter, until he later gave up sailing and sold the site to my father.

I remember Sam in my youth when growing up on Point between the 1950s, and 1970s. I later found out more about his life after Graham Hurley, the well-known local author and television film maker who first met him in the mid -1970s, made a film documentary about Sam's life. He became a great friend of Sam's, meeting up with him often in the *Still & West* pub.

Sam's house with sandbags as flood protection during a flood in 1984

Advertisement for the sale of the *Fortitude* inn in 1860

> **PORTSMOUTH.**
> TO BREWERS, PUBLICANS, & OTHERS.
> **Valuable FREE INN and Premises,**
> *Admirably situate at Broad-street Point.*
> MR. FREDERICK ELLEN has received instructions from the Proprieter to SELL by AUCTION, on the premises, on Tuesday the 21st of August 1860, at two o'clock in the afternoon, – A highly desirable
> FREEHOLD PROPERTY.
> **Known as the "FORTITUDE" INN,**
> a substantial Brick-built ERECTION, containing a capital BAR with two entrances, bar parlour, smoking room, a cheerful up-stairs sitting room with bay window, four bed rooms, and large closets. In the rear is a small paved yard, communicating with a detached kitchen and other conveniences. There are good wine, beer, and coal cellars.
> Adjoining is the "FORTITUDE TAP," which contains tap room, bar, dining room, four bed rooms, attic, store rooms, &c.
> The situation of this Property is unexceptionable, it being on the best side of the busy thoroughfare, known as *Broad Street Point*, within fifty yards of the Floating Bridge Ferry Station, near the Victoria Pier, and within a short walk of the Royal Dock-yard, the Artillery Barracks, and other Government establishments. Some of the upper rooms command fine views of the Harbour and Shipping, the Fortifications, Hasler Hospital, Gosport Victualling Yard, and various points of interest.
> The Property is in good substantial repair, and has been occupied by the present tenant, Mr. James Bartlett and his relatives, for a period of 25 years.
> Early possession may be had.
> May be viewed by permission of the tenant, and particulars, with conditions of sale, obtained by Messrs. Earle and Smith, Solicitors, or of the Auctioneer, Andover.

Sam was brought up in the late Victorian era. He had lots of brothers and sisters and recalled fondly his youth growing up on Point. His father had opened a Temperance Restaurant at No 39 Broad Street in the late nineteenth century, which is interesting when one considers that the two properties immediately adjacent to the north of the building were both pubs, the *Neptune & Mars* and the *White Swan*.

The Temperance Dining Rooms with Sam's father in the foreground circa 1900.

39 Broad Street today.

The advert for the dining rooms still visible today but somewhat weathered

Sam's father was an orphan who during his life had been a waiter, potato merchant, farmer, soldier and restauranteur.
The business on Point helped Sam in his early life and he approved of his father's diligence and hard work but it was apparent that he was a hard taskmaster and their relationship was stern, cold and formal.

His father was the living proof of where hard work and being able to spot a bargain could take you.
Sam recalled an event in his childhood when he attended a Church rummage sale and he had arrived late in the day after most of the items had been sold. The Vicar asked Sam how much money he had to spend and after Sam told him that he had four pence he was presented with a set of golf clubs for that princely sum.

When he returned home and told his father he promptly arranged to re-sell them at a local auction which he did for five shillings. He then returned the four pence to Sam and pocketed the profit, which Sam was obviously very unimpressed by: when telling this tale he said that his father was a businessman and his God was money.

Events like this helped to shape Sam's attitude to wealth creation and his father would probably have been very disappointed with the way he turned out, being solitary, unambitious and very shy.

During his upbringing he remembered the smell of his mother's cakes, the faces of the fishermen asking for credit and the price of a packet of Woodbines (five for a penny!).

During his youth he recalled two special days every week - Tuesdays and Thursdays - when the horse box as he referred to it, or cattle boat, used to disembark at the end of Broad Street at Point beach as it is known today. The cattle boat was a wooden barge and was towed by a ferry boat or small tug and they carried livestock such as calves, cows, sheep, horses and pigs from the Isle of Wight.

Sam, (pictured fifth from the right with stick) and his friends sitting on a cattle boat.

The pigs in the corral in East Street.

He recalled that often when they starting unloading the pigs they sometimes escaped and started swimming, making a bid for freedom. In the process, the large male pigs in particular, sometimes cut themselves around their necks as they swam and the sea would become red in colour from their blood. The men in charge had to set out in a rowing boat to drive them ashore. Once ashore they were herded along Broad Street to be corralled in East Street before being sold or taken off to the local slaughterhouse.

Another recollection was the fish market located near the Still & West pub which often started at 4am when the hawkers would arrive and the fish would be sold by commission agents. A vivid memory Sam carried with him from the fish market was that when he was aged 6 or 7 he saw a young man counting herring in scores from a barrel of ice. This job didn't appeal to him: he would have preferred to be like the gentleman in the Ulster coat with note book and chain with a spade guinea on it!

He really enjoyed his upbringing on Point and thought it a wonderful place to grow up with lots to do and in those days of the early twentieth century it was a very busy place centred on the Camber and its maritime trade. As children they had books to read in the winter and he remembers playing with tops, feeling that once out playing, nobody bothered you.

Point was busy and very noisy creating the atmosphere he grew up in and loved and he recalled the muffin man coming around providing an opportunity for a bit of luxury, having a muffin on a Sunday. He remembered the street criers, men selling fruit and ice cream and the hot chestnut man in the winter. Punch & Judy shows were also popular in the summer and crabbing was a regular pastime.

Part of life living on Point involved the regular tidal flooding that occurred with the water lapping at the flood boards at the front of their house in Broad Street, sometimes overtopping and causing damage.
Sam was brought up in a strict regime at home as his father permitted no swearing, which was somewhat contrary to the everyday adjectives and expletives that were part of day to day life on Point, particularly that of the stevedores, watermen and other working men.

Schooling was strict and children learned to respect their elders. Sam recalled that a local businessman had left a sum of money in his will to ensure that every year in each school the best boy and girl were presented with a silver watch. Sam was awarded one of these watches and remembers his father buying him a silver chain to go with it. He subsequently went out dressed up in his Sunday best clothes with his silver watch and chain on show but nobody asked him the time which left him disappointed!

He always fondly talked of the local working folk of Point and surrounding area, the fishermen, coal heavers and wherrymen and envied their self-reliance and good humour.

Sam attended the Dame school as a youngster and was later educated at the Portsmouth Boys school until aged 14 when he left to start his working career. Dame schools were quite varied and some of them were little more than day care facilities, while others provided their pupils with a good foundation in the basics.

During the Great War he was fortunately posted to Mesopotamia, rather than to the Western Front, which Sam thought was due to a slip of the recruiting officer's pen.

On leaving the army after the war he joined the Rating Department of the Corporation where he worked for many years, living at Cosham, but after separating from his wife he moved back to Point which he had always loved.

Sam was an active member of the Portsmouth Sailing Club during his life where he kept a sailing dinghy for many years
He would often tell the story of how he had sailed across the English Channel and after making landfall and setting foot ashore he eventually made it to Paris.

He was aged about 30 in the late 1920s and had sailed across in a small clinker sailing dinghy.

Apparently he was fed up at work, hemmed in at home and had decided on a trip to France. He'd been to France before and had loved it but due to money being tight he decided to sail across the Channel.

He set off with his French phrasebook and enough sandwiches to tide him over but after the second day the food ran out and there was no sign of France and he was wet, cold and totally disoriented. After the third day he began to see clumps of floating seaweed and decided to eat it which made him sick on the fourth day. On the fifth day he limped into a grateful landfall on the Normandy coast near Fecamp.

The following day he set off for Paris where he had a good feed (Sam's phrase), enjoyed the sights of Paris before returning to his sailing dinghy to head home. After his fateful trip to France he made sure he had sufficient food for the return trip.

He left France, heading north and after three days he sighted land and beached the dinghy on what he assumed to be a beach on the southern shoreline of the Isle of Wight. As he said, the pebbles looked familiar and the natives spoke English but he was dismayed to be told by a local fishermen, when asking him if he had reached Shanklin that he was in fact east of Pevensey Bay!

Sam then spent another week sailing against headwinds along the south coast back to Portsmouth and to his job in the Rates office. When recounting the trip he was surprised that anyone would be interested in hearing about it.

With regards women, Sam viewed them with a mixture of wariness and admiration. He regarded them as the stronger sex and he adored women. He was always very courteous to women which I recall from the numerous visits my wife and I made to his house.

Sam had been married, but his marriage had been a disaster and having heard the details, it makes one wonder why it ever took place as his wife to be had just had a row with her father and wanted to leave home. Sam thought they were in love so they married in Portsmouth and honeymooned on the Isle of Wight, where he discovered on his wedding night that they were sexually incompatible.

It also turned out they really had nothing in common and, after 30 years of misery, they separated formally with what Sam called, a messy ending, due to the incorrect-drafting of an important clause in the Separation Order by the solicitor resulting in his ex-wife hounding him to the High Court mercilessly.

Fortunately for Sam he had a much more fruitful and happy adulterous relationship with another woman for 25 years after he and his wife had separated and this relationship restored his faith in women.
Sam had two children and towards the end of his life one child lived in Gosport and another in Kenya but he saw little of one and nothing of the other.

In July 1953, Sam, still being a very keen yachtsman and now having a larger yacht, set off single handed in his Folkboat, *Edith,* bound for France during a summer cruise in favourable weather. The Folkboat, 25ft in length, was designed in Sweden in the 1940s and was an excellent sea boat that had crossed the oceans of the world.

However, on the return trip the weather deteriorated, resulting in him being caught out in a north westerly gale. He always had a reputation as being a rugged individualist in yachting circles who never asked for help unless his boat was in real danger.

On this occasion he fought a battle with the weather but was unable to sleep due to being continually buffeted in his cabin. Fortunately, he was spotted by a Norwegian tanker, the *Kosmos V* (19,000 tons), which was bound for Rotterdam.

Sam decided it was unwise to continue, so accepted help and was picked up, but his yacht, still in good condition was cast adrift and was later found by a French fisherman and was towed into Boulogne.

Sam had nothing but praise for the courtesy of the Norwegian skipper who treated him like a member of the crew. Fortunately after arriving at Rotterdam, he was able to change some francs into guilders and with the help of the British Embassy managed to arrange transport home.

He was able at a later date to retrieve his yacht from Boulogne, with a friend after having negotiated a salvage fee with the fisherman.

After his ordeal he remarked "my name has been in the paper too much lately". He was reported as taking things quietly, being none the worse for his ordeal.

Sam was a keen member of the Portsmouth Sailing Club and although not renowned for his racing skills he did win the occasional trophy and in the adjacent photo he can be seen collecting an award at the annual club prize giving.

Sam had little respect for politicians and remembered a pre-war councillor whose flagrant bending of the rules amounted to almost contempt. He thought that a lot of people were greedy, envious, aggressive and plain unkind and their lives revolved around self-interest and self-advancement at other people's expense.

He despised anything that smacked of self-indulgence and had a pity verging on contempt for the overweight, the over rich or the hypochondriac. On the other hand, Sam had great admiration for those people who felt they had a duty to help others and "gave till it hurt". He thought of them as wonderful individuals.

He had a mild obsession with death: the fact that wealth, power and good living are no guarantees of immortality gave him great satisfaction and he often remarked on the passing of some local fat cat duly recorded in the columns of the Portsmouth Evening News.

He had very strong views on independence and was dismayed in his later life at the attitude of some people who had no compulsion in going cap in hand to the Corporation or Government for handouts.

'Pointers' (dwellers of Point) were poor and rough but they were not scroungers and had a hearty contempt for the few among them who accepted Church charity in the form of grocery tickets, or coal and a blanket in winter time. "We've our pride, even if it is a mucky pride".

Sam thought it all too easy and felt that people should make more of an effort to sort their own problems out like his generation would have done. He recalled when he was younger that to be labelled as lazy was a real insult and something to be ashamed of. Once boys reached the age of 14 they would go out to work to start earning a living. He felt this was a totally different outlook to that which existed in his later life when many people had no conscience about not bothering to seek work and were content to claim benefits, which were never available during his youth.

He thought back to his youth and recalled what a marvellous spirit existed on Point and how people helped each other, whereas in his old age he found many of the younger generation greedy and selfish and were never satisfied or happy. He felt that with some people, if you gave them the moon they wanted the sun.

During his later life and into his old age Sam always helped people locally, considering himself to be lucky and in good health, so was happy to help the less fortunate. He used to rise at 6am or 6.30am and after a wash and shave would set off beachcombing on Point beach and then to the Hot walls.

He would collect anything useful, particularly pieces of wood and cuttlefish bones and any other items he could use. He would give the cuttlefish bones away to people who had budgies and he would spend hours cutting up the wood in his store and then make it up in bundles to give away to people. Some thought he should sell the wood, but it made Sam happy to give it to the less well off or less able.

When Sam gave the kindling away to people, he often also gave a large box of very long matches, ideal for lighting fires, or sometimes these would be given as presents instead of the normal gifts such as boxes of chocolates or similar items.

I remember he used to cut out and paste pictures of mountains, flowers etc. from magazines on the top of the box and on one occasion he stuck on the photo at the beginning of this chapter which shows Sam on the Point with the gold bust of the Duchess of Point which he was so fond of perched on the adjacent baulk of wood.

His house in Broad Street was inherited from his father and he let out the upper floors and lived on the ground floor in two rooms together with all his paraphernalia. On entering his house there were bundles of old newspapers tied with twine salvaged from the beach, boxes of chopped firewood, a long work bench littered with tools, ancient yellow oilskins and his 10ft dinghy chocked up with plimsolls.
Beneath the window were piles of old books, half empty tins of paint and a small mountain of driftwood. Floorboards sagged underfoot and bare electrical wires dangled from the wall and towards the back of the dimly lit store was a small grubby window leading onto a tiny courtyard.

At the back of the store was a square of living space distinguished by coconut matting, a lop sided bed, a sink, wooden draining board and a rather splendid roll top desk. Everywhere was sawdust and debris together with a smell of damp.

People used to put their old newspapers on his doorstep and he would bundle them up and take them to a local fishmonger who sometimes gave him a few pairs of kippers that he would often later give away to someone less well off.
In the summer he would launch his 10ft pale green clinker dinghy with oars and outboard off Point beach on his small trolley and set off to go fishing, usually spinning for mackerel and most of those he caught were given away to people.

Sam dragging his dinghy out of his store on its trolley.

He was well thought of by the local population who considered him a real gentlemen who never had a bad word to say about anyone and spent much of his time helping others. He was a thin upright figure with a glow in his cheeks and a smile in his eyes and a reputation for gentle eccentricity and a wonderful unforgettable laugh.

He ensured he had a healthy diet and was always fit, although very slim and thin in his old age. I always recall his love of Ryvita biscuits which accompanied much of his food. Sam ate sparingly, mainly bread, fruit, cereals and seaweed, which he'd boil and stir into one of his vegetable stews.
Health was one of Sam's obsessions in middle age and in later life he stopped smoking and eating meat.

Graham Hurley in one of his articles about Sam described his appearance so well:

> I was never quite certain whether his clothes were inherited, or just old, but his body seemed to have retreated from their outline, leaving them on his thin frame. His face, though, was marvellous spare and bony and weather – beaten and the way his neck emerged from the limp circle of ancient wool reminded me of a tortoise, old and tough and leathery.

He was very well read and on occasions would quote a passage or story from books, often by famous authors and the following tale was recounted to me by Graham:

> It was a story about a King that was lying ill in his bed surrounded by doctors who had racked their brains to think of some cure, but had come up with nothing. Finally one of them made a suggestion. If the King could wear the shirt of a happy man, he would then recover.
>
> Courtiers rode out at once to look for a happy man. For days they scoured the kingdom until at last they came across an old tramp sitting by the side of the road. He was smiling and beaming and very happy. One of the courtiers looked down at him. "The King is very ill", he said, "He needs to wear the shirt of a happy man"
>
> The old tramp nodded and smiled even more. ""It would be an honour to help", he said, "But I'm afraid I can't". "Why not?" Said the courtier. "Simple", said the tramp, "I haven't got a shirt".

I should imagine that was one of Sam's favourite tales as it sums up his attitude to life and his want to live quite frugally, like the tramp

He was never really interested in making money although his father was a true businessman. When he was 81 he had a bad fall and was left lying on his floor for 17 hours before he managed to drag himself to the door and summon help after which we was taken to hospital where he stayed for four days before being allowed home.

In the summer months he regularly went for a daily swim off Point beach, or Pickfords beach in Bath Square and, although not in the water for long, he felt it was good exercise and helped him to remain healthy. I recall him leaving his house in his white plimsolls with his red dressing gown with large white spots and wearing a dark red knitted bathing costume that hung off his thin frame.

Sam near Quebec House in Bath Square

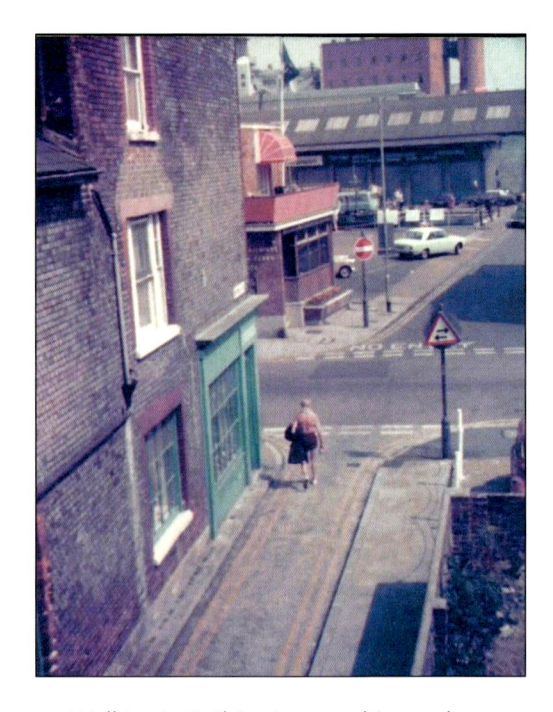

Walking in Bathing Lane on his way home after a swim.

My lasting memory of Sam is that of a real local character who took great enjoyment in helping people that he considered were deserving of being helped. He was a person with real independent views and always felt that people should sort out their own problems in life and not rely on others. Accumulation of wealth was unimportant to him and he lead his life accordingly in a frugal manner, but was happy. A rare person with views that were "old school" and synonymous with his Victorian upbringing, but a breath of fresh air in the modern world we know.

Chapter 10
The Last House on Point
(The story of 102 Broad Street (1656 - 1960))

Portsmouth Point by William Henry Smyth (1788-1865) clearly showing 102 Broad Street in the foreground © Portsmouth Museum Service.

In the Beginning

An extract from an ancient plan of the town of Portsmouth made at some time during the reign of Queen Elizabeth I shows very little development on Point and although Spice Island was almost uninhabited in the sixteenth century it was largely built up by the 1670s.

The first documentary evidence of reference to the site of "the Last House on Point" comes from the mid-seventeenth century, when "a seller of strong waters", named Nicholas Peirson was granted a piece of beach ground:

> "Grant in the fee the twentieth day of June AD 1656 made by John Tawke Esq. Mayor of the Borough of Portsmouth and the Aldermen and Burgesses of the same Borough to Nicholas Peirson, a piece of Beacon ground whereupon he hath built a wharf and two storehouses lying without the Point Gate at Portsmouth aforesaid near the new quay erecting there and containeth in length on the west side seventy-three feet, in length on the east side, sixty-seven feet, in breadth at the north side fifty-seven feet, in breadth at the south side forty-seven feet…..unto the said Nicholas Peirson his heirs and assigns for ever under the yearly rent of six shillings and eight pence payable at Michaelmas and on Lady Day and also one fat turkey at St. Thomas the Apostle…"

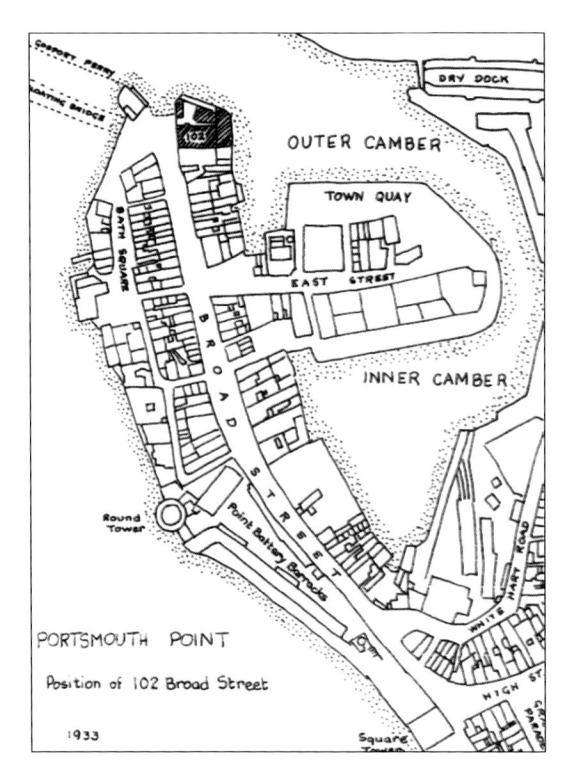

Robert East's Extracts from the Portsmouth Records tells us that Nicholas Peirson was a wealthy ship owner. He resided at the extremity of Point, where the *Star & Garter* and Baker's Wharf stood. He owned considerable property, was made a Burgess in 1645 and in 1653 issued tokens bearing his name as farthings. In 1670 he was made an Alderman and in 1672 became Mayor of Portsmouth. He died in 1677 and was buried on 29th June in St. Thomas's Churchyard.

The location of 102 Broad Street

The Board of Ordnance

The old maps of Portsmouth clearly show that the "Last House on Point "stood on an important site at the entrance to the Camber which would have been an ideal location for a wharf and storehouse for the Board of Ordnance and on the town plan of 1716 the words "Ordnance Wharfe" are written against the property. Robert East confirms this with the following entry in his "Extracts"..:

> "The Ordnance office and wharf were originally at the north end of Point, since Lindegren's Wharf (now Threadingham's)…"

There is a record that on the 20th March 1676 the property belonging to Nicholas Peirson was leased to the office of His Majesty's Ordnance for 99 years and this was to be the Town's third Gunwharf following the initial use of Portchester Castle in the fourteenth century and later the Square Tower was adapted and made into a munitions store in the late sixteenth century.

At Priddy's Hard Museum in Gosport there is stored a considerable amount of correspondence from the London office of the Board of Ordnance to Portsmouth, most of the early letters being addressed to "Mr Hooper, Storekeeper to ye Office of Ordnance at Portsmouth." One letter dealt with an incident at the stores upon which Mr Hooper had written that it related to the Point Wharfe, thus confirming that the House at Point and the Board of Ordnance store were parts of the same property.

The following letter is a typical letter that John Hooper would have received from the Office of Ordnance:

> Mr Hooper
>
> His Majesty's ship the *Adventure* being ordered into Portsmouth Harbour to be cleaned. You are to take out her Ordnance and Gunner's stores during the doing thereof and send up her Remaine as usual to
>
> Your Affectionate Friends
>
> Signed
>
> Office of Ordnance, 28th August 1701

The Remaine was a large official document listing all the supplies for which the Master Gunner was responsible, including heavy guns, pistols, shot, cartridges, pikes, swords, rammers, sheepskins, oil, tallow, needles, thread, wire, lanthorns and dozens of other necessities.

John Hooper was responsible for large sums of money. He would be sent several hundreds of pounds in order to pay the bills for repairs and supplies, especially when the Gun Wharf was being built, yet at other times he would be treated quite harshly:

> "…..We cannot but take notice of your great carelessness in relation to ye account of Powder you lately gave us and judge thereby how little you must mind other matters under your care, but hope this will be ye last time we shall have reason to complain of anything of this kind……"

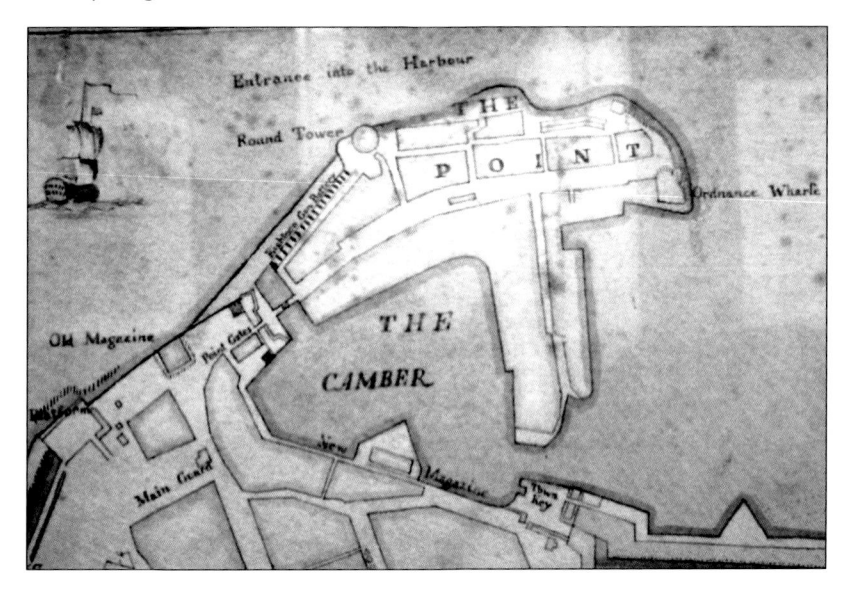

Early map clearing showing the Ordnance Wharfe at the Point.

The early Board of Ordnance dealt with many goods, not only guns and shot, but also repairs to the Fortifications, Barracks, Governor's House and God's House. So, although the powder was likely to have been stored at the Square Tower, there were many articles used on board ship and by the military such as guns and gun carriages that could have been stored at Point.

When the house was demolished in 1960 there were found to be arched vaults and stores with very solid walls beneath it that could well date from the period in question.

As early as 1699 there was concern about the unsuitability of the Point site as an Ordnance store, mainly because of the lack of water at low tide. It may well have been this factor that caused the Board to begin planning the construction of the new Gunwharf on the other side of the Camber.

The land reclamation and construction commenced in 1707 and by 1715 most of the work had been completed. John Hooper was by this time rather elderly and was not appointed Storekeeper to the new stores at Gunwharf, but continued to live in a house rented by His Majesty's Service. He died in 1723 and was buried on 30th January in St. Thomas's Churchyard.

The Dark Years

After the Ordnance stores had been removed to the new Gunwharf, the vacant property was leased on 29th September 1724 to Benjamin Whiteing. The lease was for 300 years at an annual rent of £1 2s 6d and two pair of good fat capons. The property was known as Peirson's Quay, bounded on the south by Thomas Hunt's storehouse and on the west by the house of Nicholas Peirson the Younger.

The property now occupied some 8,800 square feet, somewhat larger than defined in the original lease.

Benjamin Whiteing (or Whiting) lived in the property until about 1730 during which time his son, also called Benjamin worked as an apprentice Shipwright. This may have been the reason why, on his father's death, the younger Nicholas did not take up residence in the house. Instead it was rented to Joseph Gilbert, a victualler and a constable of the Town.

The rental on the house then seems to have passed through a number of occupants including Mrs Eleanor Gayton and family (1732), Rebecca Tooley (1745), Peter Ireland (1746) and Banister Hurst (1749). After this time Benjamin Whiteing returned to the house, dying there in 1777, his widow continuing to reside there until about 1782.

By 1783 the house had passed into the ownership of Andrew Lindegren Jnr, possibly through an association with the Whiteing family, but the process was not smooth. Although his "Wharf, Office and Store" appear in the Rate Book of that year, a report in the Salisbury and Winchester Journal for 29th December 1783 announced the bankruptcy of Andrew Lindegren and listed the Broad Street properties amongst his assets.

Somehow, though, the Lindegren family held on to the house as well as several other buildings in the Town of Portsmouth and beyond. Their business flourished thereafter.

In 1785 the history of the house was nearly changed considerably. The location of the house was ideal for keeping watch on all shipping entering or leaving the Camber, which at that time was the Commercial harbour of the town. It was considered an excellent idea to move the Customs House to the Point from its old position along the road.

The Rate Book for 1st April of that year showed the property as being "Mr Lindegren's Wharf, Office and Store", but, surprisingly, the entry for 8th April reads "Collector of Customs".

Against the old Custom House was written, "Void". Again on 20th April the rate was paid by the Customs, but by July it was back to Mr Lindegren and the old Custom House was back in business.

It appears that, because of the suitability of the site, the Customs decided to move their location, but as the cost would have been £200 more than estimated it was agreed for political economy not to continue with this venture.

The Lindegren family were very much associated with the English East India Company, one of the most powerful commercial companies ever to have existed. It laid the foundations of the British Empire in south Asia and thus lies at the very heart of the interlinked histories of Britain and Asia

Portsmouth was used as the company's leading provincial outport and the agency work there was long standing, vital and thorough. In comparison with other communities, Portsmouth was early in the field with regard to agency work, with the first agent there being noted in 1640 and agents recorded in Portsmouth until 1825, with Andrew Lindegren being recorded as being in post between 1788-1805 and Andrew and John Lindegren between 1805-1825.

Their duties were demanding and various, requiring substantial reserves. Inter personal, numerical and literary skills were required, as agents had to submit accounts to the company regarding their expenditure and write copious missives about anything and everything going on in the port which might affect company interests.

The one responsibility which gave Portsmouth agents most sleepless nights was the despatch of silver required in India for use by diamond merchants, for direct use by the company itself and for the various company mints operating in the sub-continent. This silver was sent out through Portsmouth.

The absence of banks in the town until October 1787 made retention of substantial sums of silver a real problem for the local agent and in 1708 bullion was lodged in a private house with owner being rewarded with ¼ percent of the value as remuneration.

Into the Nineteenth Century

On Saturday 24th June 1809 there occurred one of the most dramatic incidents in the history of the house. Two or three days earlier the 2nd Battalion of the 8th Regiment of Foot had disembarked at Point, leaving their baggage, including munitions, on the beach.

That morning a few soldiers were arranging the removal of their possessions when a woman, who was smoking a pipe, invited another doing her washing at the water's edge to take a whiff of her pipe. Finding it would not draw she tapped the pipe against a pebble on the beach and a spark ignited a few grains of powder that had been carelessly scattered on the beach.

This touched a cartridge which flew up into a crate, setting fire to some loose cartridges which in turn blew up a barrel of powder.

The ensuing explosion was catastrophic and in an instant the whole area was a mass of devastation, both of people and buildings. The Hampshire Telegraph reported:

> "The explosion set fire to Mr Lindegren's store, broke all the windows and many of the window frames of the *Star and Garter* Tavern, Mr Lindegren's office and Navy Post Office and upwards of 20 other houses on the street. The number of lives that were lost and of persons wounded from the instantaneous nature of the incident cannot be certainly ascertained. Three soldiers of the 8th Regiment who were standing about the baggage were killed, four were badly and five slightly burned….several of the soldier's wives and children are believed to have lost their lives"

There were reports of bodies being flung over the tops of houses with one body being blown over the houses at the lower end of Broad Street and hitting the Customs Watch House in Bath Square, being so mangled it was not possible to say whether it was a man or a woman, whilst another was thrown against the wall of the *Union Tavern* near the first floor window badly staining the bricks with blood.

In their panic, people rushed to get off the island through the Point Gate and sentries were placed there to stop sightseers coming from town. There was the possibility of further explosions from the ammunition on the beach as it was likely that Mr Lindegren had gunpowder in his stores and these were on fire.

A few brave men managed to roll the remainder of the barrels into the sea and it was not until the engines had succeeded in subduing the flames of Mr Lindegren's storehouse that the alarm in any degree subsided.

The injured were taken into the *Fortitude Tap*: these included a little drummer boy whose face was scorched beyond recognition. The Mayor opened the Town Hall as a reception centre for the soldier's wives and General Whetham sent a message by express to inform the War Office of the accident.

On the following Monday morning there was an inquest on the bodies of Corporal Aldridge and two boys who had been guarding the baggage at the time of the explosion.

Mr W Hackett, Surgeon of the Regiment, gave evidence saying that he had been informed that the cask of powder had contained sixty pound. It had been packed inside another cask and between the two had been loose cartridges and old clothes to secure the powder.

A sentry had seen a woman smoking nearby and had hastened to drive her away.

A drummer boy named Charles Burn had witnessed a woman named Fallen on the baggage reaching for a tub with a pipe in her mouth and he had seen the accident and although standing about two yards from the barrel he had only been scorched a little.

A waterman named Stephen Gregory was in his boat on the beach at the time of the explosion and with others, he had rushed to the rescue of two children who were under a chest and then helped a soldier lying on the ground. Then, assisted by another man, he pushed several boxes and an ammunition chest into the sea.

One of the survivors was the woman who had caused the accident and she related her escape to a reporter:

> "She was stooping down to take up her child with an intention to make her escape when she was beat backwards; her washing tub etc. fell upon herself and child, which nearly covered her and to this circumstance she attributed her preservation, which she bewails, because she had been the unhappy means of causing the deaths of so many others".

No one was ever quite certain how many people died that day, as estimates ranged from 17 to 40 lives. Some were probably carried out to sea and portions of bodies were even found on the roofs of houses.

The jury returned a verdict of Accidental Death.

THE EXPLOSION

When loudly cried each Spanish Lord
"Pray hasten embarkation;
"Britain! Unsheathe thy flaming sword
And save our sinking nation

When, spread along the crowded shore
To gain a moment's rest
The regiment lay, with plenteous store
In ammunition chest

Twas here a maid of Erin's Isle
Who well a pipe could quaff
And either cast a heavenly smile
Or join the boisterous laugh

High on a cask for mischief ripe
Majestic took her seat
While oft the sparkles from her pipe
She scattered at her feet

Sudden th'exploding thunder burst
Destruction marked its way
And far around the rolling smoke
Obscured the light of day

Dismay in every face appeared
Few knew from whence the sound
And Fear her dreadful form upreared
And shed her horrors round

Many a wretched wife that day
Bewailed a husband lost
Whose mangled limbs disordered lay
Along a blood stained coast

This brings an adage to my mind
Which somewhere I have read
If mischief come, you'll surely find
A woman at the head.

(A poem from "A Metrical History of Portsmouth" by Henry Slight in 1820)

The Lindegrens lived in the house for three generations: Andrew Lindegren senior was an iron ore merchant from Sweden and he died in 1783.

Andrew Lindegren junior was an able successful and well-known local merchant who had a remarkable range of business interests and activities and he was a Prize Agent for the Navy during a time of considerable naval unrest.
He died in France in 1827 and he was succeeded by his son John, who in turn proved to be a most able businessman.

The Floating Bridge.

In one of his financial ventures, John Lindegren in 1838 became a subscriber and a Director of the Floating Bridge Company, formed to create a better ferry link between Portsmouth and Gosport which hitherto had only been able to carry foot passengers by water.

The earliest plans proposed two floating bridges: the northern one was to finish at the old Gunwharf to serve Portsea and the southern one would run to Point for the convenience of the population of Portsmouth.

The original suggestion showed the landing place at Point to be Lindegren's Wharf.

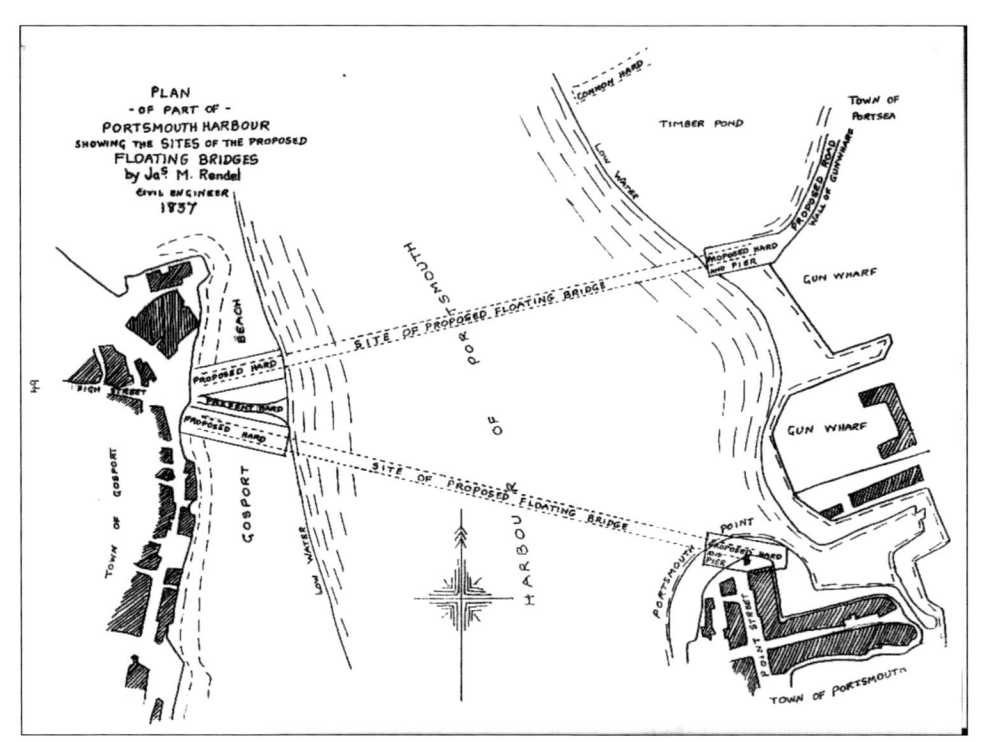

Plan showing the sites of the proposed Floating Bridges in 1837

The Admiralty opposed the building of two bridges and it was left to the residents of Portsmouth to choose the route. Portsea claimed four fifths of the population lived in Portsea, but Portsmouth stated that the Customs House, Bonding Stores and Banks were in their area, whilst the High Street was wider than Queen Street for use of carriages and in fact all the best inns were there.

Gunwharf was the most expensive option costing an extra £3000.

Eventually at the meeting to decide, after a recount, an amendment was passed allowing the Directors and Shareholders to choose and the route to Point was chosen, although the area would need redeveloping in order to accommodate it.

A Bill was prepared to go before Parliament and the Company agreed to purchase part of Mr Lindegren's premises in Broad Street to extend the slipway. After negotiating, Mr Lindegren accepted a sum of £1,950 for selling a strip of land 32 feet wide on the north side and 21ft 9ins on the south side. This strip of land formed the living quarters of the house and at that time stretched half way across Broad Street.

The artist R H C Ubsdell wrote at the time to Sir Henry Madden that:

> the house at the lower end of Point, so many years occupied by Mr Lindegren and which Parliament has ordered to be pulled down has been demolished today which gives an open view of the harbour looking down Broad Street........on crossing from Gosport to Point we have a view of the *Star and Garter* hotel and several houses up the street."

The demolition of the original property signalled a marked improvement in the social conditions in the area. Soon, the living quarters on the Point property were rebuilt in the newer and grander style which can be seen in the 1860 painting of Point on the first page of this chapter.

For some reason, however, Lindegren sold the property to Andrew Nance Jnr, a co-director of the Floating Bridge Company.

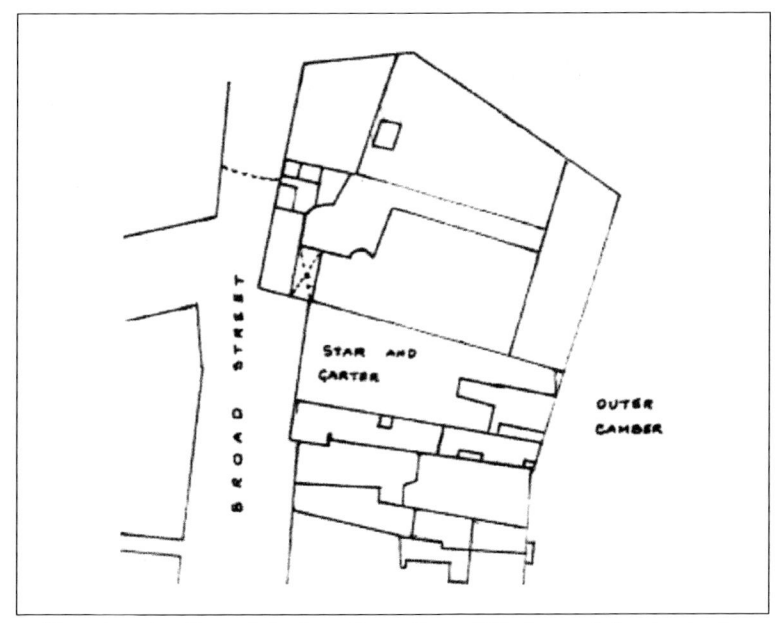

Plan showing the original configuration of Lindegren's land prior to selling off a 32 feet strip to enable the Floating Bridge venture to proceed.

John Lindegren and Andrew Nance were friends. Andrew Nance, born in 1810, was a particularly colourful character. His father, also named Andrew had two inns: the *Crown* inn in Pembroke Street and the *Blue Posts* in Broad Street.

The younger Andrew often drove the coaches for his family. He held the record for driving the "*Tantivy*" coach from Portsmouth to London and was regarded as the best four-in-hand driver in the County. He became one of the directors of the Floating Bridge Company and became a Councillor, Alderman and was elected Mayor in 1854 when aged 44.

He was a very astute businessman, becoming Chairman of the Portsmouth and Gosport Floating Bridge Company, Chairman of the Portsea Island Gaslight Company, a Director of the Southsea Clarence Esplanade Pier Company, the Landport and Southsea Tramway Company and was on the committee for the building of the Portsmouth to London railway and was even the Chairman of the short lived Southsea and Isle of Wight Steam Ferry Company that soon amalgamated with the Portsmouth and Ryde United Steam Packet Company.

He died aged 67 whilst living in Kingston Crescent Portsmouth.

Although Nance, a very well-known figure on Point, had purchased the property, he did not however live at the house, but instead rented it to George Baker Jnr., who 10 years later purchased it from Nance.

Baker had also proved adept at business and had earned enough money by 1857 to enable him to buy the *Star and Garter* hotel next door.
George Baker was now wealthy enough to move to the newly fashionable area in Elm Grove in 1861, where he lived near the Lindegren family at Elm Lodge.

The Point House was let to Elizabeth Main, who did not stay long, dying in 1863 and leaving the house to remain unoccupied for two years.
During this time, Baker, who had decided to retire, tried to sell the property to the Corporation who declined for financial reasons.
Fortunately for Baker, the Port of Portsmouth and Ryde United Steam Packet Company were in need of new premises, so in 1865 they bought the property and moved their new Superintendent, Mr Henry Threadingham into the accommodation.

The Age of Steam

When the Borough Council declined to buy the Last House on Point in 1864, the decision was made at a Council meeting chaired by the Mayor, Richard William Ford, who also happened to be the Secretary of the Port of Portsmouth and Ryde Steam Packet Company, which within 6 months had placed the following notice in the *Hampshire Telegraph:*

> "The Packet Company have taken on a lease for the whole of the wharfs, stores, etc. now in the possession of Mr Baker, Broad Street, Point. This accommodation, in addition to providing room for the repair of vessels will enable the company to have an office and Board room on the same premises"

It was a propitious time for the house at Point to enter the history of the Packet Company. The previous few decades had seen much rivalry in the business of providing ferry services to the Isle of Wight and this was not resolved until 1851, when the two principal companies operating on the route merged to form the Packet Company. Expansion thereafter was rapid and the need for a single site for all their operations must have been urgent.

Henry Threadingham was born in Portsmouth. He was aged 32 when he was appointed as Superintendent for the Packet Company and given the house on the Point as his residence and office.

He was unmarried at the time, but with his new found status, this quickly changed when he wed Mary who was at that time around 20 years of age. They had two children, Ada Mary and Alice Maud, aged 3 and 2 respectively in the 1871 Census

Henry was described as energetic and courteous, hardworking and with enthusiasm for the improvement and prosperity of the Company. He was so successful in this that only 7 years had elapsed before the Hampshire Telegraph was reporting on a presentation made to Henry at a lavish dinner for 80 employees and shareholders of the Packet Company and other associated businesses.

The toast of the evening was "Health and Prosperity to Mr H. Threadingham", an honour occasioned by his careful supervision and attention to duty.

The Railway Companies Take Over

The following years were to see a clash of interests between the companies operating the ferry services and the two companies which had brought the railway into Portsmouth. The latter were exasperated at the difficulty of providing a through service to the Isle of Wight and secretly put together a plan to take over the Packet Companies, which they succeeded in doing in 1881.

Threadingham remained the ideal man to run the combined company's operations but he was already suffering ill-heath and he died on 25th January 1885 after only 4 years in his new post. He was buried in Highland Road Cemetery in a grave that was re-used 30 years later, leaving Henry Threadingham with no permanent memorial.

Henry had already chosen his successor before he died and within a short time Robert Brown had taken over both the job and the house that went with it. He was 33 years old at the time and within 4 years had been appointed Marine Superintendent of the Joint Railway Company at a salary of £250 per annum. Brown had originally been an Engineer Officer for the Royal Mail Steamship Company but opted for a shore career after his marriage to Emily Louise. They had three children but two of them died in the house at Point both aged 12 years

Robert Brown was described as alert and resourceful and very successful in his official capacity, but beyond that little is known of his work. He must have retired early as records show that by 1904 he was living in St Ronan's Road on £100 per annum as Consulting Superintendent of Boats. Emily died in 1925 aged 72 but Robert was to survive until a week before his 86th birthday in 1933. He was buried in Highland Road Cemetery.

On the retirement of Robert Brown, the post of Superintendent and residence of the house at Point passed to Alfred Fitz-Howard Drayson who had been in the employment of the joint railway company since 1890, shortly after he had retired from the Royal Navy in which he had served for 17 years. He was joined at Point House by his wife Aileen but by this time their two children had both died.

The Draysons were thought of as a good family, well-educated and benevolent, but they were always considered "outsiders" by the local "Pointers", possibly because of an inbuilt bias against Naval Officers, whose responsibility for the Press Gangs two centuries earlier still rankled. Drayson retired in 1913 and went to live in Brading on the Isle of Wight where he died in February 1945.

The last of the Marine Superintendents to live at the house was Alfred William Langworthy who took over in 1913, the culmination of a life devoted to the railways. He had started work in 1890 at the age of 15 as a parcels clerk at Ryde Pier and worked his way upward in the company until he came to work under Alfred Drayson, eventually succeeding him. Langworthy served a total of 25 years in the post during a period that saw massive expansion in the service and one World War. He retired in March 1938 with an annuity of £1000: he had been preparing for this event as he had bought a retirement home in Waterlooville and had moved there in 1935.

Before leaving, however, he recommended that Thomas Sherwood be appointed as boatman/caretaker and be offered residency of the house, an offer which would be extended when Langworthy's successor, C.T.Pelly decided he would not need the house as he wished to continue living in his house at Warblington.

With the development of Portsmouth and the Isle of Wight there needed to be a better means of transporting larger items of equipment and livestock across the Solent and the age of the motor car was fast approaching. Even in the early twentieth century tow boat operations were still in place which could only transport a limited number of vehicles, goods and livestock between Portsmouth and Ryde.

Their last year of tow boat operation on this route was 1925 when 1718 cars were transported and later in 1926 tow boat operations were transferred from Ryde to Fishbourne with improved facilities.

Tow boats and cargo of vehicles with towing ferry at Fishbourne, Isle of Wight.

Transportation of vehicles and livestock to and from the Isle of Wight was transformed in 1927 with Southern Railway introducing the first car ferry, the *M.V. Fishbourne*, operating between Point and Fishbourne. She was 131 ft. in length and carried 18 cars with a crossing time of 55 minutes from the slipway at Broad Street to the slipway at Fishbourne.

M.V.Fishbourne

Cynthia Sherwood

When Thomas Sherwood took over the residency of Point house he moved in with his wife Elizabeth, whom he had married in 1922 at the age of 34, and his daughter Cynthia, then aged 12 years. Thomas had been born in 1888 near Leeds to a family with no connection to the sea whatsoever, and yet at the age of 17 years, much to the surprise of his parents, he joined the Navy as a boy sailor.

Thomas stayed in the Navy for nearly 23 years, rising in rank from Ordinary Seaman to Petty Officer and completing his service in 1928. He then took a number of temporary jobs, including one with Southern Railways who eventually appointed him to their permanent staff early in 1933.

During the next couple of years he worked under the Marine Superintendent Alfred Langworthy who must have realised that Thomas was a hardworking, trustworthy and sober man who was loyal to the company.

The role of Caretaker encompassed a myriad of duties, the principle one being to meet the ferries as they approached the slipway and ensure they were secured. This involved rowing out in a dinghy and securing a line from the ferry to a buoy that was sited off H.M.S.Vernon.

An early car ferry preparing to berth at Point and the man in the dinghy is probably Cynthia's father preparing to take a line on to the buoy off H M S Vernon.

During the winter months there were only three return trips a day but in the high season Cynthia recalls that her father seemed to be permanently on duty. Living so close to the job, Thomas would be called out at all times of day or night for any emergencies be they related to urgent repairs to the boats or to rescue motorists who had overshot the slipway and ended up in the water.

Thomas, Elizabeth and Cynthia stayed at Point House until 1951, with a short break for the war, when a new Marine Manager decided that he would like to make use of the house on Point.

The family moved out to a house in Laburnum Grove but Thomas died there of a stroke barely a year afterwards in 1952. Elizabeth survived him by over 20 years dying in 1973. Cynthia continued to live there until 2007 before moving elsewhere and now lives in Southsea.

Cynthia Remembers the House

I always felt that the house must have had a long and historic past...the store was full of records...everything was destroyed when the house was demolished.
On entering the double front doors there were two steps which raised the hall well above the level of the street.

This was necessary to avoid the flooding at very high spring tides. The grooves on the outside of the door were for boards that were slotted in when very high tides were imminent. On the right of the hall was the Booking Office for the Isle of Wight Car Ferries, and on the other side was a waiting room for the use of passengers (this was later to become another office)

The Booking office with flood boards deployed during a very high tide.

At the end of the hall a door led into the old part of the house and it was here that the enormous thickness of the walls could be seen.

The first of the four old vaults had been made into a kitchen; it had a semi-circular ceiling and ran the full width of the building and was divided into two rooms by a large wooden dresser. Although it was large it was always warm and cosy, being heated by a handsome range which supplied hot water and was used for cooking....During the winter it was the warmest place in the house, so this is where we listened to the radio and I did my homework.

A door to the side of the dresser led into the inside storeroom which, like several rooms in the house was without windows. During World War 2 this room had become the local air raid shelter; I suppose the thick walls were the deciding factor, and the ceiling had extra support with strong wooden posts for added safety. When the sirens sounded the front doors were opened and in came the neighbours, including any guests staying at the *Union*....although bombs fell into the sea.....the house stood still, though the upper floors developed an even greater slope.

From the hall, a flight of lino covered stairs led up to a gate marked "PRIVATE" (although we soon discovered that passengers sometimes ignored this and were found wandering about upstairs). Here the stairs divided with a flight going to the front of the house and a slightly lower one to the back. At the top of the former was a roomy landing and to the right at the corner of the building was the sitting room.

It was about 18 feet square with a window on each of the two outer walls giving magnificent views of the harbour entrance, HMS Vernon, the harbour pier and Portsdown Hill in the background. You can imagine how popular the room was when there was a Royal Review of the Fleet.

Everyone remembered where we lived and every vantage point was full of excited spectators. Even our family doctor decided it was a suitable time to call and then sat by the window to watch proceedings.

On the opposite side of the landing was the main bedroom from which there were doors leading to two small and one large unlit room. One door led to a flight of wooden steps which led to an enormous room covering the whole of the back of the house. At one time it was used as a store for furniture from the 1st Class saloons of the paddle steamers.

My bedroom was next to the sitting room. It was long and fairly narrow and had a magnificent view up the harbour. I remember sitting on the window sill watching searchlights make patterns in the sky just before the war. I was likely to awake to find a Collier aground outside my window. This happened quite often as the Camber was very narrow and the boats had to manoeuvre very carefully, often when the tide was ebbing fast.
Next door to my bedroom was the bathroom. Little did we know at the time but Henry Threadingham had died on that floor."

Some of Cynthia's most vivid memories of Point were the floods that occurred periodically. These had effected the Point for centuries and the inhabitants were generally prepared for it. 102 Broad Street had been substantially altered by raising the whole of the ground floor by two or three feet and all the houses along the street had boards that could be fitted into slots outside their doors and all possessed buckets of clay that could be used to seal any gaps in the boards.

The Green Dragon

The Green dragon was a wooden figurehead fastened to a corner of the factory looking towards the kitchen door. He was originally painted in vivid colours with red lips, white teeth and glaring eyes.
When Mrs Langworthy was living at the house she went into the yard one evening and was so frightened by this fiery apparition that she screamed and the next day it was repainted in Southern Railway green.
After Cynthia and her family had left the house the dragon was removed from his resting place and was then displayed above the front door. Some years later she found the dragon hung on the wall over the back stairs in the *Still and West*, only a short distance from his old haunts, under shelter overlooking the harbour entrance.

It is thought that the dragon had been the figurehead of a vessel named the *Dragon* that had belonged to the Admiralty in the nineteenth century and that was bought by the Joint Railway Company circa 1900 to be used as a coal hulk moored in Portsmouth Harbour, just off the Harbour Pier.

In the Southern Railways Docks and Marine Committee minutes for 28th July 1932 the following was recorded:

> Replacement of the Coal Hulk *Dragon*
>
> "The Marine Manager reported that the hulk *Dragon* which is used for the purpose of coaling the Company's Steamers at Portsmouth, and which was an old vessel when purchased 32 years ago is in need of extensive repairs estimated to cost £1500. It is not considered advisable to incur this expenditure and with the agreement of the General Manager, an offer of £2,000 has been made to and accepted by the Admiralty for a 1,000 ton coal-haul boat to replace the *Dragon*.
>
> With the acquisition of the Admiralty's vessel it will be possible to adopt a more economical method of coaling the Steamers which it is anticipated will effect a saving of £150 per annum. It is further recommended that the *Dragon* be disposed of which will result in a small additional credit being obtained".

Nine months later *Dragon's* figurehead was reported as being sold for the sum of £110.

Not long after being spotted in the *Still & West* the dragon was put up for auction and was sold for £1200, being purchased by an American from Texas.

The new owner was a collector of marine art and nautical antiques with a great sense of humour, as this extract from a letter he wrote to Cynthia in 1987 demonstrates:

> "I had planned to hang your friend on the wall at my home where most of my collection resides. However, being forewarned of the dragon's fierceness I am having a cage constructed so that he won't be able to frighten Texas ladies. This would quite naturally bring out all sorts of pseudo dragon slayers (you've no doubt heard of how gallant Texas cowboys are). The potential turmoil that would ensue is sure to bring about chaos and destruction, to say nothing of the increase in my liability insurance premiums. So, Miss Sherwood I am indeed in your debt for forewarning me of your friend's past. Should he get loose and attack someone, I now know to whom to send the medical bills."

The true story of how the dragon arrived at the *Still & West* was later told by an ex landlord, Cliff Simms. Apparently, after the figurehead had been removed from the factory wall sometime in the 1950s it was placed under sacking in the warehouse and Mr Simms had been interested in buying it but was refused. Soon afterwards it was repainted and placed over the front door of the house but was again taken down and put into storage sometime later after the wall started to bulge.

One day when the car ferry was in the harbour entrance it passed too close to the *Still & West* and some slight damage was done to the property. By mutual agreement it was decided not to report the matter either to the Brewers or the Railway Company and the factory workmen repaired the damage: Mr Simms happily accepted the dragon in compensation.

Mr Simms repainted it himself and placed it under cover for protection, painting a gold tooth each time he obtained the tenancy of another public house. At one time apparently it had 9 gold teeth!

The Final Days of the House at Point

Early car ferries dis-embarking their vehicles on Point slipway

As early as 1929 there had been a valid case for a complete redevelopment of Point. During the winter months with little traffic, the Point area coped well, but the coming of summer was a completely different matter. On a Saturday there could be 15 boats a day, all fully booked and the cars were often parked all the way up Broad Street to Grand Parade. Added to this there were still animals being driven up the street for the special cattle boats.

Livestock being loaded on to a Car Ferry at Point

One of the more exotic animals being coaxed on to a ferry

A view of the Boathouse at low water and the rear of the Star and Garter hotel and Grogan's café.

Despite being presented with detailed plans for the redevelopment, the City Council prevaricated for decades, but after World War 2 they were faced with an impossible situation and another plan was submitted in 1949.

Once again the Council put off making the vital decision which would have involved the demolition of much of the eastern side of Broad Street, including the House at Point and the *Star and Garter*, together with a section of East Street.

The initial costs were presented at £63,000, exclusive of the cost of purchasing the land, but by 1952 this had risen to £100,000 and the Council were urged to drop the plan. Instead they approved it in principle and asked the City Engineer to come up with an alternative plan.

A test boring revealed soft clay to a depth of 50-60 feet and a trial piling cost nearly £500 and yet again the plan was put on the back burner. During this period the *Star and Garter* had started to show signs of collapse and the top two stories were removed.

1955 saw a renewed effort to set a plan in motion but there was a concern that British Rail were thinking of pulling their ferries out of the Point to a new base in Gosport. This would have involved a considerable financial loss to the Corporation and rendered the redevelopment of Point much less viable.

British Rail issued a statement confirming that they were not intending to pull out of Point at this time but they envisaged a time when ferries capable of carrying 40 cars would come on stream and these would be too large for the slipway at Point. This galvanised the Corporation and new plans were drawn up for a new slipway, capable of taking 300 ft. boats to be built alongside the rear of the Broad Street properties.

The scheme was by now estimated to cost £126,800 and by June 1956, with British Railways committing itself to remain on Point, it was approved.

A site visit to the property in 1959 not long before the demolition began.

Although the plan included the use of the land where the *Star and Garter* had stood, "the Last House on Point" was not initially earmarked for demolition. However, a survey revealed that the building was in a far worse state than had been assumed. The centuries had certainly taken their toll and this had been exacerbated by the wartime bombing.

The fate of 102 Broad Street was now settled and in February 1960 it too was demolished, a process that was so thorough that all the records of the various companies that had occupied the building were destroyed along with its fabric.

With the buildings out of the way, work proceeded swiftly and the new terminal building and slipway were officially opened by the Lord Mayor, Councillor Ralph Bonner Pink on 7th July 1961. The cutting of the ribbon was a signal for the first line of cars to board the *M V Fishbourne*.

Thus began a most successful period for the car ferry service; a success story that would in the space of just 20 years outgrow its facilities. New ferries were introduced that were so long the slipway could no longer accommodate the service. Therefore in 1982 the ferry Company relocated to the other side of the Camber where they are still based today, having left the Point for ever.

The next chapter for the site of 102 Broad Street remains unknown as the site has now been abandoned and is currently fenced off, awaiting development in the future.

Chapter 11

Advertisements

Whilst researching this book I discovered and read many adverts that had been placed in local newspapers in the past, providing an insight into life on Point at that time.
This chapter of the book contains copies of a wide cross section of some of these adverts published in the eighteenth, nineteenth and twentieth centuries with their dates of publication shown beneath the adverts.

They provide useful information on existing trades at that time and those shown in this book include opticians, nautical instrument makers and repairers, naval outfitters, cork manufacturers, suppliers of beer and spirits, fish suppliers, grocers, apothecaries, druggists, clothing suppliers, ship chandlers, sailmakers, boat builders and more.

The adverts include many of the businesses one would expect to be based on Point at that time providing a service to the residents and the many maritime activities of the day.

There are copies of adverts placed by shipping agents and goods transporters such as Messrs Pickford & Son and Curtiss and Sons who throughout the years became household names.

In addition adverts are included detailing the extensive range of sailing and steam transport available for transportation of people and goods by sea to countries as far away as Australia and Canada or to locations closer to Point.

Examples of adverts placed by one of Point's well known firm of merchants and shipping agents in Bath Square, Messrs L A Van den bergh & Son, are included, whose premises were used as the headquarters for numerous foreign consuls resulting in a wide range of business interests.

Also included are adverts referring to one of the East India Company's well-known agents, Mr Andrew Lindegren, who resided at Point. Although, being an agent for the East India Company was his prime role for many years (1788 – 1815), he was also a well-known local businessman and adverts show his extensive involvement in the auction of goods and ship's cargoes.

It is interesting to note how many of the local pubs advertised in the local newspapers about other services they offered in addition to selling liquor. Many held auctions for the sale of maritime items, including boats and gear, acted as agents for both coach and boat transportation and some were used for carrying out post mortems following local deaths.

Regular adverts for auctions were placed by HM Customs & Excise held at the local Custom House and the range of goods were extensive, since boats and cargoes were often confiscated from smugglers engaged in illegal activities or for failing to pay the appropriate duties.

There are also adverts detailing information on available coach travel from Point to London and other places and listing the sale of property in the area which again provides an insight into life at that time.

In summary, it is surprising how much information and knowledge can be acquired about an area and its inhabitants by examining adverts placed in local newspapers throughout the years and the adverts selected demonstrate this well.
It should be noted that some of the adverts have been recreated for legibility.

The local newspapers from which adverts and other information were researched are listed below, with the earliest publications dating from 1772.

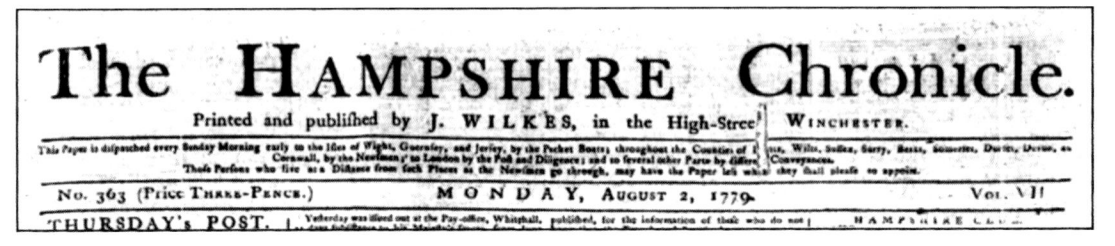

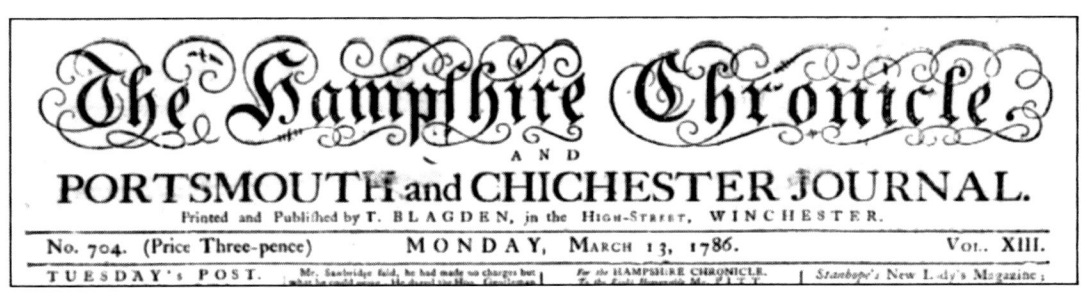

Portsmouth Telegraph;
OR,
MOTTLEY's *Naval and Military Journal*

MONDAY, OCTOBER 28, 1799. [PRICE 6D.

Portsmouth Times and Naval Gazette,
HAMPSHIRE, SUSSEX, ISLE OF WIGHT, AND GENERAL ADVERTISER FOR THE ADJOINING COUNTIES.

NO. 1046. PORTSEA, SATURDAY, MAY 21, 1870. PRICE TWO PENCE

THE HAMPSHIRE ADVERTISER
Vol. XLVIII.—No. 2531. COUNTY NEWSPAPER.—ESTABLISHED 1823. PRICE ONE PENNY
PUBLISHED EVERY WEDNESDAY AND SATURDAY MORNING, IN TIME FOR THE EARLY MAILS.
SOUTHAMPTON WEDNESDAY, SEPTEMBER 14, 1870.

The following adverts inserted by companies located on Point give an indication of the extensive range of goods sold at that time:

CHARLES MUMBY & COMPANY'S
PURE SODA WATER AND SELTZER WATER,
FOR QUALITY AND PURITY CANNOT BE EXCELLED.

H.M.S. *Serapis*, Portsmouth, 25th May, 1876.
MESSRS. C. MUMBY & CO.
GENTLEMEN,—The Soda Water supplied by you for the use of H.R.H. the Prince of Wales on board H.M.S. *Serapis* was of excellent quality, kept in good condition, and gave great satisfaction to His Royal Highness, his Suite, and the Officers of the ship. (Signed) THOS. BRADBRIDGE, Paymaster.
T. W. SCADDEN, Chief Steward.
SUPPLIED ALSO IN QUART SYPHONS.
FOREIGN ICE MERCHANTS.
A Large Stock of Pure Lake Ice always in Stock.
OFFICES,— 34, THE HARD, PORTSMOUTH;
47, HIGH STREET, GOSPORT.
ICE STORES,— EAST STREET, PORTSMOUTH.

1876

J. GIBSON, WINE AND SPIRIT MERCHANT, UNION TAVERN, BROAD STREET, POINT, PORTSMOUTH, Adjoining the FLOATING BRIDGE, and two minutes from the Victoria Pier. First-class accommodation for Tourists and Visitors. Splendid Sea View.	**WILLIAM HOOPER,** 28, BROAD STREET, PORTSMOUTH, OPTICIAN, AND NAUTICAL WAREHOUSE. Opera, Field, Telescope, and other Glasses, warranted at London prices. Instruments cleaned and repaired. Yacht and ships' brass work of every description made and repaired.
1871	1868
BARNABY, DAYCOCK & COMPY., CORK AND ISINGLASS MANUFACTURERS, 27, BROAD STREET, PORTSMOUTH.	*Wine and Porter Bottles.* NOW landing from the Leith Glass Company, a Cargo of BOTTLES, which will be disposed of on the most reasonable terms, on application to William Smith, at his Office, Bathing-house Square. Portsmouth, 4th March, 1809.
1871	1809

JAMES CHESTLE,
56, BROAD STREET, PORTSMOUTH,
LINEN & WOOLLEN DRAPER,
NAVAL AND YACHT OUTFITTER.

CLOTHS OF ALL DESCRIPTIONS CUT TO ANY LENGTH AT WHOLESALE PRICES FOR CASH.

1868

JOHN AND EDWIN GROVES,
(Successors to the late John Keet,)
IMPORTERS of FOREIGN WINES and SPIRITS, BREWERS, &c.,
WISH STREET, SOUTHSEA,
AND
EAST STREET, PORTSMOUTH.
Agents for GUINNESS'S DUBLIN STOUT, Bass and Allsopp's Pale Ale, in Cask or Bottle. Scotch and India Pale Ales, &c.

1862

Bought of W. RICKMAN,
SPIRIT MERCHANT,
Shipper of Bonded Stores,
Bread and Ship Biscuit Baker,
Wholesale and Retail
GROCER, AND PROVISION MERCHANT,
BROAD STREET.
Spices, Sauces, Pickles—Wax, Sperm, and Composite Candles, Paints—Lamp, Paint Oil, and Varnish.
LEWIS, PRINTER.

1859

PATENT FIRE LIGHTERS, 3s. PER 100.
THESE LIGHTERS surpass anything of the kind ever before introduced, and for cleanliness and comfort cannot be surpassed. The "Patent Lighters" are used in the Houses of Parliament, Government Offices, Clubs, &c., and extensively Patronised by the Nobility and Gentry, Hotel Proprietors, &c.
Agent for Portsmouth—T. STEMSON, 13, Broad-street, Portsmouth. Delivered Free in Portsmouth and Gosport. Orders by Post promptly attended to.

1874

FREDERIC HARRIS begs respectfully to inform the inhabitants of Portsmouth and vicinity he has succeeded to the BUSINESS of Mr. T. WHITE-HORN, and trusts by strict personal attendance, and vending the best drugs to merit a share of public patronage.
Sea and Family Medicine Chest Supplied and Refitted.
Teeth Extracted, Stopping, &c.
58, Broad Street, Portsmouth.

1850

NEW CRANBERRIES AND SPRUCE BEER.

JUST imported, a moderate quantity of fine New Norway Cranberries in casks of 8 gallons, and Danzig Spruce in casks of 4 gallons.
Apply to Mr. THOMAS PREW, 66 Broad-street, Point, Portsmouth.
21st November, 1851.

1851

FISH! FISH!! FISH!!!
WHITE AND HOOPER,
WHOLESALE & RETAIL,
FISH FACTORS AND SALESMEN.

Retail Business: 60, BROAD STREET, POINT.
Wholesale: At FISH MARKET, POINT, PORTSMOUTH.

All kinds of Fish in Season.
The Trade supplied with all kinds of Fish.

1874

PORTSMOUTH,
THOMAS SPEARING begs leave to inform his Friends and the Public in general that he has re-commenced his business of PLUMBER, PAINTER, and GLAZIER, at his late residence, No. 82, Broad Street, Point, (opposite the Blue Posts) and acquaints them the business will be carried on in all its branches, with diligence and dispatch, humbly solicit-ing their favour.
Wanting, an APPRENTICE and JOURNEYMAN.
N.B. Oil and Colours, Wholesale and Retail.

1816

PORTSMOUTH,
SATURDAY, MAY 25, 1811.

PORTSMOUTH.
No 50, Broad-street, Point, nearly opposite the Custom-House.
THOMAS JOHNSON, APOTHECARY. CHEMIST, and DRUGGIST, most respectfully informs his friends and the public in general, he has opened the above Shop, where every article may be purchased genuine, and he hopes by a strict and detailed attention to business, to merit their custom.
Prescriptions and Family Recipes, carefully prepared with the best ingredients. Patent Medicines, Perfumery, &c, &c.

1811

CHEAP AND FASHIONABLE CLOTHING FOR THE SPRING.
J. KEET and Co. No. 1, Broad Street, adjoining the Bridge, Point, Portsmouth, respectfully acquaint the inhabitants of Portsmouth, and Towns adjacent, they are returned from London, having purchased a prime Assortment of Cloths, Kerseymeres, Cords, Quiltings, India Nankeen, &c. of the best quality and most prevailing colors.
A handsome Suit of the best Superfine Cloth, (Mameluke Trowsers,) made to measure, for £5 1s, and at a days notice.
Irish Linens, Sheetings, striped Cottons, American Cloths, Ticks, 4-4ths Carpeting, &c. of the most approved manufacture.
A variety of ready-made Clothing, Bedding, &c.
Keet and Co. buy and sell for ready money, consequently can charge such prices as will be found well worthy the attention of the Public.
May 4, 1816.

1816

C. GROOM, Ltd., Nat. Telephone 300 Corp. Telephone 999

42, 44, 46, BROAD STREET, PORTSMOUTH

AND AT 101, LEADENHALL STREET, LONDON.

Tents and Marquees or Sale or Hire. Large Stock at Portsmouth. Any size from 25 to 200 feet. Write for Quotations.

Ropes, Paints, Oils, and Varnish. Awnings and Blinds a Speciality. Rot Covers, Horse Cloths, Linen Cloth, and all Dressed Goods.

Manufacturers of Flags & Bunting

WRITE FOR OUR PRICE OF LETTERED FLAGS.

Tents and Marquees erected any distance. Agents for the Hire and Sale of Motor Boats, Launches, Dingeys and Steam Yachts.

1908

J. N. ROBINSON, WINE MERCHANT, opposite the Custom-house, Broad-street, Portsmouth, begs to inform Gentlemen of his Majesty's Navy and Army, and Families in general, he continues to have for SALE, on moderate terms, a great variety of CHOICE WINES; consisting of fine old Port, Sherry, Madeira, Bucellas, Vidonia, Champagne, Hock, Burgundy, Hermitage, Claret, Rousillen de Grave, Sautern, Frontignac, Barsac, &c.

In addition to J. N. R.'s Stock of Wines in bottle, he has in bond, for Sale, remarkably cheap, a few pipes of very prime old Port Wine, butts of fine flavoured pale Sherry, twenty hogsheads of first growth Claret, several pipes of West India Madeira, and five hogsheads of Sautern, well worth the attention of parties who are in the habit of bottling their own wines.

A large quantity of superior Cape Madeira, Edinburgh Ale, London Porter, &c. much under the usual prices.—2,000 dozen of new Wine and Porter Bottles for Sale on Commission.—PORTSMOUTH, June 17, 1826.

1826

THE CHEAPEST HOUSE FOR DOORPLATES, VISITING CARDS, AND ENGRAVING IN GENERAL.

Plate and 50 Superfine Cards for 2s. 6d.; by post, 2s. 9d. Brass Doorplates Engraved with name and initial complete from 5s. 9d.

Arms, Crests, and Cyphers Engraved.
Silver and Plate Monograms designed.

NOTE THE ADDRESS:

A. R. EARWICKER, JUN.,
1, BROAD STREET, POINT, PORTSMOUTH.

1870

THE SOUTH HANTS ENGINEERING COMPANY

ARE PREPARED TO EXECUTE ALL ORDERS at their PREMISES in the INNER CAMBER, PORTSMOUTH,

on the most liberal terms. Agricultural machinery, brewery work, mill machinery, steam ships, marine engines, steam launches, yachts, &c., smith work, iron and founding, boiler making, &c.

Estimates and specifications prepared on the shortest notice, surveys of damage, valuations, &c.

Repairs promptly attended to.

N.B.—All descriptions of castings, in iron or brass, can be executed on the shortest notice.

1810

PORTSMOUTH.

MR. YOUNG, at the Eaft-India Muflin Warehoufe, No. 26, Broad-Street, Portfmouth Point, is juft arrived from London, and has brought with him the following Goods, which will be fold by commiffion, wholefale and retail, twenty per cent, cheaper than in any other part of England.

As his ftay will be very fhort in Portfmouth, the loweft price will be marked on each piece of Goods, and no abatement made. Any perfon buying a piece of any kind of goods may return the fame, on the fame day, if not approved of, that the public may be convinced they are not impofed on.

The Goods confift as follow:

Five hundred pieces of feven-eighths and yard-wide Irifh, at every price, from 1s to 6s per yard. 300 pieces of dark printed cottons, of the neweft and moft fafhionable patterns, 500 chintz gowns, white, blue, marble, and Mofaic grounds, from 25s to three guineas. 200 pieces of Scotch holland, from 20d. to 3s per yard. 400 pieces of Dutch ditto, from 2s 6d to 6s per yard. A quantity of Irifh fheeting, from 16d to 18d. A large affortment of diaper table linen. 50 pieces of yard-wide jaconet muflin handkerchiefs. 400 pieces of book, jaconet, ftriped and fprigged muflins of all widths and prices. A very large affortment of ftriped, fpotted, checked, and plain lawns, apron width. A large quantity of figured and corded dimitties. A great affortment of gentlemen's fancy winter waiftcoats, with great variety of gold and filver fpangled ditto.

A large quantity of rich worked aprons, handkerchiefs, and gentlemen's ruffles. 50 pieces of black and coloured double taffaties. Modes and fatins for cloaks, with a large affortment of black and white lace, and many other articles too numerous to mention.

⁎ Any lady or gentleman taking a piece or pieces of Dutch holland, or muflin, will be allowed ten per cent difcount.

1782

Other businesses that existed on Point for many years were those handling coal and several adverts are shown below:

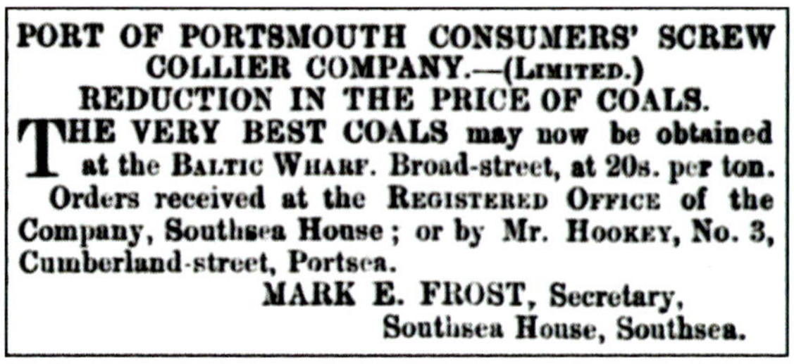

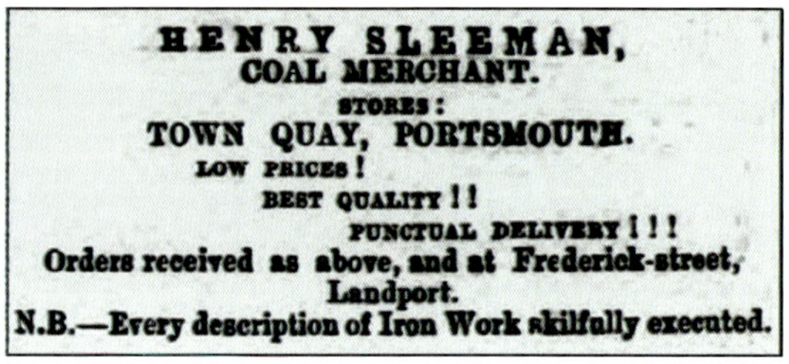

1862   1870

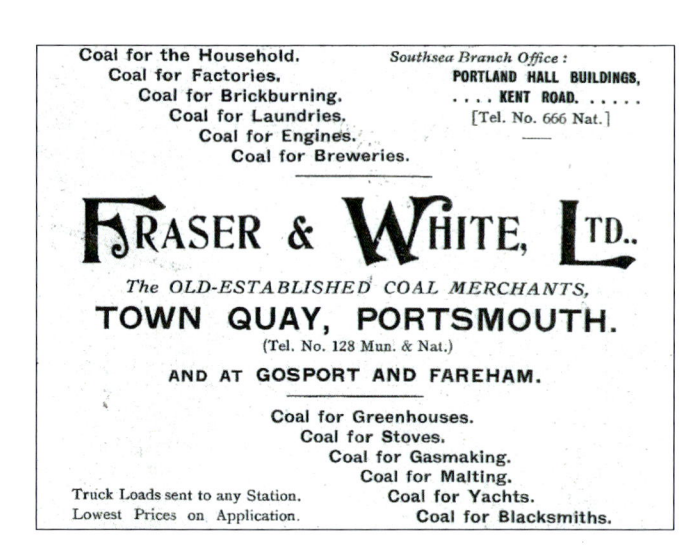

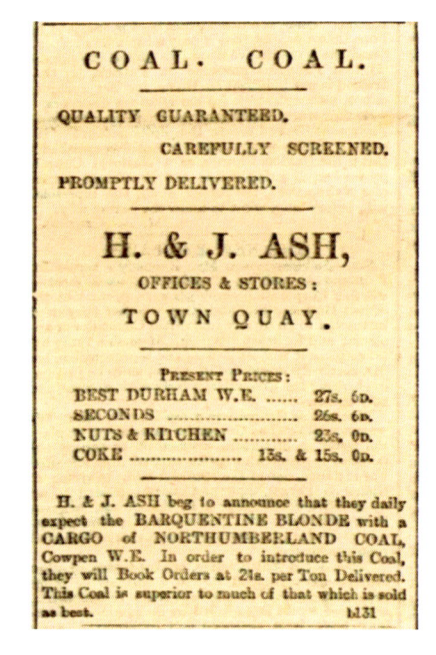

1910   1890

Two very popular companies on Point that transported goods in the nineteenth and twentieth centuries were Messrs Pickfords and Curtiss & sons.

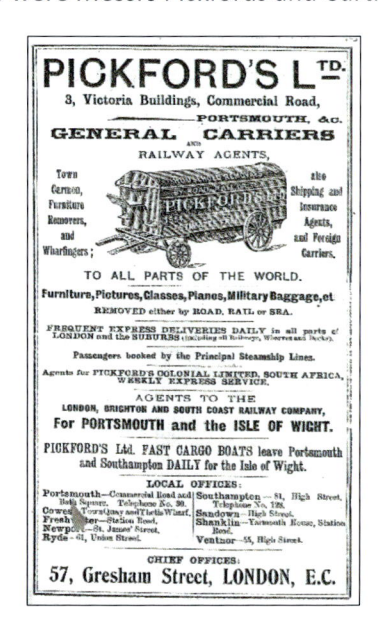

1904   1889

Transportation by water was always available on Point with vessels running regular services to nearby places like Gosport and other places in Portsmouth harbour and also scheduled services were soon established to and from the Isle of Wight. In addition, ships arrived at Portsmouth Harbour to pick up passengers travelling further afield and shipping agents organised bookings for people wishing to travel to the other side of the world. The following adverts give an indication of some of the services that were available and include passages to America and Sydney:

MAY, 1850.
PORTSMOUTH, PORTSEA, GOSPORT, and RYDE
ROYAL MAIL STEAM PACKETS

WILL, on and after WEDNESDAY, MAY 1st, 1850, run at the following hours, in connexion with the SOUTH-WESTERN and SOUTH-COAST RAILWAY TRAINS.

STEAM PACKETS TO RYDE FROM			STEAM PACKETS FROM RYDE To Portsmouth, Gosport, and Portsea Piers.
Gosport Pier.	Portsea Pier.	Portsmo. Pier	
H. M.	H. M.	H. M.	H. M.
Morning at 8 10	8 15	8 20	Morning at 6 45
9 45	9 50	10 0	9 10
11 50	11 55	12 0	10 45
Afternoon 1 20	1 25	1 30	12 15
2 20	2 25	2 30	Afternoon 1 35*
3 50	3 55	4 0	3 0
5 5	5 10	5 15	4 15
6 5	6 10	6 15	5 20
7 35	7 40	7 45	6 30

The Packet marked with an asterisk (*) will go to Portsea Pier before going to Gosport.
On SUNDAYS the Packets leave Gosport, Portsea, & Portsmouth, Morning at 8—Afternoon at 3 o'clock; Ryde ditto 9— ditto ... 4 o'clock
Coaches from Ryde to Ventnor, Shanklin, Newport, and other parts, several times a day.
A. HEATHER, 27, Broad Street, Portsmouth.

1850

CAPITAL CONVEYANCE between Portfmouth & Ryde, by a regular Poft-office Packet, carrying the mail, which will fail every morning at 9 o'clock, from the Weft India and Quebec Tavern, Bath-fquare, Portfmouth, for RYDE; and return every afternoon at half paft three, from the Bugle Inn, Lower Ryde, for PORTSMOUTH, in time to fave any of the London Coaches. There will alfo be a COACH, at Ryde, on the arrival of the Mail, to take Paffengers to Newport. The Mafter to be fpoken with at the Weft India and Quebec Tavern, Portfmouth; and at the Bugle Inn, and Hotel, Ryde. A commodious decked Veffel for the purpofe.

Early nineteenth century

PASSAGE TO HAVRE-DE-GRACE.

THE moment the French Ports are open the following Veffels will fail from PORTSMOUTH to HAVRE-DE-GRACE, and continue fo to do every week, and carry Paffengers and Goods upon the moft reafonable terms, viz.

Schooner CHARLOTTE, burthen Ninety Tons, with twelve Beds in the great Cabin.

Sloop ANT, burthen Forty Tons.

Both which Veffels are capital Sailers, and are handfomely and conveniently fitted up for the accommodation of Ladies and Gentlemen going to France. Diftance only about ten hours fail.

Enquire at Mr. CROSS's, Crown Inn, High-ftreet; or Capt. STEPHENS, Quebec Tavern, near the Bathing-Houfe, on the Point.

1820

SEASON, 1850.
REDUCTION OF FARES.

THE BRUNSWICK, Steam-Packet, Thomas Russel, Commander, will leave Portsmouth for Torquay and Plymouth, calling at Southampton, every FRIDAY, at half-past Two, P.M.; and Plymouth to Torquay, Southampton, and Portsmouth, THURSDAYS, at ONE, P.M., weather permitting.

A Stewardess to attend on the Ladies.

For Particulars apply to Mr. N. M. PRIAULX, Southampton; at the Dolphin Hotel, Chichester; Coach and Railway Office, Brighton; Castle Hotel, Hastings; 18, Cornhill, and 5, Arthur-street, Fish-street Hill; London; or to

WHEELER & HATCH,
4, Broad-street, Portsmouth, Agents to the Atlas Fire and Life Office.

1850

ALLAN LINE TO AMERICA.
LIVERPOOL TO BOSTON VIA HALIFAX,
MORAVIAN .... Nov. 18th. | CIRCASSIAN ...... Dec. 2nd.
SARMATIAN .... Nov. 25th. | SARDINIAN .... Dec. 8th.
LIVERPOOL TO BALTIMORE,
VIA ST. JOHN'S AND HALIFAX.
NOVA SCOTIAN .... Nov. 23rd. | HIBERNIAN ...... Dec. 7th.
Low Rates of Passage and Through Tickets in all points at Special Rates. Pamphlets on Canada, Manitoba, Western States of America; also Special Pamphlet, embodying reports of the Tenent Farmers' Delegates to Canada, free on application.
ASSISTED PASSAGES to Canada for Farm Labourers and Female Domestic Servants.
Full particulars on application to ALLAN BROTHERS & CO., James-street, Liverpool; or to R. W. BEALK High-street, Portsmouth; CURTISS & SONS, Broad-street, Portsmouth; J. LONG, and SON, Ship Agency Offices, Yarmouth, I. W.

1880

1870.
SOUTHAMPTON AND PORTSMOUTH TO DUBLIN AND GLASGOW.—The Steam Ships LADY EGLINTON, LADY WODEHOUSE, COUNTESS of DUBLIN, AVOCA, CYMBA, or other suitable vessels. TRADE between PORTSMOUTH, SOUTHAMPTON, PLYMOUTH, FALMOUTH, DUBLIN, AND GLASGOW.

These steamers correspond with these of the Clyde Shipping Company leaving Plymouth every fortnight.

The intended sailings for the present season are as follows (wind and weather permitting):—From Portsmouth, for Plymouth, Falmouth, and Dublin, every SUNDAY, at Eight a.m., on the arrival of the steamers, and leaving Portsmouth at Eight a.m., and Southampton at Two p.m., every THURSDAY (with liberty to tow vessels to or from any port in the United Kingdom).

FARES FROM PORTSMOUTH AND SOUTHAMPTON, including Steward's fee:—

	Main Cabin.	Second Cabin.	Deck.
To Plymouth	£0 12s 6d	9s 0d	5s 0d
To Falmouth	£0 16s 6d	12s 0d	7s 0d
To Dublin	£1 0s 0d	15s 0d	10s 0d

First and Second Cabin Return Tickets between any of the ports, available two months, for 1½ fares.

For further particulars apply to the Secretary, A. W. Egan, 5, North-wall, Dublin: James Hartley and Co., 137, Leadenhall-street, or at Miller's Wharf, Lower East Smithfield, and West Kent Wharf, Southwark, London; W. and E. C. Carne, Falmouth; R. Clark and Son, or H. J. Waring, Plymouth; Le Feuvre and Son, Southampton; or to R. Hatch, 4, Broad-street, Portsmouth, Agent to the Atlas Fire and Life Assurance Office.

1870

FOR SYDNEY DIRECT.

TO Sail direct from PORTSMOUTH, on or about the 18th DECEMBER, 1855 the Splendid Dutch frigate-built armed Ship STAD UTRECHT, 960 Tons burden, Feye Pieters Tanes Taski, Commander, lying in PORTSMOUTH HARBOUR. Open only for a limited number of First-Class Passengers. Carries a Doctor.

Fares for each Adult:—£60 for a single berth, but if two Passengers in same berth £45 each. Victualling according to Dutch Scale. Wines and Spirits not included in the above rates. Splendid accommodation for Families.

For further Particulars apply to Messrs. VAN DEN BERGH and SON, 83, High Street, Southampton, and Bath Square, Portsmouth, Agents for the above ship.

1855

SOUTHERN RAILWAY

SPECIAL NOTICE

PORTSMOUTH—RYDE STEAMBOAT SERVICE

On WEDNESDAY, 11th OCTOBER

The 11.0 a.m. boat from Portsmouth Harbour will leave at 10.50 a.m., calling Clarence Pier 11.0 a.m.

The 1.30 p.m. boat from Portsmouth Harbour will leave at 2.0 p.m., calling Clarence Pier 2.10 p.m.

The 12.15 p.m. boat from Ryde will be CANCELLED.

A special boat will leave Ryde 2.0 p.m., due Clarence Pier 2.25, Portsmouth Harbour 2.35 p.m.

PORTSMOUTH-FISHBOURNE MOTOR-CAR FERRY SERVICE

The 9.15 a.m. Ferry from Portsmouth, will leave at 8.45 a.m., and the 10.30 a.m. from Fishbourne will leave at 10.0 a.m.

By Order.

1939

The following adverts for the auction of goods are typical of those inserted by Messrs Van den bergh, shipping agents and merchants and those of Andrew Lindegren, agent of the East India Company on Point.

BOTTOMRY.

WANTED,—From £850 to £900 on the BOTTOMRY SECURITY of the AUSTRIAN BARQUE MERCURIO, of Trieste, S. A. Busanich, master, 363 tons register, her cargo of railway iron and the freight thereon, lately put into this Port in distress, on her voyage from Antwerp bound to Poti in the Black Sea, and now thoroughly repaired and remetalled.

Tenders to be addressed to Captain S. A. BUSANICH, at the I. R. Austrian Vice-Consulate, Portsmouth, on or before MONDAY, THE 3RD MAY, or to

Messrs. L. A. VANDENBERGH & SON, Agents, Bath-square, Portsmouth.

PORT OF PORTSMOUTH.
DAMAGED GOODS ex DUTCH S. S. WILLEM III.
FOR THE BENEFIT OF ALL CONCERNED.

KING & KING are instructed by Capt. Oort, of the above ship, to SELL by AUCTION, at Messrs. Fraser & White's Stores, Broad-street, and the New Dock, Camber, on Friday next, 23rd June, 1871, at Twelve o'clock precisely,—

THE FIRST PORTION OF THE SALVAGE, consisting of MANCHESTER GOODS, in calicos, prints, &c., small quantity of beef, pork, and preserved provisions, sails, rope, &c., all more or less damaged by fire and water.

Further particulars may meanwhile be had of MESSRS. VANDENBERGH & SON, Dutch Consuls, Portsmouth, or of the Auctioneers, 130, Queen-street, Portsea.

1859   1871

CABLES, ANCHORS, GUNS, SHOT, PIG LEAD, &c. &c.

FOR SALE by AUCTION, at the STAR and GARTER TAVERN, Portſmouth, on FRIDAY the 3d of January, 1800, at Eleven o'Clock in the Forenoon,

101 Iron Guns of different Calibres from 1½ to 32 prs.
Anchors from 6 to 23 cwt. each.
22 Grapnels
20 Tons Shot different ſizes.
1900 Pigs Lead.
3000 Bars Swediſh Iron.
174 Bolts Canvas.

Alſo a quantity of damaged Muſkets, Cutlaſſes, Iron Knees, Bolt Iron, Copper, Dead Eyes, Blocks, and ſundry other Ship's Stores, being ſaved from the Wreck of the Honourable Eaſt India Company's ſhip HENRY ADDINGTON, loſt on Bembridge Ledge.

The ſame may be viewed three days before the Sale, on application at the Office of Mr. ANDREW LINDEGREN, Portſmouth, where Catalogues may alſo be had.

PORTSMOUTH.

TO be SOLD by AUCTION, at the BLUE POSTS Inn, on Thurſday the 5th of April next, the Good SHIP, The COUNTESSE de BEZANCOIS, formerly the Harpooner private ſhip of war, of the port of London re-captured by his Majeſty's ſhips the Portland, Thomas Lloyd, Eſq, commander, and the Solebay, Charles Holmes Everitt. Eſq, commander, ſquare ſtern, British built, burthen 220 tons or thereabouts, a remarkable faſt failer, well found, and may be ſent to ſea at very little expence.

Inventories will be timely delivered on board, at the place of ſale, at New Lloyd's coffee-houſe, and by
ANDREW LINDEGREN, at Portſmouth.
NATHANIEL GILMORE, at Goſport.

1800   1778

Numerous pubs on Point held auctions and the adverts below give an indication of how widespread this was with examples from the *Blue Posts, Star & Garter, Thatched house, Sun and Quebec hotel*

PORT OF PORTSMOUTH.
TO SHIP OWNERS, MERCHANTS, & OTHERS

MR. C. B. SMITH has received instructions to SELL by PUBLIC AUCTION, at the Quebec Hotel, Bath Square, Portsmouth, on Thursday, July 21st, 1859, at Two o'Clock in the Afternoon, precisely, the BURNT HULL of the "*EASTERN MONARCH*," 1631 Tons Register, built at Dundee, in 1856, classed A 1, at Lloyd's for 14 years, well known in the East India trade, H. Morris, Commander, as she now lies off Haslar Beach, close to Portsmouth Harbour, together with all then remaining in her.

The Sale will be for Cash only, and the Purchase Money to be Paid upon the Lot being knocked down, and the Purchaser declared by the Auctioneer.

Further particulars may be had and the Wreck seen on application to Mr. James Garratt, Lloyds Agent, Portsmouth, or to the Auctioneer, 170, Queen Street, Portsea.

1859

This unfortunate vessel caught fire at Spithead on passage and sank off Haslar. She was regularly used on the East India trade route. Interestingly, the auction stipulated the vessel being sold in her current state as a wreck located off Haslar beach.

195

THE PRINCE WILLIAM HENRY, TOWER STREET, PORTSMOUTH.

KING & KING (late Marvin and King) are instructed to SELL by AUCTION on Friday next, the 21st day of October, 1864, at Twelve o'clock punctually, the whole of the FURNITURE and FITTINGS of the above Tavern, which will be more fully detailed in the sale bills.

On view the morning of Sale until the Auction commences.

1864

PORTSMOUTH.

FOR PUBLIC SALE, at the Star and Garter Tavern, on Thursday, twentieth September, 1810, at noon, About 100 bolts of SUPERIOR RUSSIA SAIL CLOTH, 31 inches broad, and in most excellent condition, which will be put up in small Lots for the convenience of purchasers. For catalogues and further particulars, apply three days before the sale to   JOHN MOYLE.

Portsmouth, 31st Aug. 1810.

1810

PORTSMOUTH.
TO BE SOLD BY AUCTION,

On THURSDAY, Feb. 25, 1802, between the Hours of Six and Eight in the Evening (unlefs fooner difpofed of by Private Contract, of which timely Notice will be given,) at the Houfe of Mr. Jofeph Smith, bearing the fign of the Sun, near the Point Gates,

THE good Carvel-built Cutter, called the ANT, burthen about 32 Tons per regifter.

The above veffel is well found, fails remarkably well, would make an excellent Packet or Pleafure Yacht, having good accommadations. She is at present employed as a Paffage Veffel, between Portfmouth and Plymouth.

For Inventory and Particulars, apply to Mr. Craves, 147, Queen- freet, Portfea.

1802

PORTSMOUTH,
TO BE SOLD BY PRIVATE CONTRACT,

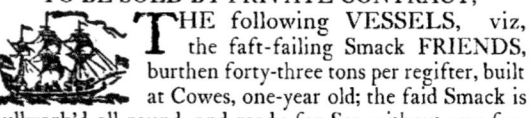

THE following VESSELS, viz, the faft-failing Smack FRIENDS, burthen forty-three tons per regifter, built at Cowes, one-year old; the faid Smack is bullwark'd all round, and ready for Sea without any further expenfe.

Alfo, the good Smack DANIEL, burthen 25 tons, built at Cowes, is eight years old, and now employed as a Paffage Veffel between Portfmouth and Plymouth.

For further particulars apply Mr. Richard Hafkell, at the fign of the Thatched Houfe on the Point, where an Inventory of each Veffels' Materials may be had.

Nineteenth century

PORTSMOUTH.
TO BE SOLD BY AUCTION,
By Mr. COLLINS,

At the STAR and GARTER TAVERN, Broad-street, on THURSDAY the 10th of JUNE, 1802, at Ten o'Clock, by Order of the Transport Board, and under the direction of Captain Charles Patton, Resident Agent at Portsmouth.

A QUANTITY of Army Clothing, Accoutrements, Sadlery, Horse Shoes and Nails, with some Carbines and Shot. Also a quantity of Old Bedding, Hammocks, and other Transport Stores.

The whole will be put up in Lots for the accommodation of Purchasers, and may be viewed three days before the Sale.

Catalogues may be had at the Transport Office, in London, or by application to Captain Patton, Agent for the Transport Service, at Portsmouth.

1802

PORTSMOUTH.
TO BE SOLD BY AUCTION,
(ON THE PREMISES)
BY MR. WELLER,

On THURSDAY the 23rd of October, 1800, between the Hours of Six and Eight in the Evening,

ALL that truly eligible and commodious FREEHOLD TAVERN and COFFEE-HOUSE, the STAR AND GARTER, most advantageously situated at the lower End of *Broad Street*.

These Premises have recently been enlarged, considerably improved, and thoroughly repaired; the Celebrity of this Tavern, and the long established Trade attached to it, is too well known to need any further Comment.

The Land Tax is Redeemed. — Possession will be given at Lady-Day next.

The FURNITURE and STOCK may be taken at a fair Appraisement.

For further Particulars, and a View of the Premises, apply to Mr. WX. CHURCHER, the Proprietor; or to MR. CALLAWAY, Solicitor, Portsmouth; and of Mr. WELLER, at his General Agency Office, Chichester.

1800

Grand View of the British Fleet at Spithead.
MARRYATT'S BLUE POSTS HOTEL,
BROAD STREET, PORTSMOUTH.
Commanding Views of Spithead, the Isle of Wight, Motherbank, St. Helen's Roads, &c.
W. E. ALEXANDER.

THE Public will find this House particularly convenient, from its proximity to Victoria Pier, the Custom House, Shipping Agents, &c., being comfortable in its arrangements, and moderate in charges.

Railway and Steam Company's General Depot. Omnibuses, Cabs, &c., to and from the Railway Station.

W. E. ALEXANDER having removed to the above Old-Established House, respectfully returns thanks to his patrons during the past Ten Years, and trusts by strict attention, with Moderate Charges to merit a continuence of the same.

N.B.—Files of the *Times* and *Bell's Life* since 1846.

1854

For the Benefit of the Underwriters.

FOR SALE by AUCTION, at the Blue Posts Inn, Portsmouth, at noon on Friday next, the 10th March, the HULL of the copper-bottomed Brig FORTUNE, burthen 129 96-100 Tons. Length upon deck, 68 feet ; breadth 21feet 9 inches ; depth, in the hold, 11½ feet ; is a fast sailing Vessel well adapted for the fruit or any other trade requiring despatch. Also her Tackle, Apparel Furniture and stores.

Further particulars may be known on application to Alex. Morison, Esq, Size Lane, London. where the inventory and Catalogues may be had two days before the Sale and the vessel and Stores viewed on application to W. Smith, Broker, at his Office, Bath Square.

1809

The adverts below published on behalf of the Customs and Excise are for the disposal of goods, most of which were confiscated from smugglers caught in the act of smuggling. The range of goods are extensive and the list includes items that were very expensive to buy legally and worth taking the risk to smuggle into the country. Wine and spirits were commonplace, but the extensive list includes many more items of a more general nature, particularly tea which was a popular item to try and import illegally.

Other goods include the auction of smugglers' vessels "seized and legally condemned" as a penalty of smuggling and one of the adverts is for the sale of a number of locally well-known sailing cutters owned and used by the Customs & Excise to run down and apprehend smugglers along the south coast. Other smaller boats and wherries were often confiscated and later auctioned as much local smuggling was carried out in smaller boats.

CUSTOM HOUSE, PORTSMOUTH.
By Order of the Honourable the Commisioners of His Majesty's Customs,

WILL be exposed to PUBLIC SALE, at this Office, on Thursday the 20th day of February, 1823, at twelve o'clock at noon, the following fine fast- sailing large CUTTERS :—

REPULSE	of	125 Tons
ROEBUCK		120
TARTAN		105
CAMELEON		75

Late in His Majesty's Revenue Service, together with their Masts, Yards, Bowsprits, standing and running Rigging, Sails, &c. as they now lie in Portsmouth Harbour.

At the same time will be sold,—The following BOATS, and their Materials, the same having been seized and legally condemned, viz.

One large Sailing Boat,
The fine Wherry called *The Challenger*,
Three other Wherries, and
Three small Boats.

Inventories may be had in due time of the Collector of the Customs, Portsmouth, and the Surveyor of Sloops, &c. Customs, London.

The Vessels and Stores may be viewed at any time before the sale, by applying at the Custom-house, Portsmouth.

By Order of the Commissioners,
G. DELAVAUD, Secretary.

1823

ADVERTISEMENT.
On Thursday, February 26. 1801, at Ten o'Clock in the Forenoon, will be
EXPOSED TO PUBLIC SALE,

AT the CUSTOM-HOUSE, Portfmouth, the fame having been feized and legally condemned,

Brandy	551	Gallons.
Rum	9	Bottles.
Geneva	1493	Gallons.
Wine	60	Gallons.
	6	Bottles.
Serges	2	Bales.
Compounds	11	Bottles
Woolen Cloth	60	Yards.
Lime Juice	4	Gallons.
Pictures	4	No.
Coffee	38	lbs.
Copper	600	cwt.
Oftrich Feathers	300	No.

A WHERRY and Materials; alfo, some OLD CORDAGE and STORES, from the Roebuck cutter.
☞ The Spirits for Private, Ufe.

May be viewed two days before the Sale, by applying to the Warehoufe-Keeper.

1801

CUSTOM HOUSE, PORTSMOUTH.

PRICE per QUARTER CASK of CHOICE and OLD FOREIGN WINES, at Her Majesty's Custom House, at the Port of Portsmouth:—

MARSALA (Finest Imported), Old Matured Wine ...	£3 10.
This with the Duty will cost about 18s. per Dozen.	
SHERRY PALE or GOLD (Good Stout Wine) ...	£5.
SUPERIOR Do. (Excellent Dinner Wine) ...	£7.
VERY CHOICE and VERY OLD REAL AMONTILLADO ...	£12.
PORT, Good full Bodied Wine ...	£7.
SUPERIOR Do (Vintage 1842) ...	£10.
VERY CHOICE (Vintage 1844) ...	£12.

A FEW CASES (Offley's Fine Old TAWNY), Many Years in Bottle, 30s. per Dozen.
Samples of the above can be had (or tasted) by applying to Mr. EDWARD COLLINS, at the CUSTOM HOUSE; or, to the Importers,

MESSRS. ALBERT RICHARDSON AND COMPANY,
QUEEN STREET, PORTSEA, and WISH STREET, SOUTHSEA.

Price List of Wines in Bottle at the PORTSEA WINE VAULTS, 130, QUEEN STREET, PORTSEA:

FULL BODIED OLD PORTS from the Wood ...	24s.	per Dozen.
VERY SUPERIOR DITTO (Vintage 1842) ...	30s.	"
OLD CRUSTED DITTO (3 years in bottle) ...	36s.	"
OFFLEY'S CHOICE OLD TAWNY and (BEES' WING)		
In Original Cases of 2 and 3 Dozen each ...	42s. & 48s.	
SHERRY PALE or GOLD (Good Quality), in Quantities not less than 2 Dozen	21s. 6d.	"
(Sample Bottles 2s. each)		
VERY SUPERIOR PALE or GOLD (Beautiful Dinner Wines) ...	30s.	"
VERY CHOICE and VERY OLD REAL AMONTILLADO, in		
Original Packages of 2 and 3 Dozen each ...	36s., 42s., & 48s.	
MARSALA (Finest Imported), old Matured Wine ...	21s.	"
BUCELLAS (Best Quality), Very Delicate ...	32s.	"
BUCELLAS HOCK (Very Choice) ...	36s.	"
CLARET LA ROSE, (2 Dozen Cases) ...	42s.	"
ST. ESTEPHE, MEDOC, VIN DE BORDEAUX, &c. ...	30s.	"

Bottles charged 1s. per Dozen—same price allowed when Returned.

1851

PORTSMOUTH.

ON Thurfday the 17th of September, at Ten o'Clock in the Morning, will be expofed to PUBLIC SALE, at the Cuftom-Houfe in PORTSMOUTH, the under-mentioned Goods, the fame having been feized and legally condemned, viz.

Green Tea,	-	-	637	Pounds,
Bohea Tea,	-	-	4885	ditto,
Brandy,	-	-	353	
Rum,	-	-	203	} Gallons,
Geneva,	-	-	591	
Nankeen,	-	-	71	
Muflin,	-	-	1	} Pieces,
China Ware,	-	-	1346	
Chip Hats,	-	-	2	No.
Sweet Meats,	-	-	42	Pounds.

Alfo will be fold at the fame Time, (for Exportation) the following prohibited Eaft-India Goods, for which Security muft be given, viz, a Parcel of Silk and Policat Handkerchiefs, Ginghams, Seerfuckers and Soofey.

The Goods to be viewed at any Time, in proper Hours, two Days before the Sale, by applying to the Ware-houfe Keeper at the Cuftom-Houfe.

1772

ON Thurfday the 21ft of January, 1773, at Two o'Clock in the Afternoon, will be expofed to PUBLIC SALE, at the Cuftom-Houfe in PORTSMOUTH, the undermentioned Goods, the fame having been feized and legally condemned, viz.

BRANDY,	117	Gallons.
RUM,	697	ditto.
GENEVA,	31	ditto.
TEA,	1360	Pounds.
COFFEE,	34	ditto.

Alfo will be Sold at the fame Time, a Parcel of CHINA WARE, NANKEEN, COCOA, WHITE and RED WINE, MUSLIN NECKCLOTHS, and MUSLIN HANDKERCHIEFS.

The Goods to be viewed at any Time, in proper Hours, two Days before the Sale, by applying to the Warehoufe-Keeper at the Cuftom-Houfe.

1773

During Point's history, there was a period of time when coach travel was very popular as a means of travelling to London and other places and the following adverts are typical of that time:

REDUCED RATE OF TRAVELLING, BY THE *BRITANNIA*, PORTSMOUTH, PORTSEA, GOSPORT, AND ISLE OF WIGHT POST COACHES TO LONDON, IN TEN HOURS.
Inside £1 10s.—Outside 15s.

EVERY morning at nine o'clock, and evening at seven o'clock, from the Quebec Tavern, Bath Square, and Britannia Coach Office, No. 46, Point, (opposite the Star and Garter) and 112, Queen Street, Portsea ; to the Bull and Mouth Inn, Bull and Mouth Street, London ; No. 11 Grace Church Street ; Cannon Hotel, Charing Cross, and returns at the same hour.   Performed by J. WILLAN.
January 11, 1816

1816

ROCKET—RESPECTABLE LIGHT COACH.

JOHN CROSS and Co. return their most grateful thanks to their numerous Friends in Portsmouth, Portsea, Gosport, and the Isle of Wight, for the very liberal support their coach has experienced, and humbly solicit a continuance of their favours; and beg to inform them, that, for their further accommodation, the ROCKET COACH will now travel EVERY DAY, Sundays included, at 9 o'clock in the Morning, from the Fountain Inn, High-Street, and Quebec Tavern, Bath-square, Portsmouth, and at the George and Red Lion, Queen-Street, Portsea, to the White Bear, Piccadilly, and Belle Sauvage, Ludgate-Hill, London :—Performed in 9 Hours, by JOHN CROSS, EDWARD WHITE, and HENRY LEVETT.

N.B.—Families accommodated by being taken up and put down at their own Residences.

Early nineteenth century

ORIGINAL LONDON POST COACH.
WILLIAM CLARK and ROBERT CLINCH,

BEG leave to inform their Friends and the Public, this Coach fets out every evening at Six o'clock, from the Two Blue Pofts Inn, and Still Tavern, on the Point, and from their Office, No. 61, Queen-ftreet, Town of Portfea; to the Spread Eagle and Crofs Keys Inns, Gracechurch-ftreet, and Golden Crofs, Charing Crofs, London; and returns from thence every evening at the fame hour. CLARK and Co. pledge themfelves that no exertions, on their part, fhall be wanting to render their Coaches equal to any on the road, and which they truft will infure them that countenance and fupport they have hitherto enjoyed the preference of. Likewife, from the above Tavern, the London Day Coach, to the Golden Crofs, every morning at Five o,Clock; and a Light Night Coach, carrying only four infides, every evening at Seven o'Clock. WM. CLARKE'S original London Waggons, as ufual, every morning at Eleven o'Clock, to the White Hart and King's-Head Inns, Borough; and, for the better accommation of his friends, wifhing their goods from the City, he has opened the White Horfe, Friday-ftreet, Cheapfide, from whence goods are punctually forwarded.

☞ Flying Waggons on the fhorteft Notice.

Early nineteenth century

WITH A GUARD
LONDON, PORTSMOUTH, and PORTSEA COACHES, to the BOLT-IN-TUN INN, FLEET-STREET, LONDON :

SET out every Evening, at Six o'Clock, from the FOUNTAIN INN, HIGH-STREET, PORTSMOUTH, and arrive there every Morning early. Alfo fet out from the BOLT-IN-TUN INN, FLEET-STREET, LONDON, for PORTSMOUTH and PORTSEA, every Evening at the fame hour. Call going and coming at the BELL INN, GRACECHURCH-STREET, and OLD SHIP INN, BOROUGH, LONDON. Paffengers and Parcels taken up at the STAR and GARTER and NAVY TAVERNS, on the Point, and at the GEORGE TAVERN, QUEEN-STREET, PORTSEA.

☞ Office and Warehoufe, No. 63, BROAD-STREET, on the POINT.

Performed by { GEORGE FIELDING, JAMES WHITE and Co.

⁎⁎⁎ Parcels above 5l. value muft be entered as fuch, and paid for accordingly.

☞ Security for any Truft.

The old original LONDON WAGGONS, every Day to the OLD SHIP INN, Borough, and CROSS KEYS, WOOD-STREET, CHEAPSIDE.—Extra Waggons on the fhorteft notice.

Early nineteenth century

These advert cards were produced by some of the boat builders that existed on Point in the twentieth century, although Vospers were founded in the nineteenth century.

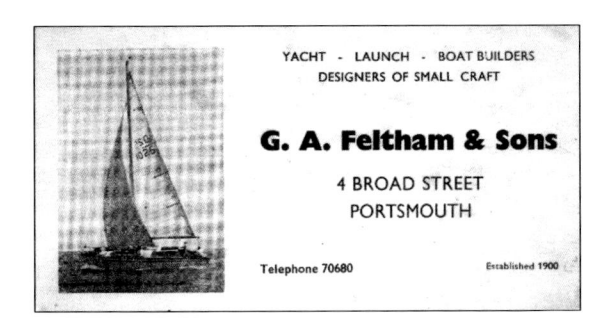

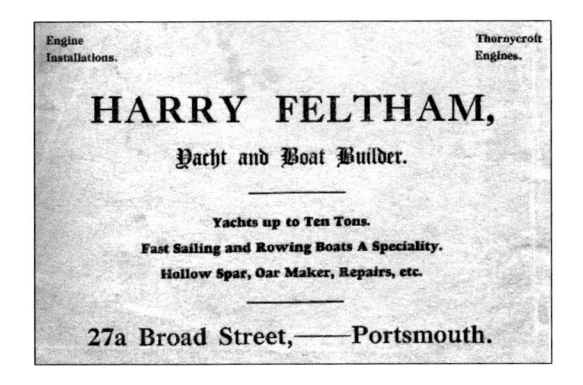

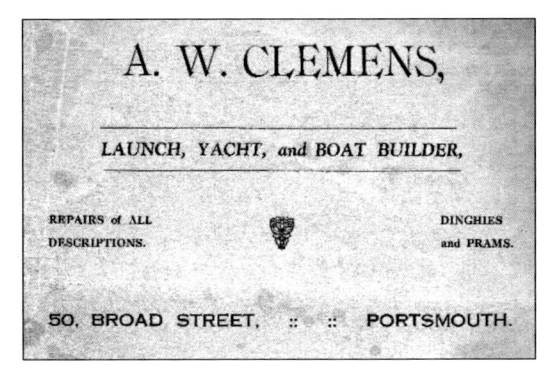

G. A. Feltham & Sons
YACHT - LAUNCH - BOAT BUILDERS
DESIGNERS OF SMALL CRAFT
4 BROAD STREET
PORTSMOUTH
Telephone 70680   Established 1900

MOTOR LAUNCHES.
Makers of Patent "SIMPLEX" STOCKLESS ANCHORS
GOLD MEDAL, PARAFFIN MOTORS.
PRIZE AT CALAIS-DOVER RACE.
FIRST PRIZE FOR MOTOR BOATS, SOUTHSEA REGATTA
GOLD MEDAL, MOTOR BOAT RELIABILITY TRIALS.
Lightest and Best.   Use Ordinary Paraffin or Kerosene.
COMPLETE BOATS or MACHINERY ONLY
Builders of all kinds of
STEAM MACHINERY OR YACHTS AND LAUNCHES COMPLETE.
VOSPER & CO., LTD., PORTSMOUTH

Engine Installations.   Thornycroft Engines.
HARRY FELTHAM,
Yacht and Boat Builder.
Yachts up to Ten Tons.
Fast Sailing and Rowing Boats A Speciality.
Hollow Spar, Oar Maker, Repairs, etc.
27a Broad Street,——Portsmouth.

A. W. CLEMENS,
LAUNCH, YACHT, and BOAT BUILDER,
REPAIRS of ALL DESCRIPTIONS.   DINGHIES and PRAMS.
50, BROAD STREET,   ::   ::   PORTSMOUTH.

Other adverts that appeared regularly in the local newspapers were for the sale of property on Point, which in some instances provide extensive detail about the area at that time. The first advert below refers to the sale of two public houses on Point, the *Lord Sandwich's Head* and the *London Tavern* and accurately describes the locations of the two premises.

Another advert in 1849 lists numerous properties to be auctioned in East Street currently occupied by various tradespeople, including two butchers, a carpenter, blacksmith and others. The butchers' shops include slaughter houses with pens for bullocks and pigs. Again, detailed locations are provided for some of the premises.

Examples of other adverts published in the early nineteenth century include timber for sale at Burridge's Wharf in the Inner Camber and in addition, adverts are shown where goods such as hemp, mess pork and rum imported from the Caribbean are offered for sale. One of the final adverts shown in the book was placed by Mr Collins of Bath Square in 1816 and refers to an auction of various goods including property, two sailing sloops, wine and seal oil.

PORTSMOUTH POINT.

TO be SOLD by AUCTION, on Thurfday the firft day of March 1781, at four o'clock in the afternoon, at the Two Blue Pofts Inn, on Portfmouth Point, in the county of Southampton, the following VALUABLE ESTATES, in feparate Lots.

LOT I.

That commodious, new built, and well finifhed Public Houfe, called The LORD SANDWICH's HEAD, now in the occupation of Mrs. Thackftone, tenant at will, being the 3d houfe from the beach or fhore, at the lower end and on the eaft fide of Broad-ftreet, on the Point of Portfmouth aforefaid and one of the firft accuftomed public houfes there.

LOT II.

That large, ftrong, and new built STOREHOUSE behind Lot I, confifting of two floors above the ground floor, 51 feet and upwards in length, opening into and at the entrance of the Camber in Portsmouth harbour, at prefent in the occupation of Meff. Robinfon and Co. and others. This ftorehoufe is too well known to need any recommendation.

LOT III.

A Meffuage adjoining fouthwards to Lot I, licenced for a PUBLIC HOUSE, by the name of The LONDON TAVERN, though at prefent ufed as a fhop, with buildings, ftore-room, and extenfive quay of near 50 feet in depth, behind and belonging to the fame, which the prefent tenant, Mrs. Mary Hufband has undertaken to quit at Lady-day next.

The fituation of all the above premifes for an extenfive trade can fearce be equalled by any in the port of Portfmouth.

For particulars enquire of Mr. James Bedford, attorney on Portfmouth Common.

1781

MESS PORK.

JUST arrived and now landing,—A large Cargo of MESS PORK—on reasonable terms, wholesale and retail, at the Baltic Wharf, by Wm. Burridge and Sons.
PORTSMOUTH, 25th September.

Swedish Timber, Christiana, and other NORWAY DEALS.

LANE, HURRY, and Co. have just landed for sale several Cargoes of the above Articles, direct from Sweden and Norway; and have also for sale on hand other descriptions of Goods in the Wood Trade.

HEMP.

FOR SALE by PRIVATE CONTRACT,—About Twenty Tons HEMP, landed from the ships *Three Sisters, Margaret, South Esk,* and *Swan,* from Petersburgh.—For particulars apply at the Office of
PORTSMOUTH, Oct. 8, 1813.   Mr. LINDEGREN.

FOR SALE, on reasonable terms,—An excellent Assortment of fine flavoured Jamaica and Leeward Island RUMS, in Puncheons, for Exportation and Home Consumption.
A. HEURTLEY & Co. 14, Bath-Square.
PORTSMOUTH, 15th Oct. 1813.

1813

VALUABLE WATER-SIDE PROPERTY,
In East-street, Portsmouth, for Sale.

TO be SOLD by AUCTION, by Mr. J. N. ROBINSON, at the Parade Coffee House, High-street, Portsmouth, on Thursday, the 11th day of October, at six for seven o'clock in the evening,—All those LEASEHOLD PREMISES, situate in East-street, Portsmouth, in the several occupations of Mr. E. Palmer, butcher ; Mr. Knott, butcher ; Mr. Knott, carpenter ; Mr. Burge, blacksmith ; Mr. Crafts, Mr. Doherty, Mr. Bricknell, and others, in the following lots:

Lot 1.—A BUTCHER'S SHOP, No. 3, East-street, with slaughter-house, piggery, and offices in the rear, in the occupation of Mr. E. Palmer.

Lot 2.—TWO TENEMENTS, Nos. 4 and 5, East-street, with a store in the rear, in the respective occupations of Mr. E. Palmer and Mr. J. Bricknell.

Lot. 3.—An extensive BUILDING, formerly used as a smith's shop, but now as a slaughter-house, and fitted with bullock stalls, pens for pigs, &c. And also two Tenements adjoining, in the occupation of Messrs. Barron and Cooling.

This is a valuable property for any mercantile purpose, being approached from the sea, where vessels may load or unload their cargoes.

Lot. 4.—A BLACKSMITH'S SHOP, on the outer Camber Quay, approached from East-street, in the occupation of Mr. Burge, blacksmith.

Lot. 5.—A DWELLING-HOUSE, approached from East-street, in the occupation of Mr. Doherty and others.

Lot. 6.—A DWELLING-HOUSE adjoining the last lot, in the occupation of Mr. Crafts and others.

And also a CARPENTER'S-SHOP, approached from East-street, situate on the outer Camber Quay, in the occupation of Mr. Knott, carpenter.

To view the premises, apply to the respective tenants, and for further particulars to the Auctioneer, 76, Broad-street, Portsmouth ; or to
C. B. HELLARD, Esq. Solicitor, Portsmouth.

SOUTHSEA.

1849

PORTSMOUTH,

TO be SOLD by AUCTION, by Mr. COLLINS, on the premises, Bath Square, on Tuesday, the 12th of March, 1816, at eleven o'clock, in lots,

Lot 1. All that convenient STOREHOUSE, Offices and Premises, occupied by Mr. Samuel Marder, Wine Merchant, &c. desirably situate for business, in Bath Square, near the beach (the water flowing nearly to the premises); are Leasehold under the Corporation of Portsmouth, for a term of which 31 years are unexpired, at a yearly rent of two pounds seven shillings.

Lot 2. The Good SLOOP *Two Sisters*, of Portsmouth, admeasures 77 tons as per register, with her apparel and furniture, well found in Stores, now lying in the Camber, adjoining the coal-yard lately occupied by Messrs. Rouse and Marder, East Street.

Lot 3. A MOIETY of the Good SLOOP *Louisa*, of Portsmouth, admeasures 34 tons as per register, with her apparel and furniture; well found in stores, now lying alongside of Lot 2.

Also for Exportation, one butt and half leager of Mountain and one leager of Sherry WINE, and twelve cask of SEAL OIL (Prize Goods) now lying in the Stores of Messrs. MARCH and Co. Gosport.

After which and the following day will be Sold by Auction on the said Premises, and at the wine Vault, Penny Street, all the STOCK and UNTENSILS in TRADE, the Counting House Desks, with mahogany tops, two Iron Book Cases &c. &c. comprising 55 dozen of old port wine, 12 dozen of sherry, and 26 dozen of Teneriffe ditto; 4 butts of porter, 1 puncheon of ale, about 400 Dozen of porter in bottles, 48 dozen of ale in ditto; about 17 gross of wine and porter bottles, large and small stone bottles, hampers, wine pipes, pulleys, hand and wheel barrows, stands; &c. Clark's hydrometer, and various other articles.

*** May be viewed and Catalogues had the day preceding the Sale, at the Office, Bath Square, Portsmouth, or the Auctioneers's, Union Street, Portsea.

1816

Deck Deals, Fir Timber and Masts, &c.

NOW landing, for SALE by PRIVATE CONTRACT, at wholesale prices,——Several Cargoes, consisting of DECK DEALS, of 20, 30, 36, and 40 feet, 3 inches; Deals, not exceeding 20 feet, of all descriptions, both from Norway and Sweden; Masts, of all sizes, not exceeding 13 inches; and Fir Timber, 12 and 14 inches square, just imported by
WM. BURRIDGE and SON.

For further particulars apply at their Baltic Wharf, Portsmouth.—*Dec.* 2. 1814. [5529

1814

The extensive amount of information contained in the adverts shown in this chapter helps one obtain a good understanding of life on Point during this time and indicates what a good reference source they are.

Bibliography.

Hampshire Advertiser 1823 – 1907

Hampshire Telegraph 1799 – 1900

Hampshire Chronicle 1772 – 1890

Portsmouth Evening News 1878 – 1955

Portsmouth Times & Naval Gazette 1850 – 1871

British Newspaper Archive

We were one: a life of W L Wyllie. M A Wyllie 1935

Yesterday in Hampshire, Sussex and Isle of Wight. No 21 January 1990

The Hampshire Magazine. September and October 1983

The Hampshire Magazine 1985: A century of sail making.

Cynthia Sherwood's personal research notes.

www.historyinportsmouth.co.uk

The Worlds of the East India Company. Edited by H V Bowen; Margaret Lincoln and Nigel Rigby.

In the footsteps of W L Wyllie. The Old Portsmouth Trail 1906 – 1931. Nigel Grundy

The Camber: Portsmouth's Commercial Port, 1565-1901. Portsmouth Paper No 80. R. C. Riley, B.Sc. (Econ), PhD.

1784 Sadler's Hampshire Directory - Portsmouth

1823/24 Pigot & Co Directory of Portsmouth

1863 Simpsons Portsmouth Directory.

1865 Harrods Postal and Commercial Directory Portsmouth.

Portsmouth in the Past. William G Gates

Bourgeois Portsmouth: Social relations in a Victorian Dockyard town 1815-75. John Langston Field B.A. (Hons)

The condition of the children of the poor in mid-Victorian Portsmouth. Portsmouth Paper No 21. Mrs Jean Stanford and Professor A. Temple Patterson.

An Early Victorian Street, the High Street, Old Portsmouth. Portsmouth Paper No 26. John Webb, F. R. Hist. S.

The Industries of Portsmouth in the Nineteenth Century. Portsmouth Paper No 25. R C Riley, B.Sc. (Econ), PhD.

D-DAY MUSEUM & Overlord website Portsmouth.

d-dayrevisited.co.uk

Hampshire archives and local studies (Messrs Fraser & White Ltd – Minutes, registers, journal and ledgers 1909-1965

National Archives Kew. Pickfords Wharf, Portsmouth 1912

lowtodunkirk.com

A short history of the Cross Solent Cargo Boats, author unknown.

Pickfords 1750-1920; A study in the development of Transportation by Gerard L Turnbull. 1972

Transport Saga 1646-1947 A History of Pickfords

A History of Portsmouth Drainage 1865-1956 Published by City of Portsmouth Corporation

Pickfords.co.uk

Reminiscences of Old Portsmouth. F. J. Proctor 1931.

Illustrated History of Portsmouth. William G. Gates 1900.

A Military Heritage – A History of Portsmouth and Portsea Town Fortifications. B. H. Patterson.

Fortifications in Old Portsmouth – a guide by Arthur Corney.

Extracts from the Records of the Municipal Corporation of the Borough of Portsmouth. Robert East 1891.

The History of Portsmouth. Henry Slight.

History of Portsmouth – A Naval Chronology. William G Gates 1931.

City of Portsmouth Records of the Corporation 1928, 1929, 1930. William G Gates.

Portsmouth and the East India Company in the Eighteenth century. Portsmouth Paper No 62. James. H. Thomas, B.A, PhD, F. R. Hist. S.

The New Portsmouth Guide, 1835.

City of Portsmouth Records of the Corporation 1835-1927. William G Gates.

Chronicles of Portsmouth. Henry Slight, Julian Slight. 1828.

Kelly's Directories of Portsmouth

MacPherson's Voyages Edited by John Scott Hughes 1944